GROWTH
IN
AMERICA

CONTRIBUTIONS IN AMERICAN STUDIES

Series Editor: Robert H. Walker

Visions of America: Eleven Literary Historical Essays
Kenneth S. Lynn

The Collected Works of Abraham Lincoln. Supplement 1832-1865
Roy P. Basler, Editor

Art and Politics: Cartoonists of the *Masses* and *Liberator*
Richard Fitzgerald

Progress and Pragmatism: James, Dewey, Beard, and the American
Idea of Progress
David W. Marcell

The Muse and the Librarian
Roy P. Basler

Henry B. Fuller of Chicago: The Ordeal of a Genteel Realist in
Ungenteel America
Bernard R. Bowron, Jr.

Mother Was a Lady: Self and Society in Selected American Children's
Periodicals, 1865-1890
R. Gordon Kelly

The *Eagle* and Brooklyn: A Community Newspaper, 1841-1955
Raymond A. Schroth, S.J.

Black Protest: Issues and Tactics
Robert C. Dick

American Values: Continuity and Change
Ralph H. Gabriel

Where I'm Bound: Patterns of Slavery and Freedom in
Black American Autobiography
Sidonie Smith

William Allen White: Maverick on Main Street
John D. McKee

American Studies Abroad
Robert H. Walker, Editor

GROWTH
IN
AMERICA *edited by*
Chester L. Cooper

WOODROW WILSON
INTERNATIONAL CENTER FOR SCHOLARS

Contributions in American Studies, No. 21

Greenwood Press
WESTPORT, CONNECTICUT ● LONDON, ENGLAND

Library of Congress Cataloging in Publication Data
Main entry under title:

Growth in America.

  (Contributions in American studies; no. 21)
  Consists of a series of essays selected from among
those prepared for a set of conferences sponsored by the
Woodrow Wilson International Center for Scholars.
  Includes bibliographical references and index.
  1.   United States—Economic conditions—Addresses,
essays, lectures.   2.   Economic development—Addresses,
essays, lectures.   I.   Cooper, Chester L.   II.   Woodrow
Wilson International Center for Scholars.
HC103.G83   330.9′73   75-35359
ISBN 0-8371-8596-3

Library of Congress Catalog Card Number: 75-35359
ISBN: 0-8371-8596-3

First published in 1976

Greenwood Press, a division of Williamhouse-Regency Inc.
51 Riverside Avenue, Westport, Connecticut 06880

Printed in the United States of America

CONTENTS

Foreword

The Woodrow Wilson International Center for Scholars is a relatively young "living" memorial to our twenty-eighth president. Created and sustained by the Congress, the center is located in the Smithsonian Institution on the mall in Washington and governed by a joint private-public board of trustees. It is unique among institutes for advanced study in its relative freedom from either the departmental structures of university-related research centers or the team approach and problem-solving focus of "think tanks" working largely on contract research.

The center seeks to include a variety of nationalities, disciplines, and outlooks among the approximately thirty-five scholars who are resident at the center, working on major, independent research at any given time. The center seeks to bring outstanding men and women in touch with the magnificent scholarly resources of the Washington area—and to ask them for tentative answers to important questions rather than definitive answers to trivial ones. There is, as well, the special Wilsonian challenge to interact the world of affairs with the world of ideas. Thus, the center promotes an active life of dialogue within and beyond its company of fellows—and is increasing the dissemination and publication of ideas and studies.

In the area of these essays, for instance, the center is also publishing an inventory of work in progress on this subject around the world. International aspects of this problem (which are not central to this volume) have been explored in three international conferences that the center has co-sponsored with Ditchley Park in England during 1974-1975. The center continues to welcome in its resident fellowship program proposals for major scholarly studies on the problems of growth within its new division of resources, Environment and Interdependence.

The essays in this collection speak for themselves—and not, of course, necessarily for the center. They do, however, fairly reflect the center's desire to periodically focus on a special area of concern, its determination to call on a wide variety of backgrounds and disciplines for perspective, and its continuing desire to ask scholars of quality to confront new problems. The essays were largely produced by outside scholars for center-sponsored conferences; and these meetings owe a particular debt to the organizing energy of Chester Cooper, the editor of this volume, and to Robert Walker, who organized the first of the center's conferences on the subject. Sincere thanks are also due to the Johnson Foundation (which funded the two conferences at Wingspread which followed the first conference, "Growth in America," at the center itself); to the Environmental Protection Agency (which funded the preparation of these essays); and to the essayists themselves (including George Brown and Arthur Kantrowitz) who gave us permission to include their papers.

JAMES H. BILLINGTON
Director

May 12, 1975

Acknowledgments

This volume of essays has been made possible by the United States Environmental Protection Agency, which funded the costs of production, and by the Johnson Foundation, Racine Wisconsin, which funded the three conferences at which preliminary versions of the essays were presented and discussed. The Woodrow Wilson International Center for Scholars and the authors as well are grateful to both these institutions.

The book is part of the American Studies series published by Greenwood Press under the general editorial guidance of Professor Robert Walker (a Wilson Fellow in 1972-1973). We are indebted to him for his counsel and his patience.

Suzanne Gerson of the center's staff had the onerous chore of administering the overall effort and riding herd on the contributors. This she did—gently, but firmly. Anna Marie Torres, in her usual impeccable, intelligent, and cheerful fashion, typed the final manuscript.

The Woodrow Wilson Center, its director, Dr. James Billington, and its administrative officer, William Dunn, made the whole enterprise possible. They obviously assume no responsibility for the views expressed in the various essays nor for any errors of omission or commission that may be evident.

CHESTER L. COOPER
Editor

GROWTH
IN
AMERICA

Chester L. Cooper
WOODROW WILSON INTERNATIONAL CENTER FOR SCHOLARS

1
Growth in America: An Introduction

I

In early 1972 the Woodrow Wilson International Center for Scholars and the Smithsonian Institution sponsored a presentation of a study on growth that had been undertaken by the Club of Rome. The study was conducted by several scholars at MIT under the direction of Professor Dennis L. Meadows. Its findings were published initially in a slim volume, *The Limits to Growth,* and in greater and more technical detail in a series of working papers.[1]

Limits to Growth addressed on a global scale the consequences of continued exponential growth in the face of finite limits. The analysis concentrated on five basic factors—population increase, agricultural production, nonrenewable resource depletion, industrial output, and pollution generation. The conclusions were melancholy: unless urgent steps are taken to slow down population and industrial growth, the global society will slide and slither into a new, but lower, distinctly unpleasant equilibrium—a process the authors describe as "overshoot and collapse."

The Club of Rome study stimulated fervent debate centering on its methodology, its conclusions, and its recommendations. And it was the starting gun for a more general debate on national and global economic and social policy. The set of issues subsumed under the rubric "growth" soon took on more urgency with increasing evidence of food, resource, and energy shortages and with an increasing popu-

3

lar sensitivity to the dangers of pollution. And the current worldwide recession added fuel to the growth-no growth debate. But a deep restiveness in many parts of the industrialized world had been manifest long before *Limits* and earlier, less well-known, examinations of growth phenomena had been published. The Club of Rome study, in short, put forward some concerns whose time had come.

The past decade may well be regarded by tomorrow's scholars as representing a benchmark in American intellectual and social history. Civil rights, Vietnam, consumerism, women's rights, environmental concerns, and prison reform were but a few of the issues that crowded the agendas of scholarly meetings, the programs of television talk shows, and the pages of popular and learned journals and of the *Congressional Record.* America has moved toward its two-hundredth birthday cynical of many old values that have long been taken for granted, skeptical of old verities that have long remained unquestioned. Indeed Americans have become wary of their own leaders and weary of the outside world.

But the cynicism and the soul searching also has its constructive side. Through the miasma of cynicism and frustration new, positive forces are perceptible. There is the beginning of a search for better as well as more. There is a growing awareness—one that cuts across age, income, and social groupings—that even the vast resources of America are discrete, that waste and plunder will have to give way to prudent husbandry, lest there be nothing for tomorrow. With the publication of the Club of Rome study, millions of Americans who, up to that point, had only a vague and inchoate sense of unease about the issues that *Limits* had raised, became more conversant with the problem of growth in a small world.

Warnings about the implications of unrestricted growth in the face of limited resources are not new, of course. In the second century Tertullian, the Carthaginian, querulously observed, "Our numbers are burdensome to the world, which can hardly supply us from its natural elements. . . . Pestilence, and famine, and wars, and earthquakes have to be regarded as a remedy for nations, as a means of pruning the luxuriance of the human race." His fears were echoed by the Reverend Thomas Malthus seventeen centuries later and have been re-echoed by both serious students of economics and self-acclaimed prophets of doom over the past century and a half. Several "growth" books immediately preceded *The Limits to Growth,* and a score or more were to follow.

II

This volume of essays on growth in America was, in a sense, conceived in the Great Hall of the Smithsonian Institution in early 1972 when the *Limits to Growth* findings were unveiled. Although the trustees, director, and fellows of the Wilson Center were wary of the methodology and of the conclusions of the study, the issues it raised and the urgency of the questions it addressed seemed to warrant serious investigation. The Center's charter, calling for the bridging of the world of scholarship and the world of affairs, made it especially appropriate to identify the broad area of growth as one warranting the attention of a selected number of fellows.

As research proceeded, it became evident that the issue to be examined was not one of *limits* to growth, as such; rather, the emphasis focused on exploring the cluster of problems involved in a strategy of *maximum feasible* growth. And this, in turn, developed into an examination of the concept of *sustainable* growth.

In the course of the research at the Center, it was decided to launch a series of conferences that would invite outside scholars to examine various facets of the American growth experience. It had become evident that a global examination of such functional factors as population and resources was both too broad and too narrow. Valuable insights into the question could be obtained by concentrating on one society and on exploring growth in its several facets, including the facet of growth as a value and as an objective. And so we asked our participants to address their attention to growth in America. Why America? Obviously because, as Americans, we felt more familiar with the substance of the problem and because Americanists are closer to hand than any other group of regional specialists. And, too, it is fair to say, because America represents an interesting case study for the purpose we had in mind. As the archtype of a Western advanced industrial society the experience of the United States may or may not be representative, but, in any case, America as a case study should be interesting to scholars elsewhere as they brood about the experience of their own societies.

Although there is a host of books available on growth and on America I believe this volume makes a unique contribution. By concentrating on growth in America from many intellectual approaches, our essayists, individually and as a body, offer some interesting, perhaps even useful, insights into America as a society and the problems Americans confront.

III

The cluster of issues subsumed under the word "growth" lies close to the American experience. In a matter of two centuries a whole continent has been domesticated, industrialized, urbanized. (Some would also add "ravaged.") Growth in America has been broadly perceived to embrace not only an impressive annual increase in the amount of goods and the number of babies, but a burgeoning in the size and quantity of virtually every type of public and private institution. For almost two centuries, to be bigger was to be better; growth became the nation's preoccupation and pride. Indeed, growth qua growth became as much an end as a means to an end—a value to be aspired to and cherished.

During the late eighteenth century and for virtually all of the nineteenth, the concept of growth was tied closely to spatial expansion—immigration from Europe to America, migration from rural areas to nearby cities and towns, and a march from the settled communities to the wilderness. For historians and for contemporary observers as well, the most dramatic aspect of this expansion was the westward trek from the towns and farms of the East.

When the wilderness became settled toward the end of the nineteenth century, it was as if the nation had stepped across the threshold from youth into middle age. In a paper read to a group of fellow historians in 1893, Frederick Jackson Turner equated the frontier with a veritable fountain of youth for American society. "Up to our own day American history has been in a large degree the history of the colonization of the Great West. The existence of an area of free land,

and the advance of American settlement westward, explain American development. . . . American social development has been continually beginning over again on the frontier. This perennial rebirth, this fluidity of American life, this expansion westward with its new opportunities, its continuous touch with the simplicity of primitive society, furnish the forces dominating American character. . . . And now . . . the frontier has gone, and with its going has closed the first period of American history."[2]

But there were new "frontiers" just over the horizon. Turner had barely written his essay when there was a tidal wave of immigration from Europe—and still to come decades hence were other waves of new settlers, not only from across the Atlantic but from the lands to the south.

Superimposed on these great movements from abroad was an internal one comprising those native Americans who regarded the pulsating industrial urban centers as their frontier. "More Americans," wrote historian David Potter, "have changed their status by moving to the city than have done so by moving to the frontier."[3] In the nation's infancy, barely 3 percent of Americans were city dwellers; only five cities had populations of more than 8,000. A century later about one-third of the population of the United States lived in towns or cities; by 1890, Manhattan and Brooklyn boasted more than two million people, Chicago and Philadelphia, more than a million each. By 1910, almost half of all Americans were urban dwellers; by 1930, two-thirds; by 1970, almost three-fourths.

But there is an important difference between expansion and growth. Thus, recent studies have seriously questioned long-held assumptions that America experienced an impressive rate of per-capita economic growth during the first two-thirds of the nineteenth century. According to Thomas Cochran, recent studies of American growth rates during this period suggest "a paradoxical reversal of the Turner frontier thesis. To [Turner] the seemingly limitless areas of open land and the continual beginning of society anew as communities stretched across the continent were major sources of American greatness, of national superiority. Recent studies suggest, however, that these far-flung settlements and this continual and sometimes fruitless movement of population joined with high fertility rates to affect adversely the rate of growth in product per capita." [4]

Frontiers are to be found not only on the boundless prairies or in the bustling cities. Within a decade of Turner's lament, even more excit-ing horizons were to be sighted and reached. Forces were gathering that would soon combine to produce an explosion of knowledge and technology. And it was this new frontier that would have a great impact on American economic growth.

Americans born at the turn of the century would witness a complete technological transformation of their society and their own lives. While more things for more people had been the driving force behind the busy mills, factories, and mines during the nineteenth century, the inventions and innovations that crowded the early decades of the twentieth gave the concept of growth even more the coloration of *industrial* growth. And with it America's economic health and prog-ress came to be measured in terms of its annual increase in goods and services. Soon the ponderous term, "the gross national product of the United States," would become familiar to millions of Americans.

It is no wonder, then, that the growth-no growth debate takes on special significance for Americans, and all the more so at this dramatic moment. The debate is occurring at a time when America faces a momentous milestone—the dawn of its third century. Such an occa-sion will be cause for national soul searching in any case. That Ameri-cans confront the moment in the aftermath of a debilitating war in Asia and with fresh memories of a disgraced President and a dishonored Vice-President add poignancy to the nation's identity quest. And, as if a further gloss were needed, the economic uncertainty that grips America on the eve of its bicentennial adds a desperate sense of urgency to the introspection about who we are and where we are going.

IV

These essays were selected from among those prepared for a set of conferences that addressed the broad subject of growth in America from three separate perspectives. Although each of the three meetings had participants from a wide array of disciplines, the principal focus of the first was on the humanities, the second, social sciences, and the third, science and technology.

The essays do not deal exclusively with economic growth; many of them deal with growth as a more generic value and process. And they are not confined exclusively to America; many aspects of growth naturally spill over to influence or to be influenced by the world beyond our borders. But, it is fair to say, the principal thrust of most of the essays takes the form of a retrospective, current, or future look at economic growth and much of the emphasis is on past, present, and future implications for Americans.

The debate among those who would limit economic growth, those who would permit growth to proceed without restraint, and those who take their stand someplace in between still goes on—in official government meetings, in university forums, in the pages and videotapes of the media. Strains of the arguments, both pro and con, can be readily perceived in many of these essays.

The ordering of the essays does not follow that of their presentation in the set of conferences for which they were originally prepared. Thus, instead of grouping them strictly in humanist, social science, and technological clusters, they have been rearranged here to provide a more coherent exploration of the issues.

The stage is set with two essays that examine growth as a value in the broadest sense. There follow several papers that treat those aspects of growth that have given rise to serious contemporary questioning and concern. Next is a group of essays that provide a historical perspective on the problem. And then there are three that project the examination of the issue into the future. The last of these, my own, was written especially for this volume. It is an effort to integrate some of the ideas contained in the others, as well as to raise some questions that Americans will have to address as they approach their third century. Finally, there are two essays in the appendix, which, while not discussed at any of the three conferences, are included here with the permission of their authors because they provide a bridge between some of the ideas raised in the body of the book and the problems of implementation.

NOTES

1. Donella H. Meadows, Dennis L. Meadows, Jorgen Randers, and William W. Behrens III, *The Limits to Growth* (New York: Universe Books, 1972).
2. Frederick Jackson Turner, "The Significance of the Frontier in American

History," *Selected Essays of Frederick Jackson Turner,* ed. Ray Allen Billington (Englewood Cliffs, N.J.: Prentice-Hall, 1961), pp. 37-62.

3. David Potter, *People of Plenty* (Chicago: University of Chicago Press, 1954), p. 94.

4. Thomas C. Cochran, "The Paradox of American Economic Growth," *The Journal of American History* 61 (March 1975): 925-942.

Part I

Growth as a Value

Sydney E. Ahlstrom
YALE UNIVERSITY

2
Reflections on Religion, Nature, and the Exploitative Mentality

I

The movement of Hebrew and kindred peoples into and out of Egypt and then into Palestine between the sixteenth and thirteenth centuries B.C. has been pieced together by historians of the ancient Middle East, but very little is precisely known. Much better documented is the process by which some of these fractious tribes gradually separated themselves from their polytheistic neighbors and entered into a solemn covenant with the storm god Jahweh, who became for them the God above all other gods, as even the oldest passage in the Bible attests:

> O Yahweh, when thou camest from Seir,
> When thou marchedst from the steppes of Edom,
> The earth quaked, the heavens also shook,
> The clouds too dripped water,
> The mountains rocked at the presence of Yahweh,
> At the presence of Yahweh, the God of Israel. (JUDGES, 5:4f.)

"With no people in ancient times," writes T. J. Meek, "did [the tendency toward monotheism] attain such full expression as it did with the Hebrews," though even among them it does not come to full

13

expression until the time of Jeremiah and the second Isaiah in the sixth century B.C.[1]

It may seem like a long stretch from this bit of ancient history to present-day worries about ecological catastrophe, but the sinews that bind the one to the other are strong and durable. And Americans, who have persistently proclaimed their manifest destiny as God's new Israel should be the last to doubt the continuing ideological significance of old Israel. We must realize, moreover, that we are not dealing with a parochial "Western" problem. Concern for the biosphere's capacity to support life is global, and the Westernization of the entire world is so far advanced that the healing springs of Eastern thought are themselves drying up.

The process of exploitation and imperialistic transformation that began with Vasco da Gama, Columbus, and Magellan has not yet seen the beginning of the end. When we listen to news on a Japanese transistor radio and hear of Marxism and nationalism in Vietnam or in China, we realize how Western thought and technics together have irreversibly created one world. And when we seek the source of the astoundingly dynamic character of Western society—as Max Weber set out to do—we are brought back (as was he) to the importance of the Judaic tradition as well as those international religious movements that derive from the Hebrew impulse: the Christian and then later the Islamic. In doing this one does no more than those bold Jewish Hegelians of the nineteenth century (Salomon Formstecher, Salomon Steinheim, and others) who saw Christianity and Islam as in some sense carrying out Israel's mission in different parts of the world. We must also understand Marxism in this sense, for its prophetic and historical passion is utterly unimaginable aside from its Judeo-Christian (and Hegelian) background. Indeed, nowhere in recorded history is there an equally astounding instance of such vast spiritual and cultural effects stemming from so small a source.

Israel's main rival, of course, would be ancient Hellas, but after the great conquests of the Greco-Roman world by Christianity and Islam, this classical heritage was itself profoundly transformed. It shall, therefore, be part of my purpose in this essay to suggest that many of the modes of thinking and acting that are generally deemed to be most distinctly Western are rooted in the faith of Israel and that many of the dilemmas so keenly felt in our own time of crisis are fundamentally religious and therefore insoluble unless carried to the profoundest levels where we reevaluate our relationship to "the whole system of existence." Before entering upon these matters in any detail, however, there are certain preliminary matters to be considered.

I focus on the United States, not because most readers of these words will be American but because this country, with its vast political, military, and, above all, economic connections, is and will continue to be more accountable for the world's ecological plight than any other. Beyond this consideration is the further fact that this country's response to the present crisis has revealed with special clarity the drastic nature of the confrontations that lie ahead and the degree to which the search for a "new ethic" by which we rearrange our priorities is at bottom a religious problem. The 1970s, as we all know, confront us with a renewal of these old debates. J. W. Forrester and the Club of Rome produce computerized warnings of exponentially advancing doom while Peter Passell and Leonard Ross in the manner of Enlightened philosophers call the evidence garbage. The script writers for Mobil and Exxon meanwhile flood us with sermons on the benign role of the multinational petroleum industry. We are lost in a plethora of ships that pass in the night. Communication falters.

II

The contemporary debate includes a transformed public consciousness of ecological distress and a worldwide awareness of crisis but no consensus on national or international policy. The problem is deepened moreover by a drastically altered religious situation that has destroyed our traditional standards of judgment. Cognitive dissonance on a vast scale undermines traditional religious attitudes or places traditionalists in isolated, threatened, and insulated communities of "cognitive deviance." Fundamentalists constitute a vast, poorly understood subculture that is alienated, resentful, and theologically and morally out of tune with the Club of Rome. Self-conscious ethnic and racial minorities accent the nation's pluralism and erode the status of the Protestant establishment. The Roman Catholic Church falls into institutional disarray and moral confusion due to the shocks of long-delayed *aggiornamento*. Jewish youth shows a new magnitude of unconcern about interfaith marriages. A new myth of the American

Indian adds to the American's discomfort with his imperialistic past. The Protestant ethic founders on a consumer-oriented economy of credit and abundance now further confounded by inflation and unemployment. Popular science and moonshots undermine supernaturalistic faith, while a powerful neoromantic current washes away many of the old landmarks of belief. Eastern religions attract not only the youthful counterculture but major philosophers and theologians. Revulsion for the war in Southeast Asia and failures to attain either racial justice, urban renewal, or tax reform combine with new forms of religious belief and disbelief to undercut traditional American forms of patriotic piety, especially the idea of the nation's providential destiny. Even the Congress, to the accolades of the tourist industry, changes our national holy days into long weekends. One may speak (as I have elsewhere done at some length) of this last decade as the closing bracket of a great Puritan epoch in our Anglo-American history.[2]

There are, of course, many superficial participants in this great debate. There are the overnight converts who declare a row of box elders sacred because they want the highway engineers to find another route for the road. Then there are the highway engineers for whom straight thinking means only to avoid curves and inclines. The debate also exposes many serious thinkers who are torn and confused by the issues; they find new threats, new fears, and new values putting pressure on old rationales and old beliefs. Whether they be biologists, economists, parish ministers, or philosophers, their thought is in transition and marred by inconsistency and indecision. Discussions of values in a world of increasing scarcity, therefore, will continue to be disrupted by profound differences at the deepest presuppositional levels, and they will continue to be rendered intractable by the prevailing religious outlook.

Disagreements on the growth question and related issues have shown a persistent tendency to be rooted in opposing views of reality. This situation is, I suppose, a function of the human condition and also a reflection of still other troubles of the present day; yet it clearly exposes the degree to which present-day debates on world and national policy raise questions about one's basic weltauffassung, one's way of putting it all together. The religious character of the debate, in fact, helps to explain the violent, absolutistic language of so many of the discussions. They quite literally involve matters of ultimate concern. One hears the thunder of world views in collision. The dean of one school of forestry and environmental science observes that students going out from the school are not so much graduated for work in a profession as ordained to a ministry.

We may safely conclude that present-day debates on the "universal crisis" require a new mode of discourse that is based on a profoundly revised world view, or at the very least an awareness of the great options presented by the traditions that come down to us. To this end, we must return first of all to a retrospective view of the world's Judaic heritage, with attention to some of its especially consequential motifs.

III

Perhaps the most celebrated feature of Israel's faith was its increasingly uncompromised monotheism and its abhorrence of any and all intimations of polytheism, syncretism, and pantheism. Here are the roots of the West's dogmatic insistence on orthodoxy, its readiness to designate heresy, its small tolerance for deviancy, its propensity for absolute judgments, and its commitment to logical consistency and rational coherence. Monotheism is stern; it exacts obedience and conformity and tends to regard compromise as immoral.

Always qualifying and giving a special character to Israel's monotheism, however, were its notions of the creation. The world is not eternal as Aristotle and the Greek philosophers would have it, but a decisive act of the one almighty and utterly transcendent God.

Closely tied to this view is the Judaic understanding of world history as *Heilsgeschichte,* as sacred history, as salvation history. From Creation to Eschaton the one true God is the Lord of History. History, as we have said, is decisive, dynamic, and significant in the highest sense. "God's eye is on the sparrow." The autumn leaf falls to its appointed place. All things, even the worst misfortunes, work together for the glory of God. Each man and woman has an appointed role and a call to obedience in two distinctive but related ways. The first of these is the powerful sense of historical direction given to Western views of the future. Time is laden with meaning. All events point to the coming of the messianic kingdom when the pain and tragedy of this world, after whatever tribulations, will be resolved. This view conduces in our time either to technocratic utopias or to apocalyptic nightmares of future famine and world conflict. Underlying any view of the past, the present, and the future is a sense of the urgency of time. Human history is understood and experienced as unilinear, unrepeatable and irrevocable; and this sense of the once-and-for-allness of human existence creates an activistic fear of wasting time or missing one's chance. Leisure, indolence, and even contemplation seem sinful.

Animating all of these themes is Israel's certainty of being God's chosen people, of being in covenant with him as his elect nation in collective obedience to his holy law. It has, thus, a collective destiny and duty. The late Jacob J. Finkelstein therefore declared Exodus 19:6—"You shall be unto me a kingdom of priests and a holy nation"— to be the "most revolutionary statement in the Bible, one which set off a chain reaction that with ever increasing—one may even say devastating—effect has continued down to our own time." In this doctrine of the "transcendent state" he sees the origins of a nationalistic movement that in due time transformed the Christian West and that is now moving into the non-Western world. Even in the Orient one can observe the "Israelization" of individual nations.[3]

Finally, and most directly relevant for our present discussion, is the biblical emphasis on the centrality of humankind, and especially *man*-kind, in God's creation of the world. Man is to have dominion over all things and to bend them to his purposes. Here one can entirely agree with John Passmore's careful and thoughtful study: "There is one point on which it [the Old Testament] is absolutely clear: nature is not sacred. And while the rejection of the view that nature is sacred does not justify an irresponsible attitude to it, it at least leaves the way open to that attitude, does not condemn it as sacreligious." He then quotes Henri Frankfort's observation that in nature there is a "mysterious life" from which the Hebrews cut themselves off. By so doing they departed from nearly every other religious tradition except, in varying degrees, Christianity and Islam. Passmore goes on to observe, moreover, that Western science "has been no less emphatic that nature is not sacred."[4] In this latter observation he ignores a scientific attitude that ever since the Romantic movement has been constantly claiming new scientific devotees. But this is to get ahead of our story. Looking at our ancient heritage in its larger, inclusive sense, one may confess to seeing many reasons for the rise of an activist, exploitative, and anthropocentric mentality that sees maximized productivity as the chief end of man.

IV

For the West, of course, it was not Israel but the Christian church that became the chief bearer of this Judaic outlook. Indeed, the early Christians—in the New Testament itself—declared the Church to *be* the new Israel and a holy nation (I Peter, 2:1-10). During the Middle Ages, to be sure, this tradition was markedly attenuated. The Church yielded to local religious practices and responded to the religious needs of new peoples. It also carried with it much of the Greco-Roman philosophical and religious heritage. The other-worldly mysticism of the neoplatonic tradition, for example, heavily conditioned Catholic conceptions of piety and perfection. "Der Menschist nateurlich catholisch," said Rudolf Sohm, with his characteristic Protestant perspective on these assimilative tendencies.

The Reformation, on the other hand, tended to see medieval Catholicism as a vast institutionalized departure from New Testament Christianity and in this way encouraged a great revival of Judaic emphases. Especially in the Reformed (or Calvinistic) tradition the reformers assigned redemptive roles to nations, peoples, and prophetic heroes. These tendencies, as well as the ethical implications of reformed theology, were drawn out with special thoroughness and intensity in England, where the Puritan movement conceived of England itself as an elect nation until the Stuart kings frustrated their plans for "Israelization."5 As the crown became more adamant, however, many Puritans transferred their hopes to holy commonwealths founded on the North American strand. Governor John Winthrop of the Massachusetts Bay Colony voiced this intention in 1630: "We shall find the God of Israel is among us. . . . We shall be as a city upon a hill." In this new Canaan, moreover, they set about with uncommon alacrity to create a social and economic order in which Puritan aims would have unhindered sway. Before a century had passed Cotton Mather lamented that prosperity was destroying the very piety that had made New England prosper.

In the American colonies generally, where old aristocratic and feudal attitudes had almost no institutional footing and where the imperialism of the popish powers raised constant threats of war and conquest, Puritanism became the overwhelmingly dominant culture-shaping power. The New England commonwealths understood themselves explicitly as God's New Israel and gradually conveyed their idea of America's providential destiny to the new republic.[6] Meanwhile the Puritan ethic, which sustained itself long after Puritanism as a doctrinal system had lost its hold on the American mind, informed the people's social, economic, and political attitudes. For the westward-moving American the Indian was from the beginning a prime example of an unethical life-style. This land of immigrants, therefore, became almost a paradigm of Puritan attitudes toward work in one's calling and on man's relationship to the natural world. Nor was this only a matter of private life-styles, for Puritan attitudes also became a major determinant of governmental forms and ideals: a commitment to individualistic egalitarianism, economic freedom, and political liberty. Puritanism, moreover, supported the view that the regulation of economic activities belonged to the private ethical realm and not to government.[7]

The "American Revolution," thus begun in the 1630s, was consummated in 1776, the year in which Adam Smith's *Wealth of Nations* was published. It became the world's fullest institutionalization of the bourgeois revolution. Nowhere did politics and religion provide a more favorable environment for economic individualism, the exploitation of nature's abundance, and the rationalization of the marketplace than in the United States where Smith's "unseen hand" almost became a stand-in for the deity. Even when the gradual collapse of Europe's peasant economy brought fifty million displaced persons (few of them Puritans) to the great American asylum (which Penn had first advertised), the Protestant establishment served as a powerful, dynamic, and self-confident reference group. Jean-François Revel was correct in insisting that the modern revolution had to occur in America and that it did not need Marx; but he was hardly right in saying "without Jesus."[8] For three full centuries Puritanic Protestantism would play a major role in America's ideological development. Perhaps one could say that the road to Manchester and the smogs of Los Angeles and Tokyo begins at Sinai. Other stops on this road might be Geneva and Wittenberg, but not Assisi or Walden Pond.

The reference to Walden Pond on this imaginary road is hardly trivial. It points to a countervailing tradition in the West that leads, one may hope, to a better world, even though no perfect city shimmers at the end of the road. Henry David Thoreau is one great American representative of a powerful modern movement that sought to reclaim a larger and more responsible relationship to nature. My reference is, of course, to that multifaceted but still strangely united religious revolution that is usually called Romanticism.[9]

V

The high tide of the Romantic movement is usually located in the period between 1770 and 1848, though romantic revivals have arisen recurrently down to the present. On the other hand, if the movement were to be dated by the ideas and attitudes that it sought to revitalize, it would extend back to Renaissance, medieval, and classical times. Romantics were alarmed above all by the mechanistic and materialistic implications of the Enlightenment. They also shared Wordsworth's fear that in "getting and spending" man would lay waste his powers and that the machine age would dehumanize society. For these reasons they often idealized the Middle Ages and dreamed of a more comprehensive, less fiercely competitive social order. For very similar reasons they became interested in primitive societies, including the American Indian.

The provocations leading to this changed view of life and the world came, of course, from many sources, not all of them entirely compatible. At the outset they were inspired by Rousseau. The rediscovery of Spinoza and pantheistic ways of thinking was promoted by Shaftesbury, Herder, and several others; and then almost simultaneously came the resounding impact of Kant and soon thereafter the current of philosophical idealism associated with Fichte, Schelling, and Hegel. Against this background many Romantics were attracted to Neoplatonism and the great mystics, including the esoteric aspect of the tradition transmitted by the Jewish Caballa, and finally to the great religions of the Orient. Dominating the whole age, from the publication of *Werther* in 1774 to his death in 1832, was Goethe's many-sided genius. Out of all this, and much more, came proposals for a basic reorientation of mind: a celebration of the inner life, a pervasive accent on the dynamic and organic qualities of reality, a new emphasis on the unity of man, nature, and God, and the immanence of the divine in all things. In negative terms, Romanticism was a protest against the exploitative and alienating aspects of capitalistic society and a critique of the utilitarianism that it entailed. It was also a modification of the radical divine-human dualism of Judeo-Christian, especially Protestant, orthodoxy.

It is this set of tendencies that led Alfred North Whitehead, in the famous fifth chapter of his *Science and the Modern World* (1925), to describe the Romantic reaction as the dawn of a new era, even in the history of science. Since that time, moreover, the process philosophy of Whitehead has provided philosophic support to advocates of more responsible concern for the earth's ecosystem.

If we seek to place the Romantic movement in Western history, it must be seen as the emergence of a new form of consciousness that expressed itself through almost every discipline and activity.

"Miracle [says Emerson in his Divinity School address] is one with the blowing clover and the falling rain. The New Teacher . . . shall see the world to be a mirror of the soul; shall see the identity of the law of gravitation with purity of heart; and shall show that the Ought, that Duty, is one thing with Science, with Beauty and with Joy." John Stuart Mill would be thrown into personal crisis by the stark alternatives this view posed for a spiritual child of Jeremy Bentham and James Mill—and it may be that his hopes for a point of human stability "beyond growth" stem from his appropriation of Coleridge. Stuart Hampshire documents a similar turning in 1973 when he dismissed the simplistic view that man is "at the very center of the universe" and that his "states of feeling [are] the source of all value in the world," and that the entire "natural order [may] be farmed for the comfort and pleasure of man without any restriction other than the comfort and pleasure of future human beings."[10]

The mere repudiation of utilitarianism, however, does not constitute a sufficient response to this planet's urgent needs. One must at least try to move on to a broader and deeper understanding of reality. And in this respect we do well to consider the American experience, for the United States, as it enters its bicentennial era, is now a "city on a hill" with a new lesson for the world. By reason of its undeviating commitment to an exploitative ethic, it has become an example for all the world to see of the wages of ecological sin. Another Great Awakening is required. One religious outlook must yield to another in which the natural world is apprehended in a new way. Traditional pragmatic modes of living, thinking, and valuing must change. Conversions of this sort have been occurring by the thousands during the last decade despite the lack of governmental leadership. But we need another

William James to describe such transformations and the kind of intellectual stimulus that would accelerate the process.

One would probably have to say that the Jonathan Edwards of America's ecological awakening was Rachel Carson, whose *Silent Spring* first appeared in 1962. Yet Edwards himself experienced in his own life a transformation of vision very similar to that of which we speak:

> *After this experience [he says in his "Personal Narrative"], my sense of divine things gradually increased, and became more and more lively, and had more of that inward sweetness. The appearance of everything was altered; there seemed to be, as it were, a calm, sweet cast, or appearance of divine glory in almost everything. God's excellency, his wisdom, his purity and love, seemed to appear in every thing; in the sun, moon, and stars; in the clouds, and blue sky; in grass, flowers, trees; in the water, and all nature.*

Given this beginning, it is hardly surprising that Edwards made it his life's work to provide the Reformed and Puritan tradition with a fully formulated system that would reflect this vision in post-Newtonian terms. In this task he was inspired by the Neoplatonism of Ralph Cudworth, though Edwards' independently developed thought would show a startling similarity to that of Malebranche, Arthur Collier, and Berkeley. But it is in his *Dissertation on the Nature of True Virtue* that he provides the grounds for an ecological ethic of great insight and value:

> *Virtue is the beauty of the qualities and exercises of the heart. . . . True virtue most essentially consists in benevolence to being in general. Or perhaps to speak more accurately, it is that consent, propensity and union of heart to being in general. . . . And if every intelligent being is in some way related to being in general, and is a part of the universal system of existence, and so stands in connection with the whole, what can its general and true beauty be, but its union and consent with the great whole?* [11]

H. Richard Niebuhr, whose *Radical Monotheism* appeared just two centuries after Edwards' *Dissertation,* also addresses our need for a more comprehensive ethic. He did not have ecological issues primarily in mind, but he defends an almost Spinozan view of reality and in his moral philosophy moves to the far antipodes from egocentrism. He would have our concern go beyond even Albert Schweitzer's "reverence for life." After depicting the community of science in its ideal sense as a paradigm of the "Beloved Community," he calls us to "the liberation of the whole groaning and travailing creation" and to the "battle against . . . what is destructive and anarchic in all accessible realms of being."[12]

VI

With these brief references to two American thinkers who, though widely separated in time, speak to our most serious dilemmas, this essay comes to an end, but not to a conclusion. Our problems are too complex and dynamic to admit of a single or enduring solution. I shall close, therefore, with only two observations. The first and most important is the assertion that the cluster of moral and technical questions that constitute the ecological problem have from earliest times to the present had many inescapable religious ramifications and that these remain fundamental. The second assertion is simply that the search for concrete knowledge remains equally important. Ecology is and should be a hard and sophisticated science. Yet just to give this entire matter one more whirl, it may be appropriate to observe that if this ecological scientific community were to be an *ideal* one in the ways delineated by Josiah Royce and Richard Niebuhr, it would become a religious paradigm of the great community, or as Royce sometimes called it, the invisible church of those who are loyal to loyalty and not to some lesser entity.[13]

NOTES

1. Theophile James Meek, *Hebrew Origins* (New York: Harper & Row, 1960), p. 184. The quoted passage from the "Song of Deborah" is in his version, pp. 99-100. See also Deuteronomy 33:2.

2. See my *Religious History of the American People* (New Haven: Yale University Press, 1972), part IX; and my article in James M. Gustafson, ed.,

The Sixties: Radical Change in Religion, The Annals of the American Academy of Political and Social Science 387 (January 1970).

3. Jacob J. Finkelstein, "The Goring Ox: Some Historical Perspectives on Deodands, Forfeitures, Wrongful Death, and the Western Notion of Sovereignty," *Temple Law Quarterly* 46, (Winter 1973): 206-207, 210, 253.

4. John Passmore, *Man's Responsibility for Nature: Ecological Problems and Western Traditions* (New York: Charles Scribner's Sons, 1974), pp. 9-10. My brief reference is no indication of the importance of this very learned and thoughtful book.

5. William Haller, *The Elect Nation: The Meaning and Relevance of Foxe's Book of Martyrs* (New York: Harper & Row, 1963).

6. On this theme see Conrad Cherry, ed., *God's New Israel: Religious Interpretations of American Destiny* (Englewood Cliffs: Prentice-Hall, 1971); Winthrop S. Hudson, ed., *Religion and Nationalism in America* (New York: Harper & Row, 1970); Ernest L. Tuveson, *Redeemer Nation: The Idea of America's Millennial Role* (Chicago: University of Chicago Press, 1968).

7. David Little, *Religion, Order, and Law: A Study in Pre-Revolutionary England* (New York: Harper & Row, 1969), is a masterly study in the Weberian tradition, with valuable commentary on the literature.

8. Jean-François Revel, *Without Marx or Jesus: The New American Revolution* (Garden City: Doubleday & Company, 1970).

9. Lynn White, Jr., in a widely read article, "The Historical Roots of our Ecologic Crisis," proposes Saint Francis of Assisi "as a patron saint for ecologists." *Science* 155 (March 10, 1967): 1203-1207. He makes Francis a representative of "an alternative Christian view" to that which has dominated the Judeo-Christian tradition. I am obviously sympathetic with his viewpoint, though I describe both the tradition and the alternative in somewhat different terms. Passmore also describes alternative views in the West but in the end says that the problem is in fact political. "A new ethic will arise out of existing attitudes or not at all." I contend that profound changes in attitude are occurring and must continue.

10. "Morality and Pessimism," *The New York Review of Books,* January 1, 1973.

11. Quoted from Jonathan Edwards, *Dissertation on the Nature of True Virtue,* ed. William K. Frankena (Ann Arbor: Michigan University Press, 1961), pp. 2-4.

12. H. Richard Niebuhr, *Radical Monotheism and Western Culture* (New York: Harper & Row, 1960), p. 89. Niebuhr acknowledges great respect for Edwards, but the differences between the two are very great, especially in their ways of describing or defining conversion or radical religious change.

13. Loyalty and the great community are concerns that pervade many of Royce's works, but see *The Sources of Religious Insight* (New York: Charles Scribner's Sons, 1912), especially chap. 7.

Charles W. Powers
YALE UNIVERSITY DIVINITY SCHOOL

3
Growth as an American Value: An Ethicist's Point of View

I

If we are coherently to consider "growth as a value," we must first ascertain what sort of "value" it is commonly understood to be. In order for some thing or some process (and growth is a process, not a thing) to be considered a value, we must deem it to be worthy of esteem and be prepared to commend it. We learn what sort of value it is by determining why or on what grounds or in what sense it is thought to be worthy of esteem and commendation. There are a number of such "grounds":

1. That the thing or process is *intrinsically* valuable, good in itself because of its own intrinsic properties. Further questions about the context in which the thing or process appears are irrelevant in determining whether it is a value. But that does not rule out other questions, such as what priority it has in a scale of values (some of which may be in conflict), or epistemological questions concerning how one discovered that such properties as constitute the thing or process were found to be intrinsically worthy of respect.

2. That the thing or process contributes to a whole that is judged to be worthy or commendable. Here the thing or process in question is not considered a value until one determines that the whole is itself a

"good" and that it is a necessary or regular component of that whole.

   3. That the thing or process is a *means to an end* that is thought to be worthy or commendable. Here the *end* is judged independently, and the thing or process is valued because it is a necessary or regularly required instrument for attaining that end.

"Growth," it seems to me, can normally be shown to be only the third type of value. If one is asked why he thinks that growth is good or commendable, it would be odd indeed for him to explain how he discovered it is good or that growth is itself a component of something else worthy of esteem. Instead the person will suggest how a/the growth process helps bring into being a state of affairs that he values. Then the discussion will center around whether growth is in fact an efficient means to the end designated, whether it simultaneously results in "bad" states of affairs, or whether the end designated is itself worthy of esteem.

If this analysis is correct, several things follow that will be of considerable importance to our consideration of growth in the contemporary discussion of growth-no growth policies. First, we shall gain nothing at all—except perhaps a propagandist's advantage—by speaking of growth in general. If we are to gain any understanding of why growth is worthy or unworthy of esteem, it must be a particular type of growth (growth *of something*) and we must be willing to carry that explanation to the end. If, for example, exponential growth of the human population and of industrial output will result in the dramatic collapse of one or more of the several interdependent life-support systems, we must be willing to specify why we abhor that result (e.g., human suffering, destruction of the human race). It is when we have specified one of the ends to which a specific type of growth is a means (collapse) and evaluated that end, and then evaluated that result in re-relation to the other *ends* that that type of growth does or is purported to help promote (remembering to be as rigorous in evaluating the efficacy of those means as of alternative ones), that we will be prepared to make an evaluation of growth of that specific type, as a value. Normatively, growth per se is a completely neutral process. It becomes normatively important only when given a context wherein its results can be evaluated. If prior to such specification we proceed to compare growth with other values of various sorts (e.g., honesty, the rights of persons, or the existence of the species), we are bound to find ourselves in conceptual confusion.

II

It would seem, however, that in America growth per se has been commended almost without specification or reservation. More is better. Bigger is better. Hence, although any analysis of growth as a value leads inexorably to the conclusion that it should be considered as an instrumental value and evaluated in terms of its purported or actual results, we might be tempted to say that in this country growth has been misunderstood as an intrinsic value. We would then seek the sources of this basic misunderstanding. But to proceed in this direction is to badly misinterpret the American mind, or better, the American peoples' perception of the historical event of which they were and are a part. It will be my contention that built into the warp and woof of the American self-understanding are a set of presuppositions, usually implicit, but frequently made explicit, which gave rise to a weltanschaaung in which growth is uncritically seen not only as the instrument of diverse but compatible valued ends, but additionally as the measure of how the country is doing in its effort to achieve those diverse ends.

We must begin with the two overriding and interdependent articles of the American faith. The first is a belief in the individual as the center or primary unit of value. Call it individualism or what you will, the American, as compared to virtually any other civilization that has yet existed, has sacralized and put its trust in the individual. But he has never been able to specify beyond a few relatively vague natural rights (i.e., life, liberty, and the pursuit of happiness) what man is. Hence, in the absence of a more complete account of man, the nature and purpose of the American institutions developed to serve him have been directed less to delivering what he basically needs than to providing him opportunity to express and pursue his interests or wants. The second article of faith is that the nation that gave space and primacy to the individual had a unique, providentially endowed destiny—a transcendent purpose and end. In sum, the national faith affirmed at its core combined and made interdependent two apparently contradictory beliefs: that by raising up the primacy of the *individual* it would be building a unique *collective* result of monumental consequence.

If we are to understand the centrality of growth in the American scheme of things, we will have to gain some understanding of why and how these two themes were thought to be synergistic and not competing ones. There are at least five factors at work:

1. The first, and perhaps least important, is that American culture is largely a reactive response to the structure of authority in European culture. A common cause of all immigration to the United States is the desire to get away from a culture considered oppressive, authoritarian, and static. America was new, free, the land of opportunity precisely in comparison to the various Europes from which everyone from the Puritans to the twentieth-century immigrants fled. A promised land is defined in opposition to the culture from which exodus is made, and the common theme in the characterizations of the several Egypts from which Americans came was that they inhibited the dynamics that made individual life worth living; whether conceived in physical or psychological terms, the space America offered meant that when you bumped you did not have to stand and chafe but could move so you would not bump again. If the old order meant restraint, a land that did not restrain was eo ipso the new Israel. Endemic to such a reactive perception was a positive valuing of growth per se as the opposite of chafing restraint.

2. If America was perceived as offering room to grow, it sustained that perception by its very physical expanse and the seeming inexhaustibility of its resources. The "material" was there to be had if one were willing to go get it. If we are to understand how the two tenets of the national faith were held together, we must understand the mentality that always assumed there would be a new frontier. In Europe obtaining power or prestige or room meant taking something away from someone else—scarcity was the determining presupposition. In America, however, no such doctrine of scarcity seemed relevant. If there was scarcity, it was due to lack of ingenuity and diligent self-application (two cardinal American virtues, as we shall see). The assumption that the land of destiny was limitless gave unspecified growth the context it needed, and the promised destiny gave it purpose.[1] To have given growth specificity in such a wilderness would

have been unnecessary peroration. Odes to the openness of both land and future (space and time) permeate the literature, folk and otherwise, of this country. The extent to which this view continues to dominate American self-consciousness can be seen in the fact that even as John F. Kennedy sought in his new frontier to redefine frontier in nonspatial terms, he seemed driven, either by his own perception of the nature of America or by political expediency (and it does not much matter for our purposes) to give the frontier a new, boundless spatial dimension in the space program.

3. Into boundless space came a people who were not only fleeing illegitimate external restraint but who were also driven by the mind and heart of Puritanism. Without Puritanism the new land deemed destinous might well not have been so blatantly defined in religious terms (the new Israel, the Holy Commonwealth where the Kingdom of God would be realized in history), but that is not the central point here. Whether in its religious or secularized forms, Puritanism gave rise to an ethic that measured the timbre of the person by his or her diligence, self-reliance, sobriety, punctuality, promise keeping, thriftiness, and willingness to work hard. And again, whether religiously or secularly conceived, meritocracy—the judging of worth and status by observable achievement—had virtually to fill the gap left by the discarded aristocracy.

But linked to the so-called minor but nevertheless operational and operative virtues of Puritanism were its "concepts of vocation," which at once bred in an imperative to civic responsibility and then differentiated the modes of fulfilling that responsibility according to the societal sector or arena (order of creation, if you will) into which one was called. The general virtues were specified, then, in terms of their arena of application. If one's place was the marketplace, one worked hard, honestly, punctually, in terms of the principles of practice operative there. Because the mark of success there was an increase in wealth, accumulation of capital signified rectitude, moral or religious. The gospel of wealth that reemerged in more virulent form in the late nineteenth and early twentieth centuries did not need social Darwinism (although it used it) to validate its basic principle. It needed only to remind Americans of their most basic Puritan beliefs. In a recent article, Henry Steele Commager suggests that this country's continuing inability to come to grips with the runaway giant corporations is partly derivative of the inability of Americans to believe that financial success can be explained as anything but the just desserts of the employment of the old economic virtues.

If an increase of wealth is a measure of this sort, then its relation to the foregoing factors in contributing to a weltanschaaung where growth is a primary instrumental value begins to emerge. A dynamic society untrammeled by Old World patterns and functioning in a context of unlimited resources will find it quite unthinkable to achieve social amelioration by redistributing goods and services by taking from some to give to others; it will come only by pressing on to the creation of more wealth (ostensibly through the conversion of more people to the Puritan ethic). Growth, then, becomes the sign of individual rectitude, and the sum of those who attain affluence measures the extent to which the society as a whole is fulfilling its destiny, not simply in material but also in moral terms.

4. If the Puritan ethic made growth the means and the measure for personal-moral reasons, the influence of English rationalism made it requisite for political-ethical reasons. The task of the framers of the Constitution was to create a framework of institutions that were weak and diverse enough to prohibit the evolution of those Old World establishments (church, state, military) from which the new nation had just extricated itself but would nevertheless be strong enough to protect the natural rights of man that had been the clarion call of the Revolution—"life, liberty and the pursuit of happiness" for all. Understandably, concern for individual liberty dominated these considerations, but it should not be overlooked that in part because they were a means to both life and liberty and in part because they were themselves a "natural right," property rights were perhaps the most important factor in actually shaping most of the institutional arrangements. Distributive justice was, accordingly, a secondary consideration. It is impossible to overemphasize the role of John Locke's thought in these considerations and in two others that were of paramount importance: (1) the concerns of justice in relation to the distribution of property were exhausted when it could be determined that all parties had had an equal chance to amass wealth (in sum, that equality of opportunity—fairness—rather than patterns of distribution—e.g., equally or "according to need"—was the concern of justice); and (2) in the economic sphere, active pursuit of one's own self-interest would lead to the appropriation of land, which would "increase the common stock of mankind." Although Locke's sympathies with mercantilism made

him a somewhat dubious guide to American economic policy, it was also the dominant view among both English rationalists and French physiocrats that if economic self-interest were permitted to proceed untrammeled by governmental meddling (except for the protection of property rights), the resultant sum and distribution of goods and services would be improved. When in 1776 Adam Smith said in his instantaneously influential *Wealth of Nations* that as every individual intends only his own gain" he is in this, as in many other cases, led by an invisible hand to promote an end which was no part of his intention," he spoke not only of the total economic revenue, but of its more adequate allocation.

Although he was no lover of luxurious consumption (by rich or poor), Smith's theory nevertheless had growth in both population and national income as its basic presupposition because he calculated growth to be the only effective means of securing full employment and high per capita wages for the poor without abrogating the natural right not to be interfered with, a right that included the maintenance of property rights.

It is hard to imagine a doctrine more perfectly suited to the requirements of the Constitution makers than this one. If they could simply locate economic enterprises in the American scheme of things so as to prevent them from becoming monopolistic (state incorporation was the device erroneously chosen), make property rights inviolable, and in other ways construct government to protect liberty, they could simply allow man's own economic self-interest to drive the economy toward an acceptable distribution of resources (automatically, in a way that would enhance equal opportunity and individually determined pursuit of happiness) and simultaneously provide the wherewithal for national security. Growth in population and income, which was the necessary operating requirement for this happy automatic mechanism for attaining these diverse desired ends, had again proved to be a welcome and costless process. That Madison shared this view with Smith, or derived it from him, is evident in the following statement to the first Constitutional Congress:

> I hold it as truth that the commercial shackles are generally unjust, oppressive and impolitic; it is also a truth that if industry and labor are left to their own course, they will generally be directed to those objects which are the most productive, and this

in a more certain and direct manner than the wisdom of the most enlightened Legislature could point out.

5. The final factor we will consider is the most vague, the most difficult to link concretely to growth, and the one about which I am least certain. I sense that it may, however, be the most important. By the middle of the eighteenth century a combination of a series of startling scientific discoveries on the one hand and a tradition of British empiricism that culminated in Hume on the other had begun to undermine, even in the common mind, the Western tradition's assumption that one could make inferences from "present space-time" to other "regions of space-time"—(the phrases are Whitehead's in *Science and the Modern World*)—from one order of being to another —because the universe could be reduced to its materiality. But in addition, the flow of thought that began with the assertion that everything in the universe could be explained in terms of the motion of inanimate objects, mechanistically related, ended with Hume in the disturbing conclusion that no causal relationships of any sort could be unequivocally justified (in Whitehead's terms, "nothing in the present fact inherently refers to past or future"). While Hume's own epistemological conclusions were not widely influential, they were indirectly so in that they shook Immanuel Kant from his dogmatic slumbers and were the catalyst for that most important modern philosophical development, the Copernican revolution. This revolution, in turn, made possible an intellectual climate that permitted both American romanticism's love affair with nature and the continuance of America's estimation of itself as an event of moral and transcendent importance to exist in a world (and more particularly a nation) that was feverishly engaged in bringing about industrial and technological developments of the nineteenth century.

How could any philosophical event have this importance? In one swift turn and many pages of specious argumentation, Kant broke the phenomenal world from the noumenal one and gave back to the former the causal certainty Newton had assumed but Hume had destroyed. At the same time, it provided the latter (the real world, the *ding-an-sich*) "room" for all manner of moral, theological, and teleological explanations. Kant, in sum, robbed materialism of its omnipotence but provided it the coherence it needed. In doing so he offered an intellectually satisfying rationale that allowed there to be logically independent "causalities" to explain the same events but that, nevertheless, did not deny those causalities their ultimate interdependence.

There were many consequences of this tour-de-force, which deserve attention (for example, the way in which it permitted history to replace nature as the primary category of interpretation). But for our purposes its importance is that it freed inquiry for the divergent but related interpretations of "higher" causalities found in Schleiermacher, Fichte, Schlegel, Hegel, Coleridge, and Carlyle. Although both the natural theologies (secular and religious) of the early nineteenth century and the ethically based theologies of the late nineteenth and early twentieth centuries were frequently more dependent on these figures than on Kant himself, it was Kant's dualism that permitted the simultaneous (sometimes grudging) acceptance of mechanistically premised technological advances even as those advances were being "transcended" by the teleological and moral interpretations of the world and America's place in it. Hence, railroads slashed across a spiritualized wilderness, but on Sunday engineers left the applied science that permitted the engines of industrial growth to churn even as they sang odes to the "real" causalities. It was precisely the logical independence but the ultimate interdependence of these realms that allowed material growth not only its unquestioned sanction but its unconsciously held priority in the world of time and space.

These five factors have not been unambiguously operative in recent American history. For example, the Puritan ethic has been under regular and increasing attack ever since the first debates that resulted at the turn of the century in labor legislation. Today differences over the value of "self-reliance and hard work" split the nation politically. Faith in the invisible hand has slowly given way as government has moved more directly into economic regulation and small-scale income redistribution. Positivism and pragmatism have radically undermined those views made possible by Kant's dualism. Tentative questioning of the assumption that the world's resources are in principle limitless has been underway for some time. (Malthus, of course, had raised the question some time earlier but got little hearing in this country.) But we have seen few indications that there is a corresponding questioning of the necessity for growth or of the assumption that it is the means of resolving our problems, whatever they may be at a particular time. Given the fact that the five factors we have discussed were present at the nation's creation or were shortly thereafter integrated into its weltanschaaung, such questioning literally had no point of entry. Parts of a world view may be questioned piecemeal but the basic suppositions of it do not come to light unless those parts are decisively rejected. Because this has not happened (at least until the 1970s) growth has never been subjected to the analysis that as I suggested in the introductory paragraphs, would normally be given to an instrumental value. America has not made growth intrinsically valuable; it has simply been committed, ideologically, to growth as the key means to attaining its most valued ends. Growth is built into the heart of America's institutional framework and of its peoples' impulse as to how to proceed as steel girders are built into the World Trade Center. As things now stand, to remove or weaken it without careful calculation of how growth's work can be done by other more complicated mechanisms would be to make American institutions into a house of cards. I challenge anyone to examine carefully *any* American institution, private or public, profit or nonprofit, and argue that its operations, purposes, and goals (if not its very existence) are not radically dependent upon growth (at least economic growth) either directly or indirectly. It is little wonder that prior to the 1970s no thoughtful American reformer (radical or moderate) who has valued any of this country's goals or achievements has ever questioned that America's ability to generate economic growth is one of the instruments he would use to build his better world.

III

We are prepared, finally, to answer some key questions:

• "What are the sources of growth as a value in America?" The combined sources of the American experience and purposes themselves.

• "How important has it been?" It has been the cement that has made all the other American values cohere.

• "Has an obsession with growth obscured other important values?" I doubt that it has been so much an obsession as it has been unexamined, taken for granted, and therefore been the value that has obscured the fact that many other American values, intrinsic, con-

tributary, and instrumental, are, in fact, rivalrous and would be seen
as such were it not for growth's promised ministrations.

• "If growth diminishes in importance, what other values are likely
to take its place?" It is to this question that I will turn in my concluding
remarks. But I would formulate the question in another way: "If
growth per se is, in fact, the means to destruction rather than the
omnicompetent mechanism for obtaining the diverse ends that undergird the American faith, how do we proceed?" (I have thus far held in
check the tendency to moralize, which is an occupational hazard of my
trade, but I fear that I will not be so successful in these final pages.)

The no-growth advocates among us have answered the "how do we
proceed" question quite straightforwardly. If it is unexamined growth
that causes us to avert our eyes from the disaster toward which growth
itself speeds us, then growth per se must be dethroned. But an attack
on growth per se can take two quite different forms, only one of which
is, I think, worthy. These forms can be stated in two different propositions:

1. "Growth as a value per se must be dethroned." Sometimes
advocates of this view seem to argue their case in the following way: If
growth per se is the instrument of our common destruction, no-growth
per se is eo ipso the means of our common salvation.

But the position need not be stated so naively. A more modest form
is that if growth per se destroys, then any time growth is rejected as a
value, in any context, the stranglehold it now has on the culture is
loosened and a gain for societal sanity is made. It is this view that seems
to lead the authors of *The Limits of Growth* to applaud the several
instances where a group or governmental unit has called a halt to
growth in areas over which they have jurisdiction. The fact that in at
least one of the instances cited the locality is attempting to protect its
affluent life-style against the projected deleterious effects of in-
migration and industrial expansion, but without any effort to reduce
the societal pressures which will cause that growth to occur elsewhere,
is ignored.

2. "Growth per se as a value must be dethroned because the role
this value plays in the culture is to keep in operation a set of assumptions about the world (its limitlessness) and many of its values (they
may be reconciled without alteration) that are dubious if not falla-

cious." This is the view that seems to be held by economist Herman Daly who recognizes the complexities involved in establishing new institutions in a stationary-state economy that will serve competing ends (e.g., liberty and distributive justice). But Daly is driven by his analysis of the role that a single-minded focus on GNP increase plays, to the conclusion that strategically the first task is to "blow the whistle on growthmania."[2] The most basic question for him is which sectors should be allowed to grow and which reduced in size within the context of an economic equilibrium.

There is all the difference in the world between these two propositions. The first ("growth as a value per se must be dethroned") leads to tunnel vision and back toward precisely the kinds of assumed synergisms that have led to our present dilemmas. The second, ("growth per se as a value must be dethroned"), however, might help us remove the ideological scales from our eyes and, hopefully, put us to work on the hard questions that we have thus far averted in this country. Is it possible to give substantive, not merely procedural, definitions of justice and liberty, or rights as distinguished from privileges (in sum, to actually differentiate human wants from human needs)? Is it possible to chart carefully the present and projected results of specific types of growth and the actual effects on the environment and for people of no-growth or reduced growth limitations on specific resources[3] in relation to the new definitions just mentioned? Is it possible to model new and innovative institutional formats and interrelationships that will be required under no-growth conditions of various sorts but will meet some substantive definitions of human needs?

In a radically pluralistic world and culture, such tasks may seem utopian. In 1787, when the world was much simpler, they seemed utopian to the most able statesmen ever to be gathered together in one place at one time—hence, as we have seen, they determined to follow the best available intelligence and let growth fill in the blanks. Now the question is, When does the bank declare bankruptcy? Assuming that the apocalypse is not already upon us (in which case, the issues that this volume is discussing are, in effect, superfluous), the task that the Constitutional framers did not undertake must be ours. But it will be undertaken only if we manage to ignore our impulse to exchange one ideological commitment to a single instrumental value for a similar type of commitment to another.

38

NOTES

1. It is noteworthy that prior to introducing money into his discussions of "property," Locke justifies his doctrine of limited appropriation by arguing that "full as the world seems," it remains true that we can find "enough and as good" in "some in-land, vacant places of America." Henry Ward Beecher still sang this song centuries later when castigating the poor: "No man in this land suffers from poverty unless it be more than his fault—unless it be his sin. There is enough and thrice over."

2. Herman Daly, "Toward a Stationary State-Economy," in *Patient Earth*, ed. John Harte and Robert H. Socolow (New York: Holt, Rinehart and Winston, 1971), p. 241. Even though Daly seems to be among the advocates of no growth most sensitive to the issues we are raising, he is nevertheless a victim of "invisible-handamania" himself when he asserts that the redistribution of resources that he favors will occur almost by itself if growth as a value disappears: "How will it be distributed, if not according to some ethical norm of equality?" Ibid., p. 237. The pages of world history seem to offer little evidence that in the absence of a morally acceptable alternative, redistribution occurs or that when faced with the task of devising a rationale for privilege, the human imagination is found wanting.

3. Recent efforts by the Environmental Protection Agency are partial steps in this direction, but in the absence of precise definitions, careful measurement of pollution levels are pitted against almost intuitive judgments about specific policy efforts on persons in various economic brackets.

Part II

Growth as an Issue

Walt W. Rostow

UNIVERSITY OF TEXAS, AUSTIN

4
Economic Growth: Past and Future

I

The notion that regular economic growth is possible is relatively new in the sweep of human history. Down to, say, the seventeenth century in Western Europe, men thought that the cycle around some relatively static norm was man's fate as a social animal, whether in the life of families or great empires. There were norms for good times often drawn from the memory of golden eras of the past when the frontiers were quiet, crops ample, taxes modest, the bureaucracy uncorrupt, state granaries full, the roads free of bandits, and (where relevant) the irrigation works well maintained. Rulers were assessed, in part, against such standards. But the society was not expected to yield a regularly rising standard of life for the people as a whole. Men accepted, more or less, Anaximander's dictum: "It is necessary that things should pass away into that from which they were born." Or, more explicitly, the great Berber historian ibn-Khaldun: "Several rulers, men of great prudence in government, seeing the accidents which have led to the decay of their empires, have sought to cure the state and restore it to normal health. They think that this decay is the result of incapacity or negligence in their predecessors. They are wrong. These accidents are inherent in empires and cannot be cured."

What changed all this was the convergence of the rise of nation-states and the policies of mercantilism, the commercial revolution, and the scientific revolution. It is the last, in all its complex ramifications,

41

that was new in the mind of man and on the face of the earth: the philosophic notion that the laws of nature were few and knowable and that they were tools for man to use to exercise control over his environment; the method of systematic experiment, linking scientists and tool makers; and the Baconian manifesto that science could be linked to invention, innovation, and economic progress. Out of this new and heady brew, interacting with the imperatives of mercantilism and the opportunities of the commercial revolution, came the industrial revolution and all that followed.

I underline this point because it was the possibilities of new technology rather than an increase in GNP that first seized the mind of modern man. And the first applications were not to increase human welfare but to increase the power of the state. The states of early modern Europe wanted an independent capacity to supply their ground and naval forces and reserves of bullion to fight wars. Mercantilist leaders like Lord Burleigh and Colbert focused on the task of increasing the power of their sovereigns. This derived demand led them to an interest in general economic expansion; and Colbert could urge peace as against Louvois, but only tactically, so he could have more time to build the economic foundations for the military power of Louis XIV.

I begin with these old times because economic growth, as measured by increases in GNP, was always and remains a highly abstract derived demand or result. In the United States, for example, Hamilton urged (and Jefferson ultimately accepted) industrialization to ensure the security of the United States, not merely its prosperity. And when public as well as private objectives shifted after 1815 to give greater weight to economic objectives, men did not seek growth; they sought concrete objectives. Before the Civil War they sought new lands to cultivate, cheaper cotton textiles, improved transport facilities. And they sought also, especially in the North, better schools for their children. After the Civil War, when the industrial system was elaborated, they accepted the fruits of the new technologies in steel, electricity, and chemicals, but they also insisted that this new heavily industrialized society be tamed by control over monopoly, concern for hours of work, and, ultimately, by the diversion of resources for welfare purposes to the state by that most revolutionary of measures, the progressive income tax. And, in Europe, starting with Bismarck, the legitimacy was accepted even earlier than in the United States of diverting large sums to programs of social insurance.

The measurement of national income in modern times arose, in fact, from a great problem of human welfare, not from a compulsive interest in growth rates. It was a by-product of the Keynesian revolution and a concern with massive unemployment. Ironically, the first exercise in the systematic control of effective demand (and the emergence of good national income data) was during World War II when the problem was inflation rather than unemployment; but we all moved on after the war to refine the tools and concepts required to maintain relatively steady levels of employment.

Something of an obsession with growth rates did arise in the 1950s from two quite different directions: the anxiety over the relative lag of U.S. behind Soviet rates of increase in GNP, underlined by Khrushchev's 1959 television talk to the American people, and, of course, efforts to measure the progress of the developing nations of Asia, the Middle East, Africa, and Latin America.

The measurement of overall growth, properly used, can be helpful. But as I argued when first presenting *The Stages of Economic Growth* fifteen years ago, it was not Soviet growth rates we had to fear but certain specific military dangers of the time; and the task for the West in the face of the Soviet challenge of the late 1950s lay, again, not in increasing our growth rates per se, but in dealing with our problems, including the further diffusion of welfare at home and assisting the developing world. As for the developing world, I concluded that as they moved forward their peoples "have the right to live their time in civilized settings, marked by a degree of respect for their uniqueness and dignity, marked by policies of balance in their societies, not merely a compulsive obsession with statistics of production."

I make this preliminary point to underline that when men have acted sensibly they have identified the problems they wished to solve; they mobilized the resources to solve those problems; and they let the GNP statistics add up to whatever the arithmetic yielded. In modern times, societies solving their problems reasonably well, using the technologies available and emerging, acted in ways that more or less regularly expanded the GNP and that had one clearly beneficial result —more funds flowed to public authorities from a given tax schedule. But the correct measure was always whether the society was dealing with or failing to deal with its agenda. GNP is too aggregate a measure, full of philosophic as well as statistical ambiguity, to serve as a touchstone for a society's performance.

This general proposition has a particular meaning in contemporary America and the world environment it confronts. We face simultaneously three phenomena, three massive problems. Our performance will be judged in the future on how well we deal with them, not on whether GNP increases regularly at 4 percent or 5 percent per annum or whether we go to zero growth. The three problems are: the transition from the stage of high mass consumption to the search for quality; the trend period we have entered as a world economy, involving the increased relative prices of certain basic commodities; and the reconciliation of the interests and objectives of the early and latecomers to industrialization in a long-term setting of finite physical resources. These problems interweave in complex ways, but I shall deal with them initially one at a time.

II

High mass consumption is the stage of growth driven forward by the diffusion of the automobile, durable consumer goods, and a suburban house to a high proportion of a nation's families. It arrives at a level of about $600 GNP per capita and persists over, perhaps, twenty years of prosperity. This stage dominated American growth in the 1920s and in the decade ending, say, in 1956. In the 1950s, as the United States was pushing high mass consumption to its limit as the basis for growth, western Europe and Japan moved fully into this stage. It is not a gross oversimplification to regard the remarkable postwar growth of western Europe and Japan as rooted in the achievement of levels of income per capita that released efficiently the stage of high mass consumption, with all its powerful spreading effects.

Putting wage-price policy aside, high mass consumption appears to create the least social tension and fewest political problems of all the stages of growth thus far experienced. It is not difficult to understand why. The affluent and sophisticated may deplore the automobile, the gadgetry of high mass consumption, and the suburban villa; but for those who have lived their lives in the narrow confines of working-class urban areas, all this means a great deal: the automobile gives a family long-range, flexible mobility; the electric refrigerator means a better and more varied diet; other household gadgetry reduces the drudgery of housework; to own a home, with a bit of grass and garden, is one of man's deepest and most abiding impulses.

High mass consumption is a real and positive social and human revolution; and while it extends to more and more of a nation's families, political tension tends to be low. The private sector is well equipped to do the job. In the past, it has sufficed in Western societies for the government to provide the roads and the suburban infrastructure required to permit high mass consumption to proceed.

But that has changed and is changing as some societies move beyond high mass consumption to a stage I call the search for quality. This new stage in North America and parts of western Europe dates from the 1960s. One can sense its coming in Japan of the early 1970s. Evidently we still have much to learn about its contours.

Although much more is involved in this stage than economics, it can be defined, like other stages of growth, in terms of key sectors with high momentum.

With respect to the disposal of private income, there appears to be a marked acceleration in outlays going to certain services—for example, in the United States outlays for medical services, foreign travel, education, religious and welfare purposes, and recreational equipment, from cameras and skis to motor boats.

On the public side, the central phenomenon is a rise in the proportion of GNP mobilized and dispersed by government—public outlays for education and medical services and for initiating the retrieval of capital lost or diminished in the form of air and water pollution and in the deterioratios of urban areas.

In the United States of the 1960s there was a remarkable, even revolutionary, shift of resources to the public sector at a time of high rates of growth, with the bulk of increased relative resources going to social services, which received 9.7 percent of GNP in 1959 and 14.2 percent in 1968, while security outlays declined marginally (11.0 percent to 10.7 percent of GNP).

The shift in the allocation of private and public outlays toward certain services has been accompanied by a searching debate on the underlying values that should control the societies of the future. Following the pattern described as far back as Book VIII of Plato's

Republic, men and women—especially affluent young men and women—have taken for granted, or reacted against, the setting to which they were born and explored objectives beyond. These have been years of criticism, confrontation, and experiment, a groping in private lives and public policies for human conditions of higher quality. Behind it all was a sense that the benefits conferred by the automobile, durable consumer goods, and living in suburbia were not enough and that man should release himself from the constraints of bureaucracy and technology.

In addition, old social problems assumed new and acute forms in a number of affluent societies. The most dramatic was, of course, the drive of the American Negro for full and unencumbered citizenship. But in Canada, Belgium, and northern Ireland the environment of spreading affluence also contributed to a new assertiveness by relatively disadvantaged segments of the population and produced demands for an altered political, social, cultural, and economic equilibrium. And, in one way or another, with more or less violence and pain, the more comfortable majorities recognized the legitimacy of these claims for equity and acquiesced, in degree at least.

To this inherently complex public agenda has been added in the United States two further problems, one domestic, the other international. At home there is evident tension between those who wish to push on with the public tasks of the search for quality and those who resent the consequent tax burden, as well as the change in social patterns and new experimental life-styles. Stages of growth are phenomena at the margin of societies; and, in this case, a substantial proportion of the American people is still focused on fulfilling the possibilities of high mass consumption—including, incidentally, most of the Negro population. The arrival of this stage in the United States at a time when Europe and Japan were coming to command fully the technologies of the previous stage, led to a second problem: a deterioration in the American trade balance. The growing services of the search for quality did not generate technological advantages capable of enlarging exports to compensate for the new virtuosity of Europe and Japan in automobiles, electronics, and metalworking. This pressure should ease as they, too, move into the search for quality; but the era of automatic, large U.S. trade surpluses is over, and we are not yet in control of a transitional problem that has shaken the international monetary system.

III

At just this time when American society was experiencing the problems and possibilities, domestic tensions, and international constraints
of the search for quality, the world economy as a whole hit what is
likely to prove to be a major inflection point in its evolution. A variety
of forces converged to produce a relative rise in the prices of foodstuffs, sources of energy, and raw materials, as, concurrently, it
became apparent that men would have to invest heavily to maintain
reasonably clean air and water, which were taken virtually for granted
in the first two centuries of industrialization.

Although there is much unique about the present situation, it bears
a family relation to inflection points that have occurred at four other
times in modern history. Phases of relatively increasing prices of
foodstuffs and raw materials came at intervals of forty or fifty years: in
the early 1790s, the mid-1840s, the mid-1890s, and the mid-1930s.
They reached peaks and gave way to phases of relatively cheap prices
of basic commodities in 1815, 1873, 1920, and 1951. The upward
phases in these long cycles or trend periods were affected by wars; but
there was more to it than that. The first reflected the rise of European
population in the latter part of the eighteenth century; the second,
once again, a catching up of European populations with existing
acreage and agricultural technology, leading to the great thrust to open
up the grain fields of the American Midwest in the 1850s and after the
Civil War; the third, the rise of American as well as European population, requiring the development of increased food supplies from
Canada and Argentina, the Ukraine, and Australia; the fourth, the
constraints on production induced by the long agricultural depression
after 1920 (including reduced U.S. farm acreage), followed by the
prewar economic expansion and war itself. In the two decades after the
opening of Korean peace negotiations, by and large foodstuff and raw
material prices were relatively cheap. The American farmer's parity
ratio (prices received relative to prices paid by farmers) fell from 107 in
1951 to a low point of 70 in 1971. It was 78 by mid-December 1972,
102 by mid-August 1973. For a generation we heard laments as well as
reasonably sophisticated arguments from representatives of Latin
America (and other developing areas) on the inherent inequity of the
terms of trade between industrial and agricultural products. In 1972
there was a 13 percent rise in Latin American export prices, an 8

percent increase in the purchasing power of exports in terms of imports. This trend accelerated in 1973.

One should not expect the dramatic changes that have been occurring since 1971 to persist at steady rates. As in the past, the trend period I suspect we have entered will not unfold smoothly or continuously. All farm and raw material prices will not move at the same rates or even in the same directions. There will be good and lean monsoons in India; ample, poor, and mediocre harvests in the Soviet Union and China. But the inexorable pressure of excessive population increase, the rising demand for grain-expensive proteins, the pace of industrialization among those catching up, and the strains of the energy crisis will persist. Given the nature of the forces operating on food, energy, and raw material prices and the costs we shall have to incur to achieve and maintain clean air and water, I am inclined to believe we are in for a long pull when the prices of these basic commodities will remain relatively high.

In other trend period upswings there have been changes in the economic environment of a quite consistent kind. Interest rates and profits have risen, as well as the overall price level; farmers were relatively prosperous; but the rising cost of living exerted severe pressure on the real income of the urban worker. For example, real wages stagnated or declined in Britain, the United States, and Germany under the trend period pressures of the pre-1914 generation. In addition, patterns of investment changed. Historically, in the period 1790 to 1914, the classic response was to open up new agricultural and raw material producing areas. The great movements of international capital during this era were, in effect, designed to help bring new supplies into the market. And surely, now, there will be an intensified search for additional supplies of gas and oil, an expansion in coal mining, and, perhaps, the bringing into production of agricultural land hitherto regarded as submarginal. But the cleaning of the air and water will require intensive rather than extensive investment; and before we have come to the other side of the energy crisis there will be large outlays to develop new technologies, as well as new energy sources. Moreover, a part of the response may well consist in reducing demand rather than increasing supply: smaller automobiles, mass transit economy in the use of electricity, and so on.

Behind all this are powerful forces operating on the world scene, which are beyond American control: the commitment of the Soviet government to its peoples to bring meat to their diet against the background of a low productivity agricultural system; the marginal position of the food-population balance in China; the failure of India and other Asian states (with a few notable exceptions) to bring down birth rates; the rapid industrial and urban expansion in large parts of the developing world, as well as the high momentum of Japan and western Europe; the virtually monopolistic position of the Middle East oil suppliers for a transitional period of considerable length until new technologies for energy production are developed.

In the trend period we are entering, the United States will benefit from its high productivity agriculture; from the bargaining power it enjoys as a large market for oil; and, if we are wise, from our capacity to generate and apply the new technologies that will be required to deal with energy and raw material problems. But as an essentially urban civilization we shall feel—as we are beginning to feel—the strains on real income that are inevitable in a world where food, raw materials, energy, air, and water are becoming more expensive.

To reconcile this economic environment with the continued search for a life of greater quality will not be easy. Think back, for a moment, to the more radical doctrines of the late 1960s. Some argued that we were a society in which scarcity was fabricated by our institutions. Affluence would be available to all if only we could cut our military budgets, release the people from the tyranny of advertising, tax the rich more vigorously, defend the environment from degradation. There was something in all this. Surely we do not want larger military budgets than we really need; advertising should be disciplined to some approximation of the truth; our tax structure falls short of what many of us would regard as equity, and I, at least, believe we require higher tax rates; the defense of the environment is not only a moral and aesthetic goal but an imperative for the survival of a decent urban civilization.

But what we have learned in the past few years—and, if I am right, we shall learn even more vividly in the time ahead—is that we are, in fact, not all that affluent; that scarcity has not been lifted from us and is unlikely to be lifted in the foreseeable future; that, like the rest of mankind, we shall have to examine our outlays at the margin, as we do in our private households. If the Brookings economists are right, the bill for decent standards will rise by 1980 to, say, $25 billion annually for water and $14 billion for air, as opposed to the $4 billion applied to control pollution in 1970. The calculus between energy requirements and environmental goals is also real. We shall have to weigh those objectives at the margin, for the conflict will not go away by wishing it nor be resolved by rhetoric. We have seen the shadow of an even more fundamental marginal decision: with food prices rising at home, should we embargo exports in a world where our exports to some nations may mean the difference between life and death for human beings? Meanwhile, we must pay our way in the world—including a mounting bill for imported oil—and meet our obligations to collective security and to the development of the latecomers to modern growth.

IV

Looking ahead, the most searching international task we face—and this includes Japan and western Europe—is our common relations with the parts of the world that have come late to the industrial revolution. The problem here is a long-range version of that we are beginning to feel in energy, food, and raw materials. It is the problem posed in *The Limits to Growth* and other projections that demonstrate that trees do not grow to the sky.[1] Although I am fully aware of its technical inadequacies and the lack of data to fill the terms of its equations, I have not joined in criticisms of *The Limits to Growth* for a particular reason. To achieve the kind of international cooperation required to deal with the tasks ahead will require profound adjustments in the way men and governments think and act. And this takes time. With all its weaknesses, *The Limits to Growth* has made a contribution to that change in perspective. Surely the long-run task will be to find the way to some more or less stable but dynamic equilibrium between man and his physical environment; and we must do so after two centuries of relatively uninhibited expansion in population and production, with all the habits of mind and action that experience carried with it. Surely, it is possible, if we are not wise, to produce yet another grandiose cycle in man's affairs and so act as to disintegrate the industrial civilizations we have built. And surely, to avoid that outcome we must design policies that permit the latecomers to move forward for a time as the presently more advanced societies go about dealing with the tasks of the search for quality.

In confronting together these questions, the nations that entered industrialization earlier and later each have serious grounds for complaint against one another. The latecomers can complain of the profligate use of finite natural resources in the past by the more advanced and their current disproportionate absorption of such resources. As representatives of the less industrialized nations stare at the computer readouts, they are bound to ask: Why should we be denied the stage of high mass consumption, whose costs and limitations are mainly perceived by those who take its blessings for granted, and denied also the uncertain adventure of experimenting with high levels of per capita income beyond?

The more advanced nations also have cause for complaint. The latecomers have eagerly absorbed the benefits of modern medicine and public health, but they have been extremely laggard in investing political, administrative, and physical capital in measures of population control. Some, indeed, have looked to vast increases in population as a future source of power in the world. Why should the more advanced nations permit themselves to be dragged down by such undisciplined self-indulgence?

Now, in fact, the world is not neatly divided, as conventional rhetoric suggests, between rich and poor nations. The so-called developing nations lie along a wide spectrum, whether that spectrum is defined in terms of the measurable but ambiguous index of GNP per capita or the harder-to-measure but more basic index of the degree to which they have absorbed efficiently the pool of modern technology. It is a long stretch from Yemen or even Haiti to Argentina, Brazil, and Mexico; and there is a sense in which India and China (at not much more than $100 per capita) are technologically more advanced than Venezuela (at, say, $1,000 per capita). Moreover, the incidence of the relative shortage of foodstuffs and raw materials will vary: some developing nations will, on balance, benefit from the agricultural and raw material resources they command; others will suffer from rising import prices, if not absolute shortages.

Nevertheless, despite these real complexities, there is latent in the world as it is a most dangerous potential confrontation between the more developed and less developed nations as they come to perceive the limits within which they will both have to work out their destinies: the more developed confronting the possibility of absolute reductions in income per capita; the less developed, the possibility that tragedy and decline might well set in before they attain the levels of western

Europe, North America, and Japan. As these shadows fall over the minds of men, we could see emerge a desperate scramble in a more intense version of the mercantilist spirit as nations once again contest for sources of foodstuffs and raw materials and markets. In a nuclear age the outcome of such a return to a kind of last ditch mercantilism could bring with it catastrophe greater, even, than that the semiknowledgeable computers project from the present pace of population increase, industrialization, and pollution.

It will evidently take a remarkable and sustained effort by men and governments at different stages of growth to avoid such catastrophe and find the terms of cooperation that will permit them to bring the human race from where it is to a relatively stable, if dynamic, relationship to its physical environment. Such terms, if they are found, must evolve from protracted joint study of the facts. The only procedural rule that has a chance of taking the human race through in reasonable safety is Jean Monnet's dictum for Europe and the Atlantic: "Bring men together to examine and solve a common problem, not to negotiate." But, also, there will—and must—be negotiations, as there have been in the West.

To advance the argument and reveal some of the issues, it may be useful to set down in a tentative and preliminary way some principles that might hold the human community together as it seeks both equity and balance.

Principle 1: The object of national and international policy is to yield by, say, the middle of the twenty-first century a situation where each of the world's citizens can enjoy on a long-term basis adequate supplies of food, full health services, the opportunity for the maximum education his talents permit, and the major amenities an industrial civilization can provide.

It would be conventional to express an objective of this kind in terms of projected or target figures for income or GNP per capita. If, for example, no Malthusian or Ricardian restraints were assumed and average GNP per capita moved for another half-century at current rates, average GNP per capita for the presently less developed world would be about 2,000 1965 dollars per capita by the mid-twenty-first century. That would be a quite comfortable figure, capable of meeting, under appropriate public policies, the objectives of the first principle. But GNP per capita, as conventionally calculated, has always been a somewhat overstated way to define standards of life. Technically, GNP includes some outputs as final products that should be treated as costs or intermediate products.

There is a second problem: GNP per capita is affected not only by the degree to which a society has modernized—that is, absorbed efficiently the pool of modern technology—but also by its endowment of good land and natural resources. Libya, for example, is a very rich but not very modern society. In ways only a little less dramatic, differences in natural endowment affect regional income per capita within national societies; and these regional differences can stubbornly persist over long periods, despite public policies designed to even things up—for example, in Britain, the United States, Canada, France, and the Soviet Union.

Third, there are relatively unexplored problems of choice. Thus far nations have chosen to allocate the increments of income provided by modern technology in relatively uniform ways, aside from the implicit decision of many of the presently developing nations to permit death rates to fall without prompt compensatory efforts to bring down birth rates. There is a rough-and-ready typical pattern one can discern in consumption outlays, urbanization, education, communications, and social services as income per capita rises.

But the average pattern from the past and present could be altered by public policy, as individual deviations already suggest. For example, more resources could be allocated at earlier stages to education and health, as certain developing nations now do, more resources might be allocated to rendering rural life more attractive, more severe constraints could be imposed on the diffusion of the private automobile.

It is particularly important that we pierce the veil and reduce the tyranny of GNP per capita measurements because we are assuming in this exercise a situation where the world community will be prepared to invest greatly enlarged resources in reducing birth rates, avoiding natural resource bottlenecks, and controlling pollution. All this will be reflected in conventional GNP calculations; but a goal of GNP per capita clearly does not suffice. The objective is a high and increasingly uniform level of human amenities capable of being sustained for long periods; and we have no simple measure for that objective. Thus, the formulation of Principle 1.

Principle 2: The reduction of birth rates so as to yield some low and agreed standards for population increase must become urgently an explicit objective of national and international policy.

This is, of course, fundamental. But it will be intellectually as well as politically difficult, as the June 1972 Stockholm meeting on the environment suggested. Here are some of the questions a global meeting of population experts, representing national governments, would have to try to answer:

- Should the long-term goal be zero population growth? Low, but positive (say 1 percent)? Or a planned population decline? Our present knowledge of resource constraints and technological possibilities is not sufficient to provide a dogmatic answer, except that radical reductions in the present global rates must be sought.
- Must population rates be reduced in the developed as well as the developing countries? Obviously the great problem lies in the developing nations where it is calculated an additional 2.6 billion will emerge between 1965 and 2000, as opposed to about a sixth of this number in the developed world (430 million); and this latter figure may prove higher than the outcome, given recent birth rate movements in the United States and the Soviet Union. Nevertheless, equity may require that the developed nations also accept policies of population constraint, since, at their present levels of raw material utilization, population expansion might further disproportionately narrow the global raw materials base. Moreover, we may well have to buy time for science and technology to generate new energy sources, raw material substitutes, and conservation measures.
- What about "empty" countries? There is still arable land to absorb population increase on a national basis in a few areas, for example, Brazil, the eastern slopes of the Andes, Australia, parts of Africa. Must these nations also accept policies of population constraint? Here again, as with the developed nations, wisdom and global equity may counsel universal acceptance of policies of population constraint. With respect to "empty" countries the case could be argued on three grounds: a slower rather than faster development of arable land would stretch out the global resource base; population increase permitted now, for whatever reason,

will translate itself later into demands on limited raw material supplies as industrialization and pollution proceed; and, in fact, the increase in population is likely to end up not on "empty" lands but in the already hard-pressed cities.

● In the critical case of birth rates in the developing world, what are the responsibilities that the developing and developed nations must assume? Governments in the developing nations must be prepared to invest vastly more political, administrative, and physical capital in pursuit of policies of population control. These might include negative as well as positive incentives; for example, regressive taxation on families above a certain size. On the other hand, the developed nations, which command greater pools of technology, research talent, and capital, have equal responsibilities: to develop more effective, cheaper, and more easily acceptable methods of birth control and to reward developing nations that have lower birth rates with enlarged flows of capital for economic and social development.

Principle 3: Despite the uncertainty of particular calculations, we must begin to act on the working hypothesis that raw material and energy scarcities are real and present global dangers.

Here past experience would appear to justify some optimism. Breeder reactors are within reach; fusion power is a reasonable possibility; cheap energy would make lower-grade natural resources more economically accessible. In general, man's ingenuity and enterprise have responded in the past rather sensitively to signals of shortage generated in the international price system. The optimists (for example, Norman Macrae in the London *Economist*, January 22, 1972) rely heavily on this historic response. And in this matter an economic historian like myself is, instinctively, an optimist. He knows of too many times in the past when Ricardian and Malthusian fears gripped men's minds only to be lifted by new resource discoveries, invention, and innovation. But optimism does not justify complacency or inaction because the price system is unlikely to do the job by itself. A good deal of the incentive and financing of research and development in recycling and other conservation measures will require government action and support. At this stage, the developed nations must, evidently, assume primary responsibility for generating the technologies and launching policies that would provide whatever economies in use, substitution, recycling, and other measures of resource conservation may permit.

The advanced nations would also have to assume responsibility for diffusing the relevant technologies (and experience with conservation policies) to the less developed. As with measures of population control, developing countries that undertook internationally responsible measures would develop a claim for increased capital assistance.

In this area, generalization can only suggest broad guidelines. What is needed is a series of international studies of the major commodity groups (including energy sources), subgroups, and key individual commodities that would explore likely future demand and supply, possible substitutes, and methods of conservation. National and international policies cannot be applied to "raw materials" on a shotgun basis.

Until such studies are carried out (we are getting a pretty good feel for the energy problem), we are justified in concern; but we are in no position to assess the problem's weight and the direction and scope for remedy.

There is another quite possibly critical saving factor we shall gradually have to assess: the tendency of high income per capita societies to shift from high rates of growth in automobiles and durable consumer goods to education, health, recreation, travel, etc. The latter lay less heavy burdens on raw material supply. It is even possible, as income per capita continues to rise in the developed nations, that an increased proportion of that potential will be taken in leisure, although that time may be further off than we sometimes think.

Principle 4: Despite the limited knowledge of pollution we now command, we must begin to act on the working hypothesis that present patterns of agricultural and industrial development, projected on the scale implicit in current rates of economic growth and population increase, carry with them potentially mortal dangers to the environment and its ability to sustain likely levels of population.

If uncertainty surrounds the prospects for raw materials, a good deal of simple ignorance surrounds the question of pollution. The critical throttling role of pollution in future projections arises from its believed relation to future levels of chemical-intensive agriculture and industrialization, combined with the projected cost of antipollution measures.

In dealing with the pollution problems of the industrialized world, as we are beginning to do, we ought to learn about both the relevant technologies and their costs. As with resource conservation measures, these ought to be made available to the developing nations, with increased capital assistance granted to those pursuing internationally responsible policies.

Principle 5: The population, raw material, and pollution prospects ahead strengthen the already overwhelming case for concerted international measures of arms control and disarmament.

Substantial proportions of national product are now diverted to military purposes: the U.S.S.R., about 10 percent; the United States, 7 percent; western Europe, 4 percent; Asia, over 3 percent; the Middle East, 9 percent or more; Africa, over 2 percent; Latin America, 1.5 percent. These establishments, their maintenance and modernization, lay a heavy claim on scarce raw materials and, for less developed nations, on foreign exchange required for other purposes. They also divert scarce research and development talent, as well as capital, from the population control, raw material conservation, and antipollution measures required to achieve global equilibrium.

To state these five principles baldly is to dramatize the gap between where we are and where we may have to be to achieve in the next half-century a tolerable and equitable adjustment. But a half-century is not much time; and we had better be up and doing. I do not expect us to act promptly and immediately as a cooperative global community. The impact of environmental constraints will not be uniform among the various nations of the world. To take marginal cases, parts of the world (for example, the Calcutta area) are right now almost strangling in the grip of the kind of pressures *The Limits to Growth* predicts for us all in a century, while Kuwait enjoys a population-resource balance that would appear to leave the skies clear for a long time. One of the great weaknesses of *The Limits to Growth* is its failure to disaggregate its equations on a national and regional basis. Moreover, politically and psychologically, nationhood and sovereignty are deeply rooted. They will, despite the conventional rhetoric of international conferences, yield only slowly and, perhaps, after a sequence of tragic but educational crises to a global perspective. But that is the direction in which we shall have to move, sooner or later, and one would hope it will be soon.

V

In the end, my point is quite simple: we shall go forward in the search for quality in a medium- and long-term environment of struggle to deal with international constraints on resources. To master those constraints and generate a viable and equitable long-term balance between man and his physical environment, a great deal of new technology will have to be developed and applied, new resources found and brought into production. As the estimated costs of dealing with air and water pollution reveal, all this will be expensive. It will generate employment and income. I would guess our GNP, conventionally measured, will continue to rise in the United States for a long time. For not the first time, but paradoxically, the leading sectors in growth may be those induced by the need to achieve balance.

Politically, as these basic household tasks are confronted, we in the United States shall have to act increasingly as a community—as a continental small town, dealing with the agenda together, ensuring that its burdens and rewards are equitably shared. And the same spirit will have to suffuse the international community if it is to avoid a mercantilist fragmentation or gross failure of the modernization process that emerged after long incubation at the end of the eighteenth century.

What about a larger issue raised by the concept of the search for quality? Why should not men and women opt out of this hardpressed, complex, highly technological, bureaucratized society and retreat to self-sufficient farming, making pottery, or other pursuits where human beings can enjoy being alive with a greater sense of control over their own destinies? That is a perfectly decent option which every individual has a right to examine and choose for himself. If a statistically high proportion of the population selected that option, our civilization would, of course, profoundly change. But I doubt that this will happen. The challenge of seeing what kind of organized life man can build in the wake of high mass consumption probably will continue to engage most men and women in western Europe, North America, and Japan; the challenge of achieving industrial civilizations, rooted in their own cultures, guided by their own ambitions, will continue to engage most men and women in the developing regions of the world; the effort will be made to find the terms on which the human community can achieve an equitable balance. Success in none of these enterprises is assured. But in seeking to move toward these goals, men and women will do things that will cause the statistics of GNP to continue to rise for a long time ahead. As I indicated at the beginning, however, that, by itself, is not a highly significant conclusion.

NOTES

1. Donella Meadows, Dennis L. Meadows, Jorgen Randers, and William W. Behrens III, *The Limits to Growth* (New York: Universe Books, 1972).

Henry C. Wallich
FEDERAL RESERVE BOARD

5
Economic Growth
in America

Economic growth has been a continuing process since the North
American continent began to be settled by immigrants some 350 years
ago. Interaction of population growth with a rich supply of natural
resources and capital has made the presence of growth clearly visible at
all times. The American experience contrasts in this with that of
Europe, where before and even after the Industrial Revolution contemporary observers might often have been unaware of the underlying
growth tendency. In the United States, it would have been difficult to
interpret the process of industrialization as implying a continuing
deterioration in the position of labor, as the equivalent British process
did in the eyes of Marx.

The evolving American condition was perceived, of course, not as
"growth" but as "progress." Progress has many dimensions. It clearly
contains the qualitative elements that today are seen to be lacking in
growth. By definition, progress is good. Growth recently has come
under increasing challenge.

The advent of the growth concept has split progress into its quantitative and qualitative components. For the purpose of economic
analysis, this is a step forward. In the dimension measured by output,
progress has become quantifiable. The growth component of progress,
to be sure, is not completely unambiguous. There can be aggregate
growth of output without per capita growth if population is increasing
at the same rate. Growth may have costs in terms of damage to the
environment, consumption of irreplaceable resources, disamenities of

industrial life, and so on. Growth not only differs from progress; it can differ also from welfare.

An effort to translate growth into welfare recently was undertaken by James Tobin and William Nordhaus.[1] In their study, the authors adjusted the conventional GNP downward for the creation of dis-amenities, for the using up of irreplaceable natural resources, and for a variety of other costs. They also adjusted it upward, however, for the increase in leisure time that has come with a rising per capita income. The authors did not attempt to qualify qualitative changes in the content of output. Automobile and airplane travel, radio and television, paperbacks and long-playing records may or may not be progress, but in the Tobin-Nordhaus analysis they do not affect growth other than through their value added to the GNP.

The quantification of progress has been on the agenda of economics for a long time. The difficulties encountered along the way indicate the quality of the intellectual achievement that is represented by the conceptualization and measurement of the GNP. Marx was almost entirely nonquantitative. Schumpeter's process of "economic development" was quantitative in that it sought to analyze the sources and behavior of business cycles. But it was only after the GNP concept had been developed that it became possible to go beyond an "index of production" and to add up the infinite variety of output in a single number.

It was a fortunate coincidence that the development of GNP concepts and data matched so closely the major revolution in economic theory of the times—Keynes' *General Theory of Employment, Income and Money*. The components of GNP isolated by the national income accountants happen to be precisely those stressed by the new theory. An immediate quantification and testing of the theory thus became possible.

When economists first began to talk about GNP, it was clearly understood that GNP was not coextensive with welfare. In popular discussion, it was customary to add a caveat to that effect, much as newspapers would add a parenthetical definition ("the sum of all goods and services produced") when they used the term for a lay readership. Both economists and the press have meanwhile dropped their respective practices. In the case of the economists, it is difficult to say whether this occurred because the distinction was taken for granted or because it began to be lost from sight.

There can be little doubt that, particularly following the recession of 1957-1958, economists began to go overboard in their glorification of growth. In part this was a political response to the slow growth of the late 1950s, in part a reflection of the impact of Sputnik. The interest of less-developed countries in catching up helped to cast growth in the role of an all-absorbing goal at that time. Only a little earlier, "stability" had occupied center stage. The Employment Act of 1946, which still stands as the nation's statement of economic purposes, speaks of "maximum employment, production and purchasing power" and does not even mention the word "growth." It was only through subsequent reinterpretation that "maximum employment" has been identified with growth and "maximum purchasing power" with price stability. Explicit "growth" consciousness is a product of the 1950s and 1960s.

During this period of exaltation of the growth objective, the question was rarely asked whether the deliberate stimulation of growth, through the tax system, through fiscal and monetary policy, and other devices, represented rational policy. Nevertheless, the question did not remain unexamined insofar as it bears on intergenerational equity. In a growing economy, each generation is richer than its predecessor. Insofar as accelerated growth requires more saving out of present income in order to raise human and physical investment that will pay off only in the future, the present generation is reducing its consumption and welfare for the benefit of the next. So long as saving and investment decisions are made through the market, this process of intergenerational transfers may reflect each generation's notion of its own maximum welfare. Even then there may be factors external to the market process that might obstruct attainment of an optimal position. But when policies are deliberately directed toward accelerating the rate of growth beyond that which the market would produce, matters become far less certain. It is by no means to be taken for granted that very rapid growth maximizes the welfare particularly of the older members of the present generation.

Problems of this kind played an important role in the growth theorizing of the 1960s. Fundamentally, this theorizing involved the translation of the classical stationary state into a stationary model of stable and endless growth. While this brought interesting insights into the nature of the economic system, it unfortunately also distracted the attention of many theorists from more immediate problems. "Golden rules" of growth contributed little to solving the pressing problems of developing countries. The assumption, implicit in most of this theorizing, that all resources, including land, could be increased without diminishing returns so that ultimately growth became indentical with population growth, was seriously misleading. Here the new ideas about limits to growth have made a valuable point. But it is not only the environmentalists and Malthusians who have raised questions about eternal growth.

Even though progress was built firmly into the structure of American thought, economists as well as philosophers have always been aware of intellectual difficulties. Doubts whether the good life really consists of the acquisition of more material goods are traditional. In a more gloomy vein, the question has been asked whether the goodness of life can be increased at all in a society where individuals are greatly concerned with their position relative to each other. If satisfaction results not from one's absolute standard of living but from one's position in the income scale, there is no way for society as a whole to improve itself. The rise of any one of its members necessarily implies the descent of another. The American emphasis on keeping up with the Joneses makes this model less implausible than appears at first sight.

Although economists have been fascinated by the growth process, they have not typically seen in it the ultimate stage of economic life. In the past, on the contrary, that ultimate outcome has been the stationary state. In it, all forces of growth have spent themselves. Population growth has come to a halt, by a Malthusian process or otherwise. Capital accumulation has ceased because accumulation of a large stock of capital—or exhaustion of complementary resources—has reduced the return to zero. It took ingenuity and readiness to abstract from the problems of land and resource shortages, to translate this model into permanent equilibrium growth. One must add, however, that stationary state theorizing also had no good answer to the problem of nonreproducible resources. Those resources could in fact not be substituted, for effectively slowing the rate of growth to zero would only postpone the day when they would run out. One is bound to suspect that somehow economists have never taken the problems of coal, oil, and metals very seriously, although they have worried greatly about food and land.

A more attractive vision of the end of growth, put forward by Keynes some fifty years ago and no doubt shared by many economists, was that some day humanity would get done with the business of providing for the physical needs of subsistence and turn its mind to higher things. This view has much in common with the changing life-styles that developed among the younger generation during the 1960s. Many young people expressed disenchantment with what they considered the extremes of materialism in America. They argued for and found for themselves different sets of goals and different forms of enjoyment. They were less farseeing than Keynes, however, who realized that some generally accepted level of adequacy would have to be achieved before this great transformation in man's outlook could take place.

The great difficulty with achieving such a level is not that there is some limit on total output that prevents mankind from reaching it. At 3 percent growth per capita, income doubles from one generation to the next. If the standard of living of one generation seems inadequate, surely the next, or the next, will achieve adequacy.

The difficulty with any level of adequacy that may be obtained is that it does not remove inequality, given our present arrangements. Those at the top of the income distribution may be quite willing to call a halt to further progress. They would probably have been prepared to do this a hundred years earlier as well. Near the top, it is always difficult to imagine how things could get much better, and it is not difficult to practice moderation. But life looks different at the other end of the income distribution. The inhabitants of the lower brackets are continually exposed to a demonstration effect from above. They know how they would spend their money if they had twice as much of it or four times as much. They would be quite unwilling to accept a ceiling on their progress unless the top brackets were cut down, by taxation or otherwise, to something approaching equality. But the leaders in the income distribution would be altogether unwilling to accept this. It is one thing to level off; it is quite another to come down.

The stationary state is superior in this regard to the unspecific Keynesian vision of putting the satisfaction of material wants behind us. In the stationary state, inequality of incomes is sharply reduced by the disappearance of a return to manmade capital. When the rate of return on capital goes to zero, so does the income share of its owners. Land will still yield a rent. Full equality of incomes could be attained only by redistributing or altogether eliminating ownership of land and by evening up inequalities resulting from unequal human endowment. But since the stationary state probably lies far in the future, if anywhere, its equalizing tendencies are of no great avail.

What applies within an economy applies, of course, across nations as well. It is perhaps conceivable that the United States, having reached a high level of income, might decide to slow up or altogether discontinue its growth to conserve resources and the environment. Its example would hardly be followed, however, by the developing countries. They would probably insist on catching up to the American level before slowing or stopping their growth. But in that case the restraint practiced by the people of the United States would have relatively little effect in holding down world demands on resources and environment.

One redeeming feature of the impasse created by inequality is that it always remains open to single individuals to drop out of the growth race. A person who wants to consume less can do so without others doing the same and without the government compelling him. He can even help others by putting his surplus earnings into the bank where his neighbors, less enlightened than he, can borrow them to consume or invest more. Or else the antigrowth oriented individual can decide to earn less by working less. In that case, he will make sure that the fruits of his labor do not become a drain on resources and environment. Anyone not satisfied with the prevalent growth scene need not limit himself to protesting. He can do something about it.

The new life-styles that arose during the 1960s as part of the protest against growth lacked conviction in other respects as well. Not only did they ignore the very human desire for some level of adequacy and for equality at that level, their proponents also weakened their cause by adopting antievolutionary attitudes and by taking the achievements of their civilization and in particular of their economy too much for granted.

They were correct in believing that American postindustrial society has risen beyond the stage of social Darwinism. Survival even in a highly competitive society need no longer be survival according to the law of the jungle. But we have hardly yet attained a level of perfection and success at which we can afford to neutralize and even contravene the many processes of natural selection built into society and into the economy. When rewards to success are withheld by the tax system, when educational efforts are devoted mainly to raising the untalented to the level of mediocrity instead of raising the talented as far as possible above it, when the thrust of the law is shifted from safeguarding society to protecting those who are probably guilty, society is undermining some of its principal protective mechanisms. In the end, if all goes well, such a society may well be a more just and humane one. But in a world in which other societies employ more positive processes of selection and survival, the anti-evolutionary society may not prosper.

Within the narrow confines of the economic mechanism, the error of taking the functioning of this economy too much for granted was perhaps understandable. Many years of prosperity, accompanied by promises of unswerving future growth, led young people to downgrade the dreary tasks of production. Existence seemed assured and not worth making a fuss over. Why worry about where the next meal was coming from? Events of the early 1970s have made painfully clear how very far we still are from that blessed state. Production still matters, and to keep it flowing smoothly still remains a challenge worthy of the ablest minds.

It was not only the recessions of the early 1970s and the dramatic miscarriages in the areas of food and other commodities, petroleum in particular; for the United States, the belief that growth had either proceeded far enough or in any event could be relied on to proceed adequately hereafter was shaken by evidence of the sharply declining role of the United States in the world economy. Once the long over-valuation of the dollar had been ended by repeated devaluations, it became apparent that per capita income in the United States had ceased to rank significantly above that of other industrial countries. These other countries, moreover, for many years had been growing more rapidly than the United States and seemed likely to leave the United States behind. In all these respects, the 1960s proved to be a poor time to conclude that growth in America had ceased to matter.

This inopportune conclusion, to be sure, was one that was arrived at and to some extent acted upon by only a small elite. The educated young and their moneyed elders represented the leadership that naturally gets to the frontiers of existence first. For the same reasons, it was the United States and a few highly industrialized countries that first reached levels of income where the usefulness of continued national growth could be questioned. For these elites and frontrunners, the question was perhaps bound to arise whether the individuals who sought new life-styles, as well as thetsocieties that have traveled the road of industrialization and resultant growth, have been on the right track. It is conceivable at least that, like many other pioneers, either or both took the wrong turn and will have to suffer the consequences. It is indeed altogether unlikely that the first roads that provided dramatic breakthroughs into the new future, be it of affluence or of contempt for it, would prove to be the right ones. Experiments and pilot projects often have to be written off. That could apply equally to the Western nations' great experiment in raising their living standards by making heavy demands on resources and environment, and to the efforts of a small elite within these nations to put a stop to that experiment during the 1960s.

There is a lesson, nevertheless, both in the success of Western growth and in recent attempts to halt it, for it has become clear that growth is a powerful process following its own laws and that it is not easy to start or to stop this process.

One need examine only the tremendous technical difficulties, quite aside from social and political ones, that stand in the way of halting economic growth. Suppose there existed a national will to prevent further increases in GNP. To begin with it would become immediately apparent that that is not really what we had in mind so long as population is still growing. To combine a constant GNP with rising population implies a decline in per capita income. Presumably then, halting GNP growth would have to mean halting GNP per capita growth.

With no great effort of the imagination one can today visualize population growth being brought to a halt. But if nothing else happens, zero population growth (ZPG) would accelerate rather than retard per capita growth. The main reason is that new savings would no longer have to be devoted, in part, to equipping the additions to the labor force with new tools. The stock of capital per worker would rise more rapidly than before. Thus, halting per capita growth would be more demanding under these conditions. It takes a greater effort of the imagination to visualize a prohibition on an increase in the capital stock. People apparently want to save in order to provide for their old age, and the more they do so, the richer they get. This saving is one of the principal sources of growth. One can visualize a fiscal system in which the government absorbs all new savings by borrowing and neutralizes them by expenditure on public consumption. The savers would still have their claims that they could draw down in old age, but the stock of physical capital would not increase. Even this, however, would not kill off all growth. As physical assets employed in production wear out, they must be replaced. If there is technological progress, they will be replaced, at no higher cost, by more efficient equipment. Growth thus could proceed without new saving. If the new technologies are resource saving or environment protecting, it might indeed be difficult to persuade people that this kind of growth should not be allowed to go forward solely in order to enforce a rigorous zero growth policy. And in the unlikely event that government succeeded in stopping all forms of growth of productive enterprises, it might still be possible for ingenious individuals to engage in private growth-oriented activities on the do-it-yourself system.

Growth is likely to prove a hardy plant. Attempts to stop it will turn out not only misguided but also futile. Departing from the pragmatic expectation that growth is here to stay, a sensible policy should try to guide it in a manner that would neutralize threats that growth supposedly carries. The question before us, in other words, is how to grow safely.

It is unlikely that agreement will be reached about the risks of continued growth. That debate has been going on since Malthus, and there will always be occasions to cry wolf. However persuasive the contrary case, it will never be possible to prove that some particular wolf will not actually arrive and stay.

Economists contend that depletion of low-cost resources will be gradual, that it will manifest itself in price increases, which will stimulate production, substitution, and resource-saving research, and eventually, if necessary, discontinuation of use. Many economists probably believe that this equilibrating process can go on indefinitely, except possibly with regard to population growth and the associated need for reproducible primary products, principally food. It is in fact immaterial whether we visualize this process as occurring within a context of continued growth or of a steady state. Unless the equilibrium mechanism functions, total exhaustion of resources and the environment will occur in a context of stability as well as of growth. The difference is only one of time. The strict logic of those who foresee doomsday requires a shrinkage of economic activity to some minimum that would be sustainable on the basis of recycling after the original supplies of natural resources have been fully used up.

Economists cannot predict what precise course events will take.

What they can do is to make sure that the adjustment mechanisms are in good operating order. Prices must be free to give their signals. Markets must be capable of responding to the signals. Where markets do not operate properly—and this may frequently be the case— devices must be introduced to make them operational. With these mechanisms in place, we can allow events to take their course with confidence. If the school that believes continuing growth is possible is right, the mechanisms will channel this growth and shift resource use in directions that insure continuity. If the opposite side is right, the same mechanisms will so increase costs on all sides that continued growth eventually becomes impossible. This would occur, however, not in the form of catastrophe and collapse. Rather, it would be a gradual slowing and eventual phasing out of growth into a stationary state. The question which side is correct can be left for events to decide. Immediate action should be directed not toward the futile effort to halt growth, but toward improving the mechanisms that will make growth safe, if it does continue.

The functioning of the equilibrium mechanism can be traced in the areas of nonreproducible raw materials, in the closely allied areas of population and food, and in the area of environmental resources. It will become apparent that the mechanism is reasonable although not perfectly effective with respect to nonreproducible natural resources, that with respect to population and food its effectiveness is substantial but not necessarily adequate, and that with regard to the environment its natural functioning is often at present inadequate but capable of great improvement.

In the markets for metals, minerals, and other nonreproducible resources the functioning of the adjustment mechanism can be observed with great clarity. A rise in the demand for or a decline in the supply of any such product tends to raise its price. This sets in motion the familiar combination of a more intensive search for supplies, a reduction in use, and the development of substitutes. The fact that raw material prices have accelerated sharply over the last year is no evidence to the contrary. As pointed out above, it reflects the coincidence of business cycle peaks in a number of leading countries. Over long periods of time, moreover, the price of unexploited reserves of natural resources, such as petroleum underground, ought indeed to rise. This is the market's way of putting a competitive rate of return on such assets. In equilibrium, their yield must be equal to the yield of any other form of capital. In the absence of such a yield, there would be no reason for holding these reserves. There would then be a tendency to use them up more quickly than their long-term scarcity would justify. The price of such resources brought above ground, of course, will reflect the cost of lifting them as well as the value of the underground reserves. If lifting costs dominate, they may obscure the secular increase in the price of the underground reserves.

The proper function of this mechanism requires the market to have correct expectations of future demand. Advancing technology may make underground reserves obsolete, as for a while seemed to have happened with respect to coal. Required also is stability of ownership rights. Fear of future expropriation of oil reserves or concern over the gradual encroachment of recreational and environmental interest on timber reserves puts a discount on these assets.

Government intervention in markets is another threat to the effective functioning of the adjustment mechanism. The U.S. government's attempt to hold down the price of natural gas along the classical lines of public utility rate regulation is a case in point. Tying the price that a monopolistic seller can charge to the level of his costs makes regulatory sense where the supply is infinitely expansible, as, for instance, in the case of telephone service. The appropriate price of a scarce natural resource, be it natural gas or oil or anything else, does not depend principally on cost of production, and it is a mistake to regulate it as if that were the case.

The appropriate price of the natural resource, the supply of which is limited, is a function of its scarcity, not of the cost of bringing it above ground. In this respect, the OPEC countries have shown a better understanding of pricing principles than some of their critics who have pointed to the minimal marginal cost of Arabian oil. The price set by monopolists may of course be—and in the case of petroleum probably is—above the appropriate long-run level, in which case the owners eventually will find themselves holding an unsalable remainder as the resource is made obsolete by advancing technology.

The role of technology in first making certain resources usable and subsequently making them obsolete deserves special comment. It will be recalled that the Reverend Robert Malthus derived his classical dilemma from the interaction of the supposedly arithmetic growth of food and the geometric or exponential growth of population. Experience over more than a century has disavowed Malthus and seems to have given the verdict to Ricardo's marginal analysis. Ricardian scarcity—which regards supply as unlimited provided ever larger resources are invested per unit of output on ever less fertile land and less productive mines—rather than the absolute supply limitations of Malthusian scarcity seems to be the rule. One may attribute this to the behavior of technology, which has made possible the exploitation of increasingly more marginal resources. To maintain an exponentially growing supply, technology must itself grow exponentially, and it has indeed been shown that this is probably a realistic view of the behavior of technology.[2]

With respect to food and population, the functioning of a corrective self-adjusting mechanism is observable also. The adequacy of its functioning, however, is less assured. Food production, too, admits the use of advancing technology and provides opportunity for massive substitutions. If owing to rising meat prices, people increasingly were to turn to a vegetarian diet, far larger numbers could be fed from the produce of the soil than under the inefficient present system, which grows food to feed animals to feed humans. Food supplies, moreover, have price elasticities that are far higher in the long term than in the short.[3] Nevertheless, sufficiently rapid population growth can bring about the Malthusian calamity.

The behavior of population undoubtedly is sensitive to technological (primarily medical) influences. The decline in the death rate demonstrably tends to be followed by a lag, by a decline in the birth rate. Population can be stable or grow at a constant rate both when birth and death rates are high and when they are low. The difference is in the average age of the population. The important questions today with regard to the adequacy of the adjustment mechanism are two: Will the decline in the birth rate follow sufficiently quickly upon the decline in the death rate that has already taken place all over the world to bring the present population explosion in the developing countries to a halt? And second, assuming the whole world to have run through the population cycle that leads to low death and birth rates, will the mounting cost of rearing children sufficiently depress the birth rate to achieve stability as per capita income increases?

Present trends in the United States suggest that the economics of child rearing tend to have this effect. Moreover, if population is to be restrained further, which seems unnecessary in a big empty country like the United States but is indeed necessary in many other countries, there is much scope for internalizing the adverse externalties of child rearing. Much of the cost of every child must be borne outside its immediate family. Internalization, through the familiar tax mechanism, would probably reduce the indulgence in the consumer good "children." But this mechanism seems to have its greatest potential strength in a country like the United States where it need not be invoked at present population levels, while it may be ineffective in developing countries where children still are regarded as "producer goods." Population probably is the sector where the world is most seriously vulnerable to unconstrained growth. This is hardly a problem of growth in America, however, which is the theme of this paper.

It can be argued, of course, that even the American population is excessive in those areas that now are badly crowded. Because this crowding is unnecessary, given the supply of space in the United States, it becomes necessary to inquire why the equilibrium mechanism that presumably governs the geographical distribution of people does not lead to a more even spacing. That mechanism takes the form of rising rents and rising disamenities for city dwellers. Apparently the prevailing costs and disamenities are not sufficient to keep people from coming to the city or to induce enough of them to leave.

The economics of urban immigration and emigration require more study than they have so far received. It may turn out that the familiar price mechanism is operating adequately and that this has been obscured in the past by a very long lag. But the conclusion might also be that the mechanism is not operating with sufficient strength. In that case, a tax to internalize the adverse externalities generated by an immigrant into a crowded area, or a subsidy to internalize the positive ones generated by an emigrant from the city, would be appropriate. The immigrant raises rents and crowds the sidewalks not only to his own disadvantage but also to that of all the previous residents. In contrast to the behavior of most other markets, where an increase in price calls forth an increase in supply, immigration into the city does not increase the supply of available space, although it may, because of higher rents, lead to an increase of the supply of shelter. This might make public intervention in the market for urban real estate more appropriate than it would be in markets with a different supply mechanism. Different views are sure to emerge concerning the appropriateness of such policies. What matters for the purposes of the present analysis is that if the equilibrium mechanism that operates in the market for urban space is not considered adequate, the means are at hand to make it adequate without interfering with the free choice of the market participants.

Where environmental resources are concerned, for which at present there is no market, such as clean air and water and attractive views, the principle just enunciated with respect to urban space applies with even greater force. Almost all use of environmental resources generates mainly externalities. The users of these environmental resources, polluters of water, air, and scenery, suffer little from the damage that they do. This is a serious defect of the market system, fundamentally resulting from the fact that these environmental resources are not appropriable. Recent environmental legislation has sought to cope with the problem by regulation and prohibition. We have set standards for automobile emissions and for the emissions into the air and into rivers by utilities and manufacturing installations. This approach is not internalization, and it is highly inefficient. A better procedure would be to levy a tax on emissions and thus deflect the costs of environmental damage upon the polluter himself or on the supplier of the defective equipment. By setting the tax at an appropriate level, any desired standard of environmental cleanliness could be achieved. It would be achieved efficiently, however—that is to say, those who could reduce pollution at little cost would do so to a substantial degree while others, for whom the cost was higher, would continue to pollute substantially.

A similar result could be achieved by offering a subsidy to those willing to cut back pollution. Economically, the immediate results of tax and subsidy could be made identical. In the long run, however, a subsidy would probably attract more polluters into the industry or other activity. That, of course, would be counterproductive. An even more efficient device than a tax on pollution would be the auctioning of licenses to pollute. This would make it unnecessary to guess the level of tax by which pollution would be reduced to a tolerable level. That level could be controlled simply by the volume of licenses.

The process of internalizing adverse externalities does not, to be sure, completely replicate the process of a free market. A political process is needed to set the admissible level of pollution, and hence the required tax. Nevertheless it is evident that the threat that growth poses to the environment, through pollution, can be controlled by these means. If pollution should rise very rapidly, the tax will have to be very high. It may have to become so high that an increase in production becomes unprofitable. Further investment then will come to a halt. If this process repeats itself in all lines of economic activity, the marginal return to capital will have been reduced to zero and growth will come to an end to the extent that it is dependent on an increase in the capital stock. This is the stationary state, which economists have long envisioned at the end of a shorter or longer period of growth. Properly handled, this end should be a "soft landing." There is no need for the hard landing of global catastrophe envisioned by the critics of growth.

The environmental conditions that would be brought about through this process would not, to be sure, be those of ideal purity and cleanliness. It is theoretically possible to achieve such standards of perfection, but only at very high cost. The internalizing taxes would have to be very high. Substantial growth otherwise possible would have to be foregone. It is not likely that people would be willing to pay this price unless new technologies could be developed that would reduce it. An ultimate stationary state, therefore, if it is reached by this route, must not be envisioned as one of great environmental perfection. Air and water will still be dirty although short of the level dangerous to health. Not all views would be beautiful, not all cities spacious and uncrowded. In this respect, the future that we are preparing for our children may be poorer than our present. But thanks to higher income it will be a richer one in other respects. That seems to be the likely outcome of growth in America.

NOTES

1. James Tobin and William Nordhaus, "Is Growth Obsolete," Cowles Foundation Paper 398 written for *Measurement of Economic and Social Performance,* Milton Moss, Editor, Studies in Income and Wealth Series, Vol. 38, National Bureau of Economic Research, New York, 1973.

2. Chauncey Starr and Richard Rudman, "Parameters of Technological Growth," *Science Magazine,* 182 (October 26, 1973): 358-364.

3. Luther Tweeten, "The Demand for U.S. Farm Output," Food Research Institute Studies, 1967, Volume VII, pp. 343-369.

Eugene B. Skolnikoff

MASSACHUSETTS INSTITUTE OF TECHNOLOGY

6
The Governability
of Complexity

I

Growth, particularly economic growth, has recently come under challenge as a convenient symbol of the cause of many of our social problems. Particularly in the United States, where growth is so often used as a measure of success and where the results of economic growth have been so obvious in material prosperity, has it been held up for reexamination in a new light and with more skeptical attitudes (at least in the media and in academic circles).

But "growth" is not a precise concept and in fact can often be misleading or meaningless if used with excessive generality. Moreover, it is not growth (however one defines it) that is the problem but its effects; and growth of anything is itself not an independent phenomenon but a product of many other events. Thus, it is hard to know whether to treat growth as a dependent, an independent, or an intervening variable; or whether to think of it as process, objective, value, or characteristic; or even what kinds of growth are worth dealing with.

I am interested here primarily in the effects, and particularly the political effects, of rapid growth of almost any kind. For the arguments I wish to make, it is not necessary to distinguish among kinds or even rates of growth but only in the magnitude and character of the effects of growth. A few preliminary remarks are in order, however, in order to see the American growth ethic in some perspective.

There seems little question that growth related to the economy and to many characteristics of the physical environment has been seen as a positive value in the United States for most of its history. This did not mean that economic growth was treated as an overriding value or objective. Growth was understood as natural, as needed, and as the appropriate criterion for evaluation of industrial, national, and even individual performance. But other values have often been in competition, or apparent competition, with a growth ethic; growth has not always been the victor. Antitrust legislation, regulatory agencies, national parks, were accepted even though they did not appear to contribute to the simple objective of economic growth. Growth was never thought of as the supreme economic or political goal.

This is important to recognize today. The current challenge to a growth ethic, except for some largely academic groups, is not so much a move for rejection of growth as for a rediscovery and reemphasis of other objectives. In fact, I do not believe that the larger part of the nation sees the problem as growth versus quality of life, or more leisure, or other alternatives. Rather with considerable perspicacity, the public at large wants economic growth now to serve these other objectives relatively more than simple material prosperity; it remains to be seen what happens when there are a growing number of obvious trade-offs that imply direct and obvious reduction in personal material standard of living in order to achieve other amenities. The energy problem may present those trade-offs sooner than was expected.

What we have now come to appreciate are the growing conflicts in values—the realization that growth may not always be compatible with other societal objectives. In a more operational sense, we are developing a better appreciation of the costs as well as the benefits of some of the objectives we took for granted, and we are in the process of trying to understand just what those costs are.

Here the problem with the loose use of "growth" is obvious. Some kinds of growth are certain to be incompatible with almost any definition of quality of life: unconstrained expansion of unmodified automobile use in the Los Angeles basin, continued dumping of growing amounts of untreated waste in most rivers, or unregulated access to parks and beaches. Other kinds of growth may not only be compatible with improved quality of life but essential to it: a growing economy to pay for higher costs of improving amenities, expansion of recycling industries and energy generation to ameliorate resource scarcity, growing leisure time and resort industries. Moreover, the time scale becomes critical. Concern out to, say, 1985 may lead to quite different conclusions about various forms of growth than attempts at a far longer look to the future.

The essence of the matter is simply that all changes in social systems, of which growth is one kind, bring in their train problems. One need not accept the poorly based claims in the apocalyptic literature that growth inevitably will bring about social collapse as a result of approaching the physical limits of the globe. But that is not to deny the reality of the problems growth will bring (and has brought) nor to ignore the very real benefits growth will bring (and has brought).

There is, however, one critical problem that has been largely ignored in the growth debate and that may well overshadow all others before the end of the century. It concerns the political problem of governance and thus the kind of political society that is possible and acceptable.

II

Much of the literature on the problems of growth has focused on physical or economic or social questions; very little has looked at the political dimension. These dimensions are all interconnected, of course, but analyses have tended to neglect the political implications that in fact present some of the crucial *root* problems that are already before us and about which it is extremely difficult to be optimistic. The political questions are obviously related to growth of all kinds and certainly are steadily more exacerbated by continued growth.

To sum up the problem in one sentence: Is man capable of designing social institutions that will be able to govern a world of incredibly growing complexity and scale without sacrificing values important to the society?

There is much assumed by and subsumed within that question, and many uncertainties of definition: What is meant by "govern"? Whose values are to be served or sacrificed? Is the nation-state the basic unit? What value changes are assumed? Rather than attempt to make the question more precise, it would be more useful to elaborate some of the problems and their implications that lead to the conviction that governance is a (perhaps the) key issue. Many of the problems are overlapping, and all are related to each other, but they deserve separate, if somewhat arbitrary and abbreviated, statement.

The old belief that growing *interdependence* among nations would breed at least a sense of common purpose, and more hopefully a genuine community of values, has proven a weak reed at best. Unexpectedly rapid growth in the relations and dependencies across national borders has not reduced strife but rather has sharpened divisions and distinctions. Much of the change can be traced to the more rapid development and application of technology than was or could have been predicted, a phenomenon that still appears to be accelerating, and to which I will return.

The pattern is not unidirectional, of course; many old disputes have withered. And at catastrophic levels of power, the very logic of modern weapons has forced at least some recognition of common objectives among large nations. But as a whole, increased openness and interconnectedness had led to new areas of dispute, breakdown of consensus within nations with regard to external objectives, multiplication of nations and national interest groups, growth of independent international power in multinational corporations, and politicization of an ever-larger number of issues. At the very time when previously isolated ecosystems are, in Kenneth Boulding's phrase, merging to become a single global ecosystem, the social system is fragmenting into a multitude of decision centers, suspicious of each other, and each with strident claims of independence and self-interest.[1]

National political processes must, as a result, cope with an enormously enlarged international agenda of issues. But nations all too often have little background or competence in subjects that must be dealt with, have inadequate trained manpower resources, and reflect a fragmented internal society with new aggressive assumptions about national self-interest. To top it off, the international environment in which governments must act itself generates few grounds for trust.

In that international environment, one of the unavoidable implications of a single global ecosystem, or of interdependence, is the growing need for corporations and other nongovernmental institutions able to carry out "governmental" functions of regulation, enforcement, management, adjudication, and allocation of resources. Increasingly, such international activity will be concerned with issues that directly affect domestic policies and in effect create constraints on internal actions. The power and performance of international machinery is now and will be of considerable, and growing, political salience.[2]

Evaluation of existing international institutions and of national attitudes toward international decision making makes it clear that this is an area of continuing inevitable controversy. By and large global institutions are only occasionally adequate for the tasks they now have, and the direction of change more often than not is negative. If present trends continue, the global and even regional regulation required will be carried out through (disputed) dominance of a few countries achieved largely by their economic, technological, and physical power, or carried out by nongovernmental entities of great economic power: the multinational corporations. It is unlikely that either will be a politically acceptable pattern to the rest of the world. It should be added that it is not at all clear that the alternative of increasing delegation of power to genuine supranational institutions will be any less conflictual; little in experience to date gives confidence that nations know how to or are willing to design and operate supranational governmental machinery successfully.

The level of international interdependencies adds enormously to the load placed on the political process of all countries and on the global political process. Can the process as we know it, or as we can modify it, sustain that load?

Within societies, as within the global system, a *process of fragmentation* is and has been underway—a fragmentation closely related to numbers, to erosion of accepted assumptions and values, to new awareness of individual possibilities, to disappearance of old power blocs and sources of legitimacy, and to confusion in a new world of exploding technology little understood and seemingly autonomous. Harold Isaacs has said it well:

> This process of fragmentation and re-fragmentation can be examined in any day's news, indefinitely multiplied now any day, any week, anywhere in the world, whether in East Pakistan or East St. Louis, South Africa, or South Bronx, northern Luzon or northern New Jersey, Alaska, or Ceylon. . . . We are experiencing on a massively universal scale a convulsive ingathering of men in their numberless groupings of kinds—tribal, racial, ethnic,

religious, national. It is a great clustering into a separateness that
people will, people think, improve, assure or extend the group's
power or place, or keep it safe or safer from the power, threat, and
hostility of all other groups similarly engaged.

. . . This fragmentation of man is one of the great pervasive
facts of contemporary human affairs. It forms part of one of our
many pervasive great paradoxes: the more global our science and
technology, the more tribal our politics; the more we see of the
planets, the less we see of each other. The more it becomes
apparent that man cannot decently survive with his separateness,
the more separate he becomes.[3]

It is a matter of argument, and research, as to the causes of this
fragmentation. Certainly part of the motivation, as Isaacs says, is a
search for security and identity in an increasingly complex and impersonal world. There is no reason to think that continued growth of
population and complexity of life will do other than stimulate this drive
toward tribalism.

Coupled with the interdependence of modern society and with the
erosion or disappearance of old assumptions, tribalism creates enormous strains on a political process. These ethnic or religious or national
tribes no longer accept the simple notion of elites, nor any longer are
willing to give up voluntarily their claims for participation in social
decision making, nor can a society operate by ignoring them. And
communication between them becomes more difficult as cultural
development diverges. The result is growing competition and conflict
and less, rather than more, unity of purpose, just when physical
realities call for the opposite.

Perhaps this fragmentation is the necessary prelude to a new, higher
form of integration, but there is little other than idle hope to sustain
such a prediction. Rather it is much more likely to be one of the societal
characteristics with which political processes will increasingly have to
cope. It goes to the heart of politics, since these groups will be battling
for their share of power. And thus it will add greatly not only to the
agenda of politics but also to the background noise and conflict within
which the process will have to work.

The most significant value of the market in the economic organization of society is as a self-regulating mechanism to provide for efficient

allocation of resources and distribution of income and to organize consumption and production. Shortcomings in the functioning of the market, as measured by other social objectives, have led to the need for new forms of regulation and to modification of the market in all market economies. In turn, this implies a need for *central planning and economic direction* by political authority once the automatic nature of self-regulation is modified.

It is beyond question that present market mechanisms cannot adequately represent all the objectives of a society. The arguments about the need for production of public goods, for recognizing the weakness of the market in weighing externalities or signalling long-term irreversible shortages, for providing "appropriate" incentives for R&D, for enabling "equitable" as opposed to efficient distribution of income, are all well known. Clearly political authority has assumed, and will have increasingly to assume, the burden of complementing and regulating the market, and thus of central planning and allocation of resources.

But how capable is political authority of performing that task? What will be the social costs and what reductions will there be in efficient use and distribution of resources? The problems of the political authority "alternative" are also well known.

Planning mechanisms are not yet models of competence. The very complexity of society makes a planning task exceedingly difficult, even if there were no other problems. Everything affects everything else so that it is no longer possible to isolate subjects in neat independent boxes. In addition, domestic regulation and planning must be carried out in a setting in which independent decisions abroad directly affect internal issues.

Planning, because it deals with allocation of resources and thus with distribution of power, is a political task. It requires establishment of priorities through the political process and is subject to the pressures engendered by the social fragmentation and competition discussed above.

Moreover, the legitimacy of the political authority is at stake unless often strident new demands for participation are met. But participation is usually inimical to efficiency because of increased competition for resources among more groups, increased time necessary for resolution of issues, difficulties of communication, and varying levels of competence and information.

The information that is needed for planning—the nonquantitative indicators or projections that the market does not produce—is not necessarily available or understood or is contentious. How should preferences be determined when needed? Questionnaires? Ad hoc elections? Instantaneous electronic feedback systems? Under what conditions and with what information?

And, as noted, the growing importance of external events may mean planning bodies have only a portion of the subject actually under their control.

Regulatory agencies and mechanisms also share these problems and have some of their own: public interest in the subject, and, hence, in the agency wanes, reducing public pressure and awareness; the only groups consistently interested and thus able to exert continuous pressure or to infiltrate are those to be regulated; often the commercial interests to be regulated are able to organize political and economic power more effectively than the more diffuse groups affected by the commercial interests; the original political objectives and setting that led to a particular regulatory institution may have changed, but the statutory base and historical development make change exceedingly difficult; and the knowledge on which to base regulatory decisions is often uncertain and controversial.

The problems inherent in bureaucracy itself must be added to all of these, especially since a concomitant to increased complexity and scale in society is expanded bureaucracy. The difficulties of generating adequate information and analysis, of modifying the status quo, of integrating action, of developing competence, of providing a sense of participation, of influencing permanent bureaucracies, and of reaching effective and timely decisions are all well known and grow along with bureaucratic expansion. The situation is further complicated by the growing need for more international bureaucracies, which are on the average an order of magnitude less satisfactory than U.S. domestic bureaucracies.

Finally, the information and analysis problem must be stressed. Increased scale and complexity of society and of its artifacts, especially their technological complexity, greatly multiplies the difficulty of providing adequate, comprehensible, and timely information for decision making. Society is much more vulnerable to the parochial views of the small groups able to understand facets of the issues, and the difficulty of developing alternative policy choices is enormously compounded. Informed public debate over the consequences of planning choices becomes rare, at best.

Thus, the great benefit of the market for self-regulation must increasingly be sacrificed because it is not adequate to serve social goals. But the capability of political institutions to carry out the planning and regulation thereby required is also in question.

Accelerating advances in *science and technology* and their social applications have been central movers in the rate of growth and in some of the value and societal changes of recent years. They have made possible, or were the direct "cause," of the population explosion, upheavals in international relationships, rural depopulation, totally new industries, changed resource uses and availability, drastic changes in communication patterns and knowledge, shortened decision time scales, and innumerable other effects. The complexity of modern life and the level of technological sophistication necessary to understand everyday appliances, let alone other artifacts with which man comes into daily contact, have fundamentally altered his view of his surroundings. The pace and seeming autonomy of technological change have contributed critically to the sense of inadequacy and of alienation that have become significant hallmarks of advanced technological societies.

Technology has made possible the unparalled conveniences and resources available to all citizens of technological societies, just as it has come to raise psychological and social issues. The possibility (and actuality) of resource substitution made feasible by technological change has already greatly extended the time when there may be limits to growth. Whether, or when, that possibility will no longer be available is a contentious issue. There are other problems raised by application of advances in science and technology that deserve attention. They can be summed up, again, as problems that complicate or load the agenda of political choice.

One of these is technology's continued contribution to the growing complexity of society. Likely computer, communications, and transportation developments alone will have such effects, and many others in other fields are in prospect (weather modification, genetic engineering, medical technology), let alone those that have not yet been thought of. Many, perhaps most, will involve public regulation with all the difficulties already indicated, exacerbated by the ever more abstruse nature of scientific and technological knowledge.

Another set of problems complicating the political agenda arises from the need to direct technological development for public ends. Though "technological fix" is a much abused term, it is true that we will be looking to technology to cure or bypass some of the environmental, resource, and related issues now coming so prominently to attention. These problems necessarily are often in areas where the market is not an adequate allocator of resources, so that public authority must be involved. This is particularly relevant to R&D where development times force decisions long in advance of provable need or economically certain advantage.

A third consequence of science and technology is the shortening of the time scale for the making of public policy decisions. More and more often the time needed to develop consensus among competing interests is simply not available, with consequent effects on the decision itself, on its effects, and on the attitude of affected interests toward the resulting policies.

Another problem mentioned earlier grows out of increasingly sophisticated technology that places new requirements for expertise and information in policy making. Meeting these requirements either puts increasing distance between the lay public and the expert, with increasing implicit delegation of power and growing frustration, or else results in enormous reduction in efficiency of decision making as all interested groups attempt to become knowledgeable and influential on complex technologically related issues. The legitimacy versus efficiency problem in the overloaded public sector becomes a critical issue.

Last, the effects of technology on social values and objectives may continue to be of central importance to social viability. The sense of inadequacy in the face of complexity and of impersonal technology have already been mentioned. Increased intrusions on privacy are inevitable whether as a result of surveillance for benign purposes—for example, the collection of needed data, inspection to avoid social disruption, or monitoring to enforce social policies—or as a result of more malign activities of public authorities and private groups with new tools available for intrusion into individual lives. Complex societies are also vulnerable societies, vulnerable to low-level violence or disturbance that can have greatly amplified and disastrous effects. Protection against such disruption may involve public authorities in activities now considered well outside present norms of behavior in the United States.

Again, it is the increasing demand on the political system that is the chief concern, rather than the more highly touted physical problems raised by advancing technology.

A wide variety of significant *changes in the political process and in underlying beliefs* have been taking place in the United States, some of which have already been referred to in other contexts. Some are the effects of the physical changes and growth in modern society; others may have more autonomous roots. All are undoubtedly to some extent both cause and effect. It would be futile to attempt to list all such changes, but a few peculiarly relevant to the process of growth in the past or future are worth mention.[4]

The rise to power in the political process of new groups, often without the assumptions of the past, is a significant phenomenon likely to continue and to become more pronounced in the future. The loss of consensus that results, and the abandonment of convenient beliefs that helped to make possible a reasonably stable social system, serve to load even further the political process. The erosion of beliefs such as the trust in elites, or the conviction that rewards are earned only by performance, or the voluntary renunciation of claims for participation, or the conviction that all problems are capable of rational resolution, has gradually brought about a quite different political setting that lacks the relative unity and agreement on objectives that characterized the United States in the past. The strains of continued growth will surely exaggerate this pattern.

Other changes in the social setting also have had major effects on the political process and are likely to be emphasized by the effects of growth: increased levels of education and their impact on forms and styles of participation (and on organization and acceptance of work patterns in industry); increased importance and politicization of the media; monopolies of knowledge skills by professional groups; the rise of ad hoc, single-issue political movements; the growth of coalitions of powerful interests on specific issues with considerable bureaucratic control of policy; rising importance of technocratic planning struc- tures; growth of international corporate empires; increasing disposition of governments to use technological tools to "manage" dissent and manipulate public opinion.

The list could be lengthened, though it should also be noted that the effects of some of these changes may in fact be contradictory. But all add to the agenda and difficulty of political choice.

This imposing catalog of social changes could be considerably extended and elaborated in detail, but the message is clear. One of the central problems of growth far into the future is a political problem: *can the political process cope with the demands on it that arise* directly, or through second and higher orders of effects, *from growth of all forms?* I characterized these critical first and higher order effects of growth as enormously increased complexity and scale, with the emphasis on complexity.

It would be more precise to ask what changes in the political process will be necessary, or will in fact come about to cope with the effects of growth. The problems will be dealt with somehow. But that "somehow" may include fundamental changes that would be inimical to our present values.

Many scenarios are possible. On one end of the scale is political breakdown under a crisis that grew out of the growing clumsiness of government unable to reach timely decision, develop consensus, or anticipate problems. The result could be the imposition of authoritarian rule, or a reaching out to foreign confrontation by a frustrated government looking for a means of developing consensus on a single overriding issue, or more likely both. On the other end of the scale (possibly also arising out of the crisis), one can imagine "post-postindustrial" restructuring of institutions and values that was able to strike compromises among competing interests and develop trust sufficient to allow decisions without full participation.

Without attempting to develop alternate scenarios, it can legitimately be concluded that the first scenario is the more likely prediction of the future unless we find ways consciously to move toward the other end of the scale. What are some of the changes (or direction of change) that appear to be required?

1. Development of "self-regulating" mechanisms where possible. The beauty of the market is its automatic character; to the extent it can be made more sophisticated and sensitive to presently nonquantita-

tive, noneconomic signals, the greater relief will there be on the political process. Other such self-regulating mechanisms may be possible, for example, with regard to income distribution, foreign trade, economic incentives, fertility, and others. To the extent feasible, the externalities of growth should be dealt with in this way.

2. Institutional development of all kinds is obviously required. In particular I would single out the need to develop planning and dispute-settling mechanisms able to function more rapidly and with more authority at as local a level as an issue allows. The problem of legitimacy cannot, of course, be avoided by this means alone, but over time trust in political institutions must be reestablished, and it takes time if it can be done at all.

3. One critical element in the functioning of planning and dispute-settling mechanisms, which is woefully inadequate today, is the availability of adequate information and analysis. Two kinds of information and analysis are needed: that available to interest groups for advocacy and adversary purposes and that which is sufficiently disinterested, and is seen to be disinterested, to be accepted by disputants as decisive. Both are essential; both are in short supply; both require special institutional form and resources. And the availability of both could contribute substantially to a willingness of fragmented groups to accept the decision of an adversary process seen to be "fair."

Another important purpose of adequate information and analysis is to provide early warning to society to allow longer time for consideration, debate, and the development of consensus.

4. Regulatory devices and agencies clearly also need thought and attention. Since I can only assume that the fragmentation of interest groups will be with us for a long time, mechanisms are needed that allow, even encourage, interest group participation and alliances and yet can function with reasonable efficiency. The reality of being able to fill that need will critically depend on social attitudes as well as ingenuity. But attitudes will also be affected by actual achievement of more equitable distribution of resources.

5. On the international scene, institution building is even more obviously needed and even less likely to happen without substantial shifts in national attitudes toward international competition. This is a subject crying for leadership from those nations (or that nation) that should see the problem most clearly.

6. Value modifications are necessary. Trust, willingness to subordi-

nate or defer claims on resources, concern for equity in the distribution of resources, and acceptance of other similar values are essential
to the reduction of strife and achievement of compromise. These
developments are not likely to come about autonomously, but rather
through creative institution building and policies that meet some of
the real demands and concerns. But that brings us back again to the
enormous load being placed on the political process.

It should be noted in passing that economic growth that allows
income distribution that is not simply redistribution will be a necessary, though obviously not a sufficient, condition to bring about value
changes. Growth may all too often be the solution as well as the
problem.

Crisis may also be a means of inducing value changes. The danger, of
course, is that the costs of crisis in today's technological world may be
too great, even if the aftereffects of crisis were expected to be benefi-
cient.

These are a few of the weak and not very hopeful reeds on which to
meet the political problems associated with governance of "incredibly
growing complexity and scale." Others can and need to be spelled out.
Perhaps the analysis is too pessimistic, and our society will in fact
muddle through without major crisis or undesirable changes in values
and structure. My guess is that we will know the answer well before
the physical constraints on growth are predicted to be upon us.

NOTES

1. K. E. Boulding, "What Went Wrong, If Anything, Since Copernicus?"
AAAS Symposium on Science, Development, and Human Values, Mexico
City, July 2-3, 1973.

2. E. B. Skolnikoff, *The International Imperatives of Technology: Technological Development and the International Political System,* Research
Series 16 (Berkeley: Institute of International Studies, 1971).

3. H. R. Isaacs, *Group Identity and Political Change: The Politics of
Retribalization,* Bulletin 31, (Tokyo: The International House of Japan, Inc.,
1973).

4. L. N. Lindberg, "A Research Perspective on the Future of Advanced
Industrial Societies," (unpublished manuscript), p.7.

John Holdren

UNIVERSITY OF CALIFORNIA, BERKELEY

7

Technology, Environment, and Well-Being: Some Critical Choices

I

The complex relationship between the uses of technology and human well-being is at the heart of what has aptly been called "the predicament of mankind."[1] At the most elementary level of analysis, it is apparent that prosperity and indeed survival for human beings are contingent on uninterrupted flows of a variety of resources—including food, energy, fiber, water, and metals—and that maintaining these flows and deriving services from them is what technology is all about. There has been a persistent tendency to view malfunctions or potential malfunctions in this process largely in terms of shortfalls of the individual resources—the existence or prospect of a food shortage, a fuel shortage, a water shortage, and so on. The essence of the real predicament, however, resides not in the question of theoretical adequacy of one or several resources but in the interactions of the resources and their associated technologies with each other and in the impact of the entire enterprise on the nontechnological environment.

The consequences of even a temporary energy shortage, for example, reverberate through all sectors of economic activity, generating or aggravating materials shortages, food shortages, unemployment, and inflation, all of which in turn may exacerbate the initiating event itself. Massive diversion of investment capital and technical resources to

89

meet the crisis of the moment—attempting to compensate for lack of foresight with brute force applied too late—weakens the system elsewhere and thus promotes crisis in other sectors later. Apparent solutions seized in haste and ignorance cut off options that will be missed only in future predicaments. (Consider the "solution" to finding housing for a swelling middle class disenchanted with central cities: building suburbs on the best agricultural land.)

The most fundamental difficulty of all is the environmental one, and it exists even in the unlikely event that foresight and organization are flawless. Simply stated, it is this: while the intelligent application of technology fosters human well-being directly, a reducible but not removable burden of environmental disruption by the same technology detracts from well-being. The negative effects may include not only damage to health, property, and human values, but perhaps most importantly, disruption of public-service functions of natural systems (for example, nutrient cycling, climate regulation, pest control, water management, and ocean fish production). These indispensable services are often not replaceable by technology at all; when they are replaceable it is generally at great expense and as part of a vicious circle—the side effects of more technology disrupting more natural services that must be replaced with still more technology.

This line of argument is not intended to suggest that technology per se is undesirable. The benefits of technology in support of human well-being have often exceeded the liabilities, and the expansion of some existing kinds of technology—and the development of needed new kinds—will continue to be warranted in the future by a favorable balance of benefits versus risks. I suggest, however, that a point will eventually be reached in the expansion of *any technology of production* where the incremental gains in well-being from further expansion do not compensate for the incremental losses caused by the technology's environmental impact. That such a point always exists follows from fundamental physical and biological principles; the encounter with it may be postponed by innovation, but it cannot be indefinitely evaded. I am convinced, moreover, that for some of today's important technologies of production—particularly in the areas of food and energy—the point beyond which further expansion is counterproductive has already been passed.

The problems that would be associated with this situation, even in a politically homogenous, economically unstratified, and physically nongrowing world, are enormously multiplied in the real world of deep ideological divisions and territorial disputes, staggering inequities between rich and poor both within and among countries, and rapid growth in population and material consumption per capita (distributed in such a way as to enlarge even further the existing disparities). The competition among nations for access to resources and the political tensions that arise as a result, and the wasteful and dangerous diversion of human and material resources into military enterprises, are inextricably a part of the resources-technology-environment predicament. Just as these elements cannot be disentangled, moreover, the fate of the United States cannot be disentangled from that of the rest of the world; it is not plausible that our end of the boat can be made to stay afloat if the rest sinks.

If the foregoing is a reasonable outline of the characteristics and dimensions of the predicament, then the resolution for the most part is not to be found in devising and deploying bigger and better variations of the same basic kinds of technologies. This approach, which has comprised the knee-jerk response of most industrial nations to the symptoms they perceive and which seems to be the first choice of many developing countries seeking a path to prosperity, will intensify the underlying stresses, not relieve them. The aim of this essay is to identify some elements of an alternative approach—some nontraditional goals and criteria for shaping technologies and institutions that will ameliorate, not aggravate, the contemporary predicament. But to make the need for such change persuasive, I shall first return in more detail to some of the main aspects of the present situation.

II

That the technologies of exploiting different resources are far from independent is clear from a moment's reflection. It takes water and steel to produce fuel; fuel and water to produce steel; fuel, water, and steel to produce food and fiber; and so on. The higher the level of technological development, in general, the more intimate and demanding are the interconnections among different resources. Agriculture in the United States, Europe, and Japan, for example, uses far more energy, steel, and fertilizer per unit of output than does agriculture in India or Indonesia. (In exchange for the additional investment and complexity, one obtains more output of food per unit of land and per unit of labor.) All else being equal, the interconnections among different resources also become more intense as the quality of the resource base diminishes. The amount of steel invested in securing petroleum, for example, is relatively low for onshore, shallow fields near centers of use, relatively high for fields offshore or deep or remote from centers of use.

That the physical links among resources are already tight enough to be very troublesome for rich countries and poor countries alike has been particularly vividly demonstrated by the worldwide petroleum squeeze of 1973 and 1974. Poor countries such as India can now scarcely afford to pay for imports of energy-intensive fertilizer, the price of which has soared upward with the price of petroleum; nor will India long be able to afford the imports of petroleum needed to run its own fertilizer factories and other agricultural functions. Indeed, the energy-fertilizer-food linkage is now making itself felt worldwide as an important contribution to the rising price of food.

In addition to the direct, physical interconnections among resources, there are also indirect but very important economic links. It is hard to doubt, for example, that the United States' need to increase food exports in order to pay for growing and increasingly expensive oil imports has contributed to the continuing upward spiral of U.S. domestic food prices.[2] The same phenomenon assures that there will be no uncommitted food reserves in the rich countries to alleviate prospective famines in countries too poor to pay for food on the world market. Hardly surprisingly, the United States government has also called attention to the possibility of using quotas or higher prices for exported food as retaliatory weapons against the oil-exporting nations. (No such policy has actually been effected, but the prospect is illustrative of the seamy side of resource interdependency.)

Other dimensions of the connection between resource problems and international relations are equally appalling. The United States exports not only food but also military hardware to generate the foreign exchange needed to pay for imported raw materials, as do many other industrial nations. The intensity and indiscriminateness with which the arms exporters hustle their wares in the international market seem to be increasing as resource-related balance-of-payments problems worsen. The result is encouragement and sustenance for the spiralling arms race in the poor countries, which is both a pathetic diversion of funds desperately needed there to increase the standard of living and a profoundly destabilizing force operating against world peace.

Apparently, foreign-exchange-hungry industrial nations are also unwilling to refrain from exporting nuclear reactors, even though in practice this has the effect of introducing the capacity to manufacture nuclear weapons into the most politically volatile regions of the world. Historically, proliferation of fission bombs has been limited principally by the nonavailability of suitable fissionable material (which only the largest industrial nations have had the technical resources to produce) and, probably to a much smaller extent, by "good intentions" (as reflected in the Non-Proliferation Treaty of 1970). Proliferation has not been limited by lack of knowledge of how to construct a fission bomb, for such knowledge has been obtainable with modest effort by virtually any country for many years.[3]

The spread of nuclear reactors means we are left relying only on good intentions to prevent proliferation. Even a single reactor per country is significant: one of the size promised to Egypt by the United States in 1974 (600 electrical megawatts) produces enough fissionable plutonium each year to make about twenty-five fission bombs of the size dropped on Nagasaki. The "safeguards" provided by the Non-Proliferation Treaty and administered by the International Atomic Energy Agency, moreover, provide only for detection (not physical prevention) of diversion of reactor-produced material for explosive purposes, and even this for only nations that have signed and ratified it. (Many have not.) It hardly needs emphasizing that good intentions or fear of international censure provide a thin reed to grasp indeed. If there were any doubts about the reality or the immediacy of this issue, of course, India's nuclear explosion in May 1974 should have dispelled them.

If the energy-balance-of-payments squeeze has made industrial nations more eager to sell reactors, it has also made some developing countries more eager to buy them. This issue is so instructive as an example of present trends in technological development and their implications that it will be considered again in more detail later. Suffice it to say at this point that, although there is some semblance of a case for fission in developing countries without indigenous fossil fuels or hydroelectric potential, the intense desire to "go nuclear" may have other than economic origins in a country with developed but unused hydro capacity (like Egypt) or one with some of the cheapest oil in the world (like Iran).

In sum, the world outlook with respect to resources and politics in the next several decades is far from encouraging. A continuing set of interlocking shortages is in prospect, which will generate not only direct adverse impact on human well-being but also increased political tensions and (perversely) increased military wherewithal for poor countries to relieve their frustrations aggressively. Resort to military action is possible not just in the case of poor countries unwilling to suffer quietly, but, with equal or greater likelihood, in the case of industrial powers whose high stardard of living is threatened by denial of external resources. Conflicts over access to resources of undefined ownership, such as seabed minerals, comprise a potential tinderbox of growing magnitude; the confrontations over ocean-fishing rights that have already occurred may be but a feeble precursor of problems of this general nature yet to come. The probability that conflicts of *any* origin will expand into a nuclear exchange, of course, can hardly fail to be greater in a world of perhaps fifteen or twenty nuclear nations than it has been in the recent world of five.

III

The traditional technologist's dream is to banish such nightmares by fashioning a world of abundance for all: we will produce more of everything and do it cheaply enough that the poor can become prosperous. There are unfortunately several defects in this cornucopian vision, some of which have already been alluded to. The first two stumbling blocks, which are related to each other, are logistics and economics. (By logistics is meant the scale and rate with which technology can be brought to bear.)

Cornucopians generally are preoccupied with the apparent theoretical capacity to supply a large (but fixed) population with basic raw materials over long spans of time. They refer to the vast stores of minerals available at low concentration in sea water and the first few miles of the earth's crust, and they argue that cheap and abundant energy from fission breeder reactors or controlled thermonuclear fusion will make these dilute mineral resources economically accessible (as well as permitting large-scale desalting of sea water to make the deserts bloom with food crops). Weinberg and Hammond, for example, have argued that breeder reactors could supply a world population of 20 billion with twice the present U.S. per capita energy consumption for thousands of years and that this is enough energy to squeeze a decent living from common rock and desert soils.[4] (Note that even ardent cornucopians do not postulate continued growth of population or material consumption per person beyond a few more doublings, for that cannot be sustained under *any* assumptions.)

Logistics is crucial, however, because civilization confronts not an "equilibrium problem" (is there an imaginable world in which 20 billion people could be supported?) but rather an "initial-value problem" (how can we get from here to there, and especially with such a bad start?). Technology is not providing adequately for the present world population, and indeed the available data for the 1950-1970 period indicate that the rich-poor gap in prosperity has been *widening*.[5] What new evidence is there to suggest that technology can now be mobilized (and paid for) quickly enough to begin to rectify this situation at a meaningful rate?

A particularly instructive perspective on the logistics issue has been provided by Harrison Brown, in emphasizing the importance of the capital stock of various materials (as distinguished from annual material throughput) as a measure of well-being.[6] (That is, the capital stock of ten tons of steel per person in the United States—tied up in automobiles, buildings, bridges, productive machinery, and so on—is a more informative measure of well-being than the annual U.S. per capita "consumption" of steel of 600 kilograms.) To match the material prosperity of the United States in a poor country, using the same kinds of technology that have been used in the United States, one must essentially match this per capita capital stock for all the major raw materials of technological society. Now, consideration of logistics requires us to ask not merely whether enough material to do this worldwide exists, but how quickly it can be provided. In this connection, Brown has calculated that to provide the 1970 world population with the capital stock of industrial metals, per person, that prevailed in 1970 in the ten richest nations would require, on the average, about sixty times the 1970 world production of these materials. (Production may grow above 1970 levels, of course, but so will population; and, under present patterns of consumption, most of the production will go not to establishing the material basis of prosperity in the poor countries but to replacing losses and further increasing the standing crop in the rich ones.) The real message of the calculation, and almost certainly that of any more careful consideration of logistics, is that present materials-intensive technologies would offer little hope of early prosperity to the poor countries even if global allocation of materials flows were to change dramatically.

On grounds of logistics, then, the cornucopian vision is of little immediate relevance. But even its ultimate relevance may be questioned on grounds of economics, for its economic viability seems in virtually every version to be predicated on the assumption that energy will be very cheap.[7] Examination of the actual prospects suggests that this assumption is most unlikely to prove valid. The advanced energy technologies with the greatest potential in terms of abundance—solar energy, controlled fusion, and fission breeder reactors—are all characterized by raw fuel that is free or nearly so, but the high capital costs likely to be associated with these technologies will lead to high overall energy costs despite free fuel.

The construction costs of today's water-cooled fission reactors are $500 to $600 per kilowatt of capacity, despite estimates little more than ten years ago that this figure would fall from $200 then to about $125 now. Inflation accounts only for part of the discrepancy. Breeder reactors are intrinsically trickier than the water reactors just described, with more severe operating conditions and correspondingly stringent demands on materials. They will probably be significantly more expensive to build, more than offsetting the cheapness of the fuel.

No one yet knows exactly what a fusion reactor will look like, but the operating conditions will be extreme: plasma temperatures of one hundred million degrees, a meter or so from superconducting magnets that must be kept within a few degrees of absolute zero; stresses near the failure point of the strongest alloys; magnetic fields a hundred thousand times the magnetic field of the earth; and destructive neutron-fluxes even more intense than in breeder reactors. Coping with these conditions may require the use of exotic materials in limited supply, and it will be expensive.

Solar energy on a large scale needs large collectors. Efficient collectors need exotic materials, which are expensive and may be scarce; less efficient ones (including photosynthesis) need more land area, another resource characterized by competing uses and rising prices. These points are not made to disparage solar energy; it has important advantages over the alternatives, but it is not likely to be cheap.

Of course, even *free* energy would not constitute a sufficient condition for making the cornucopian vision economically possible because the technologies for extracting other raw materials, the technologies for transforming these materials and energy into useful goods and services, and the skilled labor to run these enterprises are and will likely remain expensive. Perversely, energy is important enough as a fraction of the cost of industrial activity that rising energy costs would doom the cornucopian vision but not important enough that falling energy costs alone could bring it to pass.

IV

Even if the defects of the cornucopian vision with respect to logistics and economics could somehow be made to vanish, the attempt to realize it would surely founder on the environmental constraint. This would not be so, of course, if environmental damages consisted only of nuisances such as befouled beaches and roadside litter, of isolated threats to obscure species of plants and animals, and of a modest incidence of pollution-related disease in the most urbanized and industrialized regions. The conventional wisdom, although rarely so bluntly stated, has been that these are not unreasonable costs to pay in exchange for increased material abundance.

But the real environmental dilemma, as already noted, lies much deeper. Services even more fundamental to human well-being than those now provided by technology are supplied by biological and geophysical processes in the natural environment, and these services are susceptible to significant disruption by contemporary technology. Rising population and material consumption, relying on this technology, increase the demands on the "public service" functions of ecosystems while simultaneously reducing the capacity of these systems to meet the demands.

The character and vulnerability of natural "public service" functions have been discussed at length in the technical literature,[8] so only the most cursory listing of the main points will be undertaken here.

1. The greatest apparent potential for harm in the near future is by disruption of agricultural productivity. Agriculture depends on natural systems for control of most potential crop pests (through natural enemies and environmental conditions), for maintenance of soil fertility (through natural nutrient cycles and regulation of the pH of surface water), and for maintenance of favorable climatic conditions. The critical dependence of food production on the weather, in a world with virtually no food reserves, would be cause for serious concern in the face of natural climatic change alone; but worse, the activities of civilization can in principle superimpose faster change on the natural cycles, and there is considerable evidence that this is either already occurring or is possible soon.[9]

2. Production of protein in the sea, of great importance because of the shortage of protein in the global diet, is vulnerable to disruption by overexploitation, disruption of coastal habitats, and pollution. The latter factors are particularly effective because marine systems are most productive and most sensitive precisely in the shallow near-shore waters where the human impact is greatest.

3. Beyond the loss of food production, the principal threats to human well-being from disruption of ecosystems consist of accumulation of toxic substances (including carcinogens, mutagens, and teratogens) in the environment—owing to overloading or circumventing natural chemical cycles—and alteration of environmental conditions governing agents of epidemic disease and the vectors that spread them.[10]

4. Scientific knowledge of the operation of environmental systems and the influence of civilization's activities is not adequate to predict in detail when, where, and in what forms the conceivable human environmental disasters will take place; but it is adequate to show that some such disasters are plausible at present or apparently soon-to-be achieved levels of technological activity. At the simplest level, this conclusion follows from a wide variety of studies comparing the impacts of our technology against the yardstick of global natural processes: we are equal to six to twenty times nature as a source of oil in

the oceans, half of nature as a source of sulfur in the atmosphere worldwide (and many times nature over regions of millions of square kilometers), 5 percent to 50 percent of nature as a source of particles in the atmosphere, perhaps equal to nature as a source of mercury in the environment, and we have increased the atmospheric concentration of carbon dioxide by 10 percent since 1900. Intervention on this scale is clearly capable of triggering regional and global consequences.

The widespread tendency to underestimate the environmental constraint comes not only from a lack of appreciation of the magnitude of the threat to human well-being, but also from excessive optimism as to the ease with which modest adjustments can ameliorate contemporary technology's environmental impact. This is of course not to say that reduction of the impact of technology is impossible—to the contrary, the possibility and indeed the necessity of doing so is one of the principal burdens of this essay. But the task will entail far more than the largely cosmetic and generally uncoordinated measures that today pass for environmental protection.

Although a good many of the "technical fixes" that have been envisioned to clean up contemporary technology would be worthwhile, the shortcomings indicating that such measures alone will not be enough are easily identified. The main such shortcomings are suggested by the following questions (logistics and economics again loom large):

1. How fast can the fix be implemented (compared, for example, to the rate of expansion of the offending technology)? The answer depends on whether the fix can be retrofitted to old units (like some smog control devices) or whether instead its market penetration is limited by the rate of introduction of new units and the "death rate" of old ones (consider the problem of a completely new type of automotive engine).

2. What degree of control does the fix provide, and what will we do for an encore after the gains have been erased by further growth? (For example, an 80 percent degree of emissions control permits a fivefold expansion in the technology involved before total emissions reach the initial uncontrolled value again.)

3. How much will the fix cost, and who will pay for it? As a general

rule, extracting pollutants becomes disproportionately expensive as the degree of control required becomes higher. (Going from 90 percent to 95 percent control may cost as much as going from 0 percent to 90 percent). The larger the population and the consumption per capita, the larger the degree of control needed to maintain some fixed level of total emissions; the larger the degree of control, the larger the cost per person.

4. Will a "fix" for environmental impact in one form and one place aggravate the impact in other forms or other places? Shifting to electric automobiles would shift part of the environmental burden of personal transportation from the central cities to the vicinities of electric power plants. Use of tall stacks to reduce ground-level pollution by sulfur oxides in European cities has spread acid rain over the European countryside all the way to Scandinavia. Generating electricity with nuclear fission instead of with fossil fuels reduces air pollution at the expense of a still undetermined risk of catastrophe from accidents, sabotage, or terrorism.

For the most intractable environmental impacts, there appear to be no ultimate "fixes" short of controlling the level of use of the offending technologies. Carbon dioxide is produced by combustion of fossil fuels in quantities too large to contain, and it may already be influencing climate. Particles below one micron in diameter—emitted by combustion of fossil fuels and to a lesser extent by mining operations and agriculture—largely escape available controls; unfortunately, the size range below one micron is the most serious both in terms of human health and the disruption of climate. The human factor may make designing foolproof safeguards against nuclear-fission disaster impossible. Conversion of an ever larger fraction of the earth's surface to intensive technological management in direct support of civilization's use of resources simplifies ecosystems, apparently decreasing *their* ability to perform their indispensable supporting functions for civilization. Finally, heat is the ultimate pollutant—it would eventually stop the growth of energy use, by generating major climatic disruption, in the extremely unlikely event that nothing else stopped such growth first.[11] This outcome is the result of the laws of thermodynamics; it can be postponed somewhat by technological cleverness, but it cannot be averted.

V

Most of the foregoing discussion has been framed in a global context, as the character of the problem seems to require. It is nevertheless useful at this point to focus more closely on some specific aspects of the situation in the United States, both because of the particular intensity and special dimensions that the enormous levels of resource use and technological complexity here lend to these problems and because of the continuing role of the United States as an international model for sophisticated technological development.

The disproportionate share of global resource use accounted for by the United States and our correspondingly large share of responsibility for many forms of environmental impact have been widely noted. [12] The case of energy use is particularly instructive: the United States, with about 5.5 percent of the world's people, accounts for about a third of the world's annual energy use, the per capita rate corresponding to fifty times India's and twice Sweden's. [13] This means that modest percentage increases in U.S. energy use have a large absolute impact on global requirements and, correspondingly, that modest percentage reductions in wasteful uses of energy here would have a significant absolute impact.

The high level of use of energy and other resources already attained in the United States also means that increasingly difficult problems of logistics and economics will be associated with maintaining a high growth rate on this large base. A fixed growth rate implies a constant doubling time, and it is transparently more difficult to double from twelve to twenty-four million barrels per day of petroleum refining capacity (for example) than it was to double from six to twelve million barrels per day in the same length of time. One common approach to this problem is to make each new individual unit larger than were the units in the previous generation. This may offer economies of scale, but, all else being equal, it has the disadvantages of decreasing the number of firms with the resources to tackle the job, increasing the amount of capital that must be raised in one lump sum, increasing the amount of environmental damage that must be absorbed at one location (thus making sites harder to find), and increasing both the economic and environmental risk associated with making a major technological mistake.

As economists are wont to point out, of course, the pressure of growth stimulates substitution and technological innovation that can circumvent the limitations of resources and technologies previously relied upon. This, too, is a two-edged sword. In the case of the energy situation in the United States, for example, it is difficult to escape the impression that desire to sustain rapid growth and increase self-sufficiency has motivated firms and the government to gamble ever larger stakes on unproved technologies. Some of these hasty technological gambles will fail expensively in economic terms and others may present high risks of grave environmental errors that will be identified too late.

As noted above, the links between different resource sectors become tighter and more demanding as the sophistication of technology and the overall level of resource use increase. Many manifestations of this phenomenon can be identified in the United States. Some of them are: competing pressures for land, particularly coastal land, constraining the siting of large technological facilities; rising taxes resulting from commercial valuation of suburban agricultural land, leading to higher food prices and/or the conversion of the agricultural land to residential and industrial use; competing demands for water constraining the development of coal and oil-shale resources in the West; and growing uses for hydrocarbons as chemical building blocks, cutting gradually into the availability of hydrocarbons as fuels. The increasing importance of interactions among different technologies and between technology and the environment underlines the necessity of ever more sophisticated evaluation of technological alternatives before decisions are made. The environmental and economic stakes grow higher; the degree of reliance on elusive technological perfection to avoid disaster becomes greater; but the extraordinary pressures of growth itself operate against time-consuming deliberation. Witness the mounting pressure to "streamline" environmental-impact evaluations and licensing procedures for technological enterprises in this country and elsewhere.

VI

The development and deployment of nuclear fission reactors for the commercial generation of electricity—in the United States, in other industrial nations, and most recently in the developing regions of the world—provides a striking illustration of many of the troublesome issues associated with the connection between technology and well-being.[14]

The technology is complex, capital intensive, economical only in large unit sizes, and unforgiving of carelessness in manufacture, inattention in operation, or malicious intervention. Its great attractiveness lies in the cheapness, abundance, and compactness of the raw fuel and in the absence of conventional air pollutants at the nuclear power plants themselves. The uniqueness of the technology's hazards lies in the quantity, toxicity, and longevity of the radioactive by-products, which must be isolated from the human environment with extraordinary diligence, and in the direct connection between power-reactor technology and the capacity to manufacture nuclear weapons.

The early history of the commercial deployment of fission power plants in the United States, encompassing the years 1957 to 1970, was characterized by a variety of government subsidies and special regulations: government enrichment of fuel and purchase of by-product plutonium on very favorable terms; limitation of liability in the event of a major accident by act of Congress, and assumption of most of the limited liability by the U S. Treasury; and large government research expenditures on reactors and peripheral facilities, to the near exclusion of funding of research on alternative energy technologies. At the same time, commercial manufacturers of nuclear reactors understated their costs and sold early models as "loss leaders." All these measures were presumably justified in the minds of their supporters in industry and government by the vision of the great benefits to human well-being that cheap electricity from fission would eventually deliver. Without these measures, of course, fission reactors would not have been economically competitive at the time with fossil-fuel burning power plants; with them, fission was made so alluring that electric utilities did something virtually unprecedented in this conservative industry's history and perhaps in the recent history of industrial technology—they ordered dozens of large power reactors, at a capital investment of billions of dollars, before a single example in this size range had operated commercially.[15]

In mid-1974, with forty-five U.S. power reactors in operation, sixty under construction, and 105 more on order, it still cannot be known for certain whether these installations will operate reliably for the twenty or more years necessary to return the utilities' investment. No large commercial reactor has yet been retired and "decommissioned," so the costs of this cumbersome procedure are largely unknown. No scheme has yet been shown to be feasible for the isolation of the long-lived radioactive wastes from the environment for the necessary thousands of years. A controversy continues in the technical community as to whether safety precautions against catastrophic accidents in the principal U.S. reactor types are adequate. The possibility of diversion of fissionable materials from reactors for the production of nuclear bombs, not merely by nations but also by subnational groups of black-mailers or terrorists, has only in the past year begun to receive wide discussion in the general technical community and the public. And the "commercial nuclear fuel cycle" is not a cycle at all because no commercial fuel-reprocessing capacity is in operation in the United States; a small reprocessing plant in upstate New York is out of commission until at least 1977 for modifications, and a new, larger General Electric plant, which has not worked after an investment of $60 million to $80 million, is apparently being abandoned.

It is difficult to escape the impression, then, that the pressure of growth (in this case the notion that a doubling of U.S. electricity generation every decade is necessary and desirable) and the vision of a technological panacea (cheap, clean energy from the atom) have led this country into a massive commitment that is at least premature. An objective reevaluation of the problems and prospects of fission, together with those of the alternatives, would likely lead to a postponement of further reliance on fission until the major uncertainties concerning it are satisfactorily resolved—if they can be. In practice, such a reevaluation is made highly improbable by the enormous financial, intellectual, and emotional investment that the government and the influential supporters of fission already have made in this technology. What is likely to occur instead is a transition to a still more capital-intensive, complex fission technology—the Liquid Metal (cooled) Fast (neutron) Breeder Reactor (LMFBR). The technological, economic, and environmental uncertainties surrounding this reactor are, if anything, greater than those associated with the fission technologies relied upon today.

If expanding reliance on fission and the entrenched nature of the commitment to this technology are troublesome issues in industrial nations like the United States, the corresponding issues are even more disturbing in the context of the poor countries. It is hard to imagine a technology less well suited to the conditions in most such regions. The required capital investment per unit of capacity is high, but capital in poor countries is in exceedingly short supply. The economies of scale for nuclear plants dictate large units, but the capacity of the poor countries to absorb electricity is usually small and dispersed. The level of technical sophistication required for operation, maintenance, and monitoring is high, and malfunctions are costly and difficult to repair. Most poor countries will have to rely on industrial-nation suppliers for enriched fuel and other peripheral services, in a world where such dependence is increasingly perceived not only as unfashionable but threatening; and countries that elect to invest in their own fuel-reprocessing plants obtain, along with this ingredient of independence, the capacity to fuel a nuclear-weapons program.

One must conclude, then, that poor countries are buying reactors for one or more of four main reasons: (1) the industrial nations are pushing their expensive fission technology for export with exceptional vigor; (2) for those countries with no economical indigenous energy resources, imported nuclear technology from industrial nations is preferable economically or politically to imported oil from Arab nations; (3) having a nuclear reactor is a sign of technical progressiveness (the influence of the rich-country role model); and (4) the temptation to become a nuclear-weapons power is irresistible. This picture inspires little confidence in the pattern of technology transfer by which the poor countries are ostensibly to become better off.

VII

The foregoing survey has presented a pessimistic view of the present human predicament and the prospects that contemporary trends in the application of technology will improve it. Indeed, I must conclude with Kenneth Boulding[16] that much of what we have regarded as technological progress can most charitably be described as "suboptimization"—determining the best way to do that which ought not to be done at all. The realistic prognosis must now include continuing worldwide inflation, further widening of the prosperity gap between rich and poor, increased incidence of famine and quite possibly other environmentally related increases in death rates, heightened social unrest characterized by strikes, riots, and terrorism, more frequent international confrontations over resources, a general level of international tension aggravated by all these factors, and a probability of nuclear conflict that increases not only in proportion to this level of tension but also in some (probably nonlinear) relation with the growing number of possessors of nuclear weapons.

What, then, must we do? Some thoughtful elements of a program have been separately set forth by a variety of authors, among them Sakharov, Platt, Illich, the Ehrlichs, Harrison Brown, the Meadows group, and Daly.[17]

It is clear, first of all, that no combination of policies and technologies can significantly ameliorate the predicament unless it confronts and overcomes the nontechnological roots of the problem: population growth, competitive nationalism, the maldistribution of wealth and opportunity, the illusion that economic throughput and material well-being are directly proportional, and the environmental hubris that supposes civilization to be self-supporting without help from natural ecosystems. The highest priority must therefore be given to measures that directly attack these driving forces.

The cornerstone of a rational program should be a great reduction in the growth of throughput of energy and materials in the rich countries. This approach would permit, in principle, an *acceleration* of the application of energy and materials to meet the genuine needs of the poor countries *within a context of declining global growth*.[18] In this way, the rich-poor gap in prosperity could begin to be removed—a prospect that supporters of rapid growth overall have often held out to the poor but never delivered. At the same time, the slower growth in the global rate of mobilization of energy and materials, and the much slower growth in the rich countries where certain environmental impacts of energy and materials technologies are now most severe, would significantly reduce the grave environmental risks that accompany continuation of recent trends.

The success of such a scheme of course depends strongly on the success of programs to limit the growth of populations. Only at lowered population growth rates can the relatively high growth in use of energy and materials per capita that is needed in the poor countries be achieved within an economically and environmentally sustainable rate of total growth. In the rich countries, the effect of multiplying even small population increments by the very high per capita resource use and environmental impact already prevailing there makes it essential to approach a zero rate of population growth as soon as possible. [19]

Another essential ingredient of the approach advocated here is a massive, coordinated worldwide campaign of research, development, and implementation aimed at increasing the amount of human well-being actually delivered for each unit of throughput of energy and raw materials, while decreasing the amount of adverse environmental impact per unit of throughput. This proposal should be recognized as a prescription not for *less* technology but for better technology—more frugal, better focused on the most compelling needs, more compatible with the fabric of the physical and social environments.

Some useful insights into how to attack the problem emerge from economist Herman Daly's concept of "ultimate efficiency" or the ratio of service to throughput. [20] It is instructive to write this as the product of two more ratios:

$$\frac{service}{throughput} = \frac{service}{stock} \; x \; \frac{stock}{throughput}$$

Here "service" means a contribution to human well-being, and "stock" refers to the accumulated collection of artifacts that serve as the intermediaries between throughput of energy and materials on the one hand and services on the other. Clearly one can increase this efficiency by reducing the stock of materials needed to provide a given service (a simple example is making automobiles smaller) or by reducing the amount of throughput needed to maintain a given stock (making the automobiles more durable). There are abundant opportunities of both kinds in heavy industrial processes, in the design and packaging of consumer goods of all kinds, in the construction of residential and commercial buildings, in transportation, and in the substitution of communication for transportation, indeed throughout the economy. A cohesive literature of this subject—how to do more with less—is only now beginning to emerge, [21] but one can surmise that sustained application of the sorts of ingenuity and technical skills that have been devoted in the past to weapons and space exploration would reap enormous rewards. (No doubt the major reason so little effort has historically been devoted to this task is that "throughput" has been cheap—or we thought it was—compared to the inputs of skilled labor and ingenuity needed to maximize the physical ratios defined above.)

The potential of increased technological efficiency notwithstanding, its pursuit must be tempered by two concerns. The first is that even the most efficient technology must be applied and expanded cautiously lest the environmental impact of its throughput disrupt environmental services or social relationships of greater importance than the services the technology provides. (This consideration, as well as the interaction of different technologies with each other, can be embodied in Daly's formulation by noting that it is the ratio of all services—including environmental and social ones—to all technological throughput that is to be maximized.) The second concern is to avoid the pitfall of trading away too much diversity in the single-minded pursuit of efficiency. One must generally pay something extra in throughput for diversity—in this sense it is "inefficient"—but natural ecosystems seem to have "discovered" that diversity is good insurance against uncertainty about the future, and civilization would probably do well to learn from the example. Just how much of this insurance civilization should buy and what it will cost are questions that need further study.

Within these constraints, the potential for favorably altering the ratio of service to throughput by a major directed effort means that prosperity in the poor countries can be increased at a rate greater than the rate of growth of resource use itself and that, even in rich countries where a drastic slowing of growth in energy use is called for, ingenuity can reduce the impact on the economy and on the prospects for increases in actual well-being. This possibility, together with increased awareness in the rich countries that their own well-being is imperiled by the social, economic, and environmental consequences of continuing present trends, comprise the only real basis for believing that the technological changes and rich-poor reallocations envisioned here can actually take place.

Obviously the best approach to increasing the physical efficiencies will not be identical for all regions. It seems clear from the difficulties enumerated earlier in this essay that new technology for the developing regions must be tailored to specific local conditions rather than transferred willy-nilly from industrial nations. Rather than centralization, technical complexity, standardization, and interdependence, the characteristics of new technologies for developing regions should be dispersal, simplicity, diversity, and independence. Durability and reliability, which often go hand in hand with simplicity, are also essential. It is evident that the technologies of industrial nations as well should in many instances now evolve away from complexity and centralization, and in all instances away from reliance on a standard of perfection in manufacture, maintenance, and operation that is not attainable in practice.

Industrial nations, rich as they may seem to be, must also face up to the fact that they are not rich enough to do what must be done and waste resources on frivolous economic fiascos as well. Supersonic transports, overbuilding of subsonic airbuses, the proliferation of unfillable luxury hotels and vacation condominiums—all these are economic blunders that will cause some well-deserved bankruptcies but, unfortunately, only after desperately needed technical and economic resources have been wasted.[22]

Military expenditures are in a category by themselves. No one can afford them, the poor even less than the rich, but everyone makes them—to a total of more than $200 billion per year worldwide.[23] This cannot be considered *merely* a waste, inasmuch as the expenditures profoundly threaten human well-being through what is bought even more than through what is not bought. The most powerful single lever at the disposal of industrial nations for narrowing the prosperity gap is to shut off uniformly all sales and gifts of military hardware to the poor countries, replacing these with offerings of technologies selected for their ability to contribute to genuine increases in well-being. Naturally the gesture will be a hollow one if the industrial nations do not at the same time divert their own expenditures on weaponry to productive purposes.

I am regularly informed in all solemnity that the sorts of drastic changes proposed here are economically, politically, and socially impractical or unrealistic. No one has yet devised a plausible scheme, for example, to see that reductions in throughput of resources in the rich countries (if this could actually be achieved) are translated into increased availability of resources for rational development in the poor countries. Little real progress has been made on global disarmament by the superpowers, and extensive proliferation of nuclear weapons is widely (if quietly) held to be inevitable. The issue of population growth continues to be widely underestimated or misperceived by scholars and governments alike. I believe it is past time for the social science community to devote its full attention to the resolution of these obstacles, just as the physical science and engineering community must devote theirs to the transformation of technology. The alternative of proceeding along our present course is not only even less practical economically, politically, and socially than the demanding changes that are required, it is also impractical physically. The real question for those concerned about "realistic" solutions is whether our scholars and decision makers can devise ways to bring human behavior into harmony with physical reality in time.

NOTES

1. Donella H. Meadows, Dennis L. Meadows, Jorgen Randers, and William W. Behrens III, *The Limits to Growth* (New York: Universe Books, 1972).

2. Kenneth E. F. Watt, *The Titanic Effect* (Stamford, Conn.: Sinauer Associates, 1974).

3. Mason Willrich and Theodore Taylor, *Nuclear Theft: Risks and Safeguards* (Cambridge, Mass.: Ballinger Books, 1974).

4. Alvin Weinberg and Phillip Hammond, "Limits to the Use of Energy," *American Scientist* 58 (July-August 1970): 58.

5. Harrison Brown, "Population Growth and Affluence: The Fissioning of Human Society," *Quarterly Review of Economics* (Spring 1975).

6. Harrison Brown, "Human Materials Production as a Process in the Biosphere," *Scientific American* (September 1970).

7. The technologies on which the cornucopian vision rests—for example, extraction of raw materials from sea water and common rock, desalting sea water for irrigation, and cultivation of marginal lands—are much more energy intensive than typical contemporary practices, in which energy at 1974 prices already accounted for 10 percent to 20 percent of the cost of basic raw materials. For insight into the role of energy in contemporary industrial processes, see, for example, Office of Emergency Preparedness, Executive Office of the President, *The Potential for Energy Conservation* (Washington, D.C.: Government Printing Office, 1972). If energy use per unit of raw material triples without a concomitant drop in the price of energy, then raw material prices will rise steeply. But to permit realization of the cornucopian vision, raw material prices would have to fall.

8. Study of Critical Environmental Problems, *Man's Impact on the Global Environment* (Cambridge: MIT Press, 1970); The Institute of Ecology, *Man in*

the Living Environment (Madison: University of Wisconsin Press, 1972); Study of Man's Impact on Climate, *Inadvertent Climate Modification* (Cambridge: MIT Press, 1971); John P. Holdren and Paul R. Ehrlich, "Human Population and the Global Environment," *American Scientist* 62 (May-June 1974): 282-292.

9. R. A. Bryson, "A Perspective on Climatic Change," *Science* 184 (May 17, 1974): 753-760.

10. Jacques M. May, "Influence of Environmental Transformation in Changing the Map of Disease," in *The Careless Technology: Ecology and International Development,* ed. M. Taghi Farvar and John P. Milton (Garden City, N.Y.: The Natural History Press, 1972).

11. The hope is sometimes expressed that the cooling effects of extra particles in the atmosphere and (perhaps) a natural climatic cooling trend may fortuitously be counterbalanced by the warming effects of civilization's heat dissipation and addition of carbon dioxide to the atmosphere. Unfortunately, the most likely and imminent forms of climatic change involve not so much global warming or cooling as disruption of the circulation patterns that govern the *distribution* of temperature and rainfall. For this class of problems, the various influences of civilization are extremely unlikely to cancel and indeed are quite likely to reinforce each other.

12. See, e.g., Paul R. Ehrlich and Anne H. Ehrlich, *Population, Resources, Environment* (San Francisco: W. H. Freeman, 1970).

13. United Nations Statistical Office, *Statistical Yearbook of the U.N., 1972* (New York: United Nations Publications, 1973).

14. For a more extensive discussion of the technical difficulties of fission than is given here, see John P. Holdren, "Hazards of the Nuclear Fuel Cycle," *Science and Public Affairs: The Bulletin of the Atomic Scientists* (October 1974).

15. An interesting discussion of this point is given in chapter 6 of Resources for the Future, *U.S. Energy Policies: An Agenda for Research* (Baltimore: Johns Hopkins Press, 1968).

16. Kenneth Boulding, "Fun and Games with the Gross National Product— The Role of Misleading Indicators in Social Policy," in *The Environmental Crisis,* ed. Harold W. Helfrich, Jr. (New Haven: Yale University Press, 1970).

17. Andrei D. Sakharov, *Progress, Coexistence, and Intellectual Freedom* (New York: W. W. Norton, 1968); John Platt, "What We Must Do," *Science* 166 (May 16, 1969): 1115-1121; Ivan Illich, *Celebration of Awareness: A Call for Institutional Revolution* (New York: Doubleday, 1970), and his *Tools for Conviviality* (New York: Harper & Row, 1973); Ehrlich and Ehrlich, *Population, Resources, Environment;* Harrison Brown, "Scenario for an American Renaissance," *Saturday Review* (December 25, 1971): 18-19; Meadows et al., *Limits to Growth;* Herman Daly, ed., *Toward a Steady State Economy* (San Francisco: W. H. Freeman, 1973).

18. To see quickly why this is so, note for example that the richest third of the human population accounts for 85 percent of global energy use, leaving 15 percent to the remaining two-thirds. Thus, a reduction of only 18 percent (15/85) in the total energy use of the "rich" would permit a doubling of the total energy use of the "poor" without any increase in the global total. A more detailed and perhaps more realistic example of the potential of reallocating the growth of energy use is given in John P. Holdren, "Energy and Prosperity," *Bulletin of the Atomic Scientists* (January 1975).

19. John P. Holdren, "Population and the American Predicament: The Case Against Complacency," *Daedalus* 102 (Fall 1973): 31-44.

20. Herman Daly, "The Economics of the Steady State," *The American Economic Review* 64 (May 1974): 15-21.

21. Energy Policy Project of the Ford Foundation, *A Time to Choose* (Cambridge, Mass.: Ballinger Publishing Company, 1974), chs. 3 and 4; Holdren and Ehrlich, "Human Population."

22. Watt, *The Titanic Effect.*

23. Stockholm International Peace Research Institute, *World Armaments and Disarmament: SIPRI Yearbook, 1974* (Cambridge: MIT Press, 1974).

Part III

Growth as a Factor in American History

Samuel Hays

UNIVERSITY OF PITTSBURGH

8
The Limits-to-Growth Issue:
A Historical Perspective

I

Environmental conservation problems are persistently moving toward a context of the limits to growth. The writings of Forrester and the Meadows have given an overall formulation to a set of predispositions and hunches that have been rather widespread in a variety of more disparate and piecemeal issues.[1] The impact has seemed rather astounding. The Meadows' writings especially took us off guard, so much so that at the start they were considered in an atmosphere of transient sensationalism. Yet there is a persistence to the insights in all this that has remained and will remain for a long time to come. As the sensationalism of the initial impact wears off, the relevance of the idea becomes more concretely pervasive. A frame of mind is developing in which environmental conservation problems are defined in terms of the tension between a finite physical environment and increasing human pressure upon it.

What sense can a historian make of all this? These moods of thought and outlook, of course, are relatively new, and it would be a major temptation simply to look back and contrast the old and the new. In the nineteenth and early twentieth centuries a sense of optimism pervaded American society that the nation's physical environment had no limits, that resources were infinitely exploitable, and that America was technologically capable of transforming at will the physical world around it. There was little thought of limits, for although some of that physical world was destroyed there was more of it to be had "out there." Even in the days of revulsion against the massive timber cutting in the late nineteenth and early twentieth centuries the sense of having reached limits was only temporary. In fact, the conservation movement of the early twentieth century carried with it far more a sense of optimism about the vast and unlimited potential of technology, applied science, and large-scale system than about environmental limits. It was only a pause toward a new variant of continued physical development.

But to contrast the human perception of limitlessness in the past with that of limits in the present would not help much to understand where we are today. It is far more important to focus on the process by which the change came about. Let us assume that the task of history is to understand the processes of long-run social change, the transformations in societies as they change over long periods of time. In the current instance the problem is to understand the present perception of limits in terms of the evolution of a frame of reference, to identify the process by which a sense of limits grew and developed out of a past when a different frame of mind prevailed. The task in this essay, therefore, will be more modest than a sweeping panorama of historical wisdom. It will be confined to some observations about social change in twentieth-century America, which may provide some insight into the changing perceptions of the nature of our environment.

Let me make one other point by way of introduction. The context of what follows will be political. We are speaking here of human choices and the values and perceptions that lie behind those choices. It is true that the relevant conditions of life can be described variously as economic or social or cultural, that the substance of the issues concern how we make a living, what we produce in goods and services, what we prefer to consume with personal and social resources. Yet all this still involves choices, which, in turn, reflect preference and values. The shift from a concern with food and clothing to a concern for material goods to a concern for nonmaterial services to a concern for environmental quality involves values and choices that can be understood fully only as political phenomena. What values, perceptions, and preferences are operative, and how is the interplay of the variety of conflicting preferences worked out in the form of social decision and social action? We are dealing here with emerging preferences and emerging choices, and all this requires a form of social understanding at that fundamental level.

II

As an initial backdrop let me contrast the earlier twentieth-century conservation movement with the more recent environmental concerns. There are continuities that I shall dwell on later, but it is important that we first understand the differences.

Prior to the 1960s the conservation movement was dominated by the perspective of "efficient production."[2] The term "conservation" arose initially to describe new approaches to resource management that involved the application of science, technology, and planning to the development and use of those resources. In its origin the movement was closely related to the practice of scientific management, not only in its concepts but also in its leaders. There was some emphasis on the limits of resources and the need to save resources to live within those limits, but that emphasis was minor and ephemeral. The major focus was on the way in which science and technology could eliminate waste and increase the material base of human life. The movement affirmed, and did not seriously question, the perspective of an abundant and unlimited future if the methods of science and technology were used to manage resources "wisely."

Three different focal points of activity illustrate this approach. First was multiple-purpose river development. Unharnessed rivers flowing to the ocean without being used by man were deplored as wasteful; they could be made far more productive if brought under control by large-scale public works such as dams and reservoirs. Moreover, if located and constructed with multiple uses in mind, entire rivers could be harnessed for multiple benefits of navigation, flood control, irrigation, and hydroelectric power production. Engineers extolled the seemingly unlimited possibilities if the manifold uses of a single resource, water, could be dovetailed according to concepts of efficiency and under centralized planning and direction by experts. Glimmerings of this approach began in the first decade of the twentieth century; by the 1920s it had begun to jell and by the 1930s projects

118

were in full swing. The Tennessee Valley Authority was the most dramatic consequence.

Sustained-yield forest management reflected a similar focus. Wasteful lumbering practices could be prevented and future supplies of timber could be assured if timberlands were managed according to the scientific principles of sustained yield, that is, the annual cut should be balanced with annual growth. This was the spirit of "scientific forestry" that Gifford Pinchot popularized and instilled into the minds of young foresters whom he attracted into the new profession. Pinchot was committed to the forests as commodity resources that should be developed for commercial purposes, and he vigorously opposed efforts to allocate lands in the national forests for parks and other noncommercial purposes. Hostile to what he called "preservationists" he played a major role in establishing the dominant mood of conservation as efficient, scientific, economic development.[3]

The new contribution of the 1930s—the soil conservation movement—continued this approach. The immediate problem it tackled was soil erosion and in doing so it generated the new movement of scientific soil management. Erosion was easily construed as an economic problem; it depleted the capital base of agriculture. A new science and a new technology could reverse that trend and both stabilize and restore that capital. Focusing on the intricate relationships of soil and water, the movement, of which Hugh Hammond Bennett was the symbolic and de facto leader, continued to inject into the conservation impulse its traditional theme of efficient production. Forest, soil, and water became a complex of perspectives and interests that readily dovetailed in the "conservation movement."

Throughout all these years a quite different perspective persisted, but in a subordinate and often obscured role. This was the park and outdoor recreation movement. Its major focus was the "preservation" of lands from commercial development or production in order that they might be enjoyed for their natural beauty. The development of national parks and the growth of the National Park Service, established in 1916, represented this focus.[4] At the state level programs for fish and wildlife "conservation" constituted a different but related focus.[5] And the outdoor recreation movement, represented by hiking clubs, trail riding organizations, and camping groups, was another.[6] All of these came into sharp conflict, at one time or another, with the efficient development perspective and played a subordinate role to it through the 1950s.

In the 1960s all this came to be modified or often superseded by the "environmental movement," with a strong connotation of "quality" or "amenity" rather than efficient economic development.[7] New concepts arose that went beyond production to the enjoyment of life and concern for the quality of the environment necessary for that enjoyment. Air, water, and land each came to be conceived of not as a commodity to be molded into a material product or as a public facility for the disposal of waste, but as the environment in which people work, live, and play. The "environment" was not a thing to be used for material purposes, but the context of life and the enjoyment of life required that the context be of one kind rather than another. The phrase "environmental quality" arose, embedded in such public action as the "Council on Environmental Quality," and soon began to compete with the older word "conservation."

This amenity focus is increasingly at odds with the earlier production focus of conservation, and many heroes of the conservation past have become villians of the environmental present. As opposition to river "impoundments," dams, and reservoirs has grown, not only the U.S. Army Corps of Engineers and the Bureau of Reclamation, but also the Tennessee Valley Authority, have come in for sharp attack.[8] TVA, the conservation hero of the 1930s, is rapidly becoming a major target of environmental criticism, not only for its dam building proclivities but also for its role as a major purchaser of strip-mined coal. The Soil Conservation Service, changed from a protector of soil from erosion to a developer of undeveloped lands through wetland drainage and stream channelization, has become equally a villain in the current scene. The U.S. Forest Service, with its dominant focus on commodity timber production and its close, "incestuous" relationship with the timber industry, has come under more than usual attack. The issue of clear-cutting, offensive to aesthetic sensibilities among environmental conservationalists, has presented the Forest Service with one of the major crises of its history.[9] Even the National Park Service, because of its increasing involvement in mass, developed recreation, has been severely criticized.[10] But it, more than the other agencies mentioned, has begun to make sharp adjustments in its thinking under the stark realization that increasing human pressure is threatening its scarce resources with destruction. On the whole, it has been painful for the old "conservationists" to adjust to the new "environmentalism" because the two emphases are, more often than not, incompatible. Quality or amenity is a direct challenge to efficient production.

Echoes of the distinction in perspectives between production and amenity persist within the environmental quality movement itself. For many, environmental quality means primarily "clean production" with the emphasis, as much as in the old conservation movement, on production, including an acceptance of the ideology of material growth. They would simply add the word "clean" to "efficient" production. For others, however, environmental quality means a sharper, more direct, and more thorough emphasis on "quality" as a goal coordinate with and not derivative of production. Amenity or quality should not merely guide the manner in which production goals are carried out but should become a fundamental goal itself, coordinate with production goals.[11] This difference in approach is an important, but as yet not widely manifest, aspect of the controversy over the "environmental impact" or "102" statements now required of all federal construction agencies. Production-oriented agencies such as the U.S. Forest Service, the U.S. Army Corps of Engineers, the Department of Transportation, or the Energy Research and Development Administration view these as merely examining environmental consequences of their primary production mission. Most controversy over the statements has focused on the adequacy of that examination. But much of the environmental quality movement demands that "quality" enter in decision making in the initial planning not as consequences but as goals. Clean production is not enough; basic production goals must be restricted to make way for "quality-of-life" goals.

The concern for the limits of growth emerges from this "amenity" sector of the environmental conservation movement. Clearly it is vastly at odds with the older emphasis upon large-scale, efficient production. But it also rarely finds much support among those more modern environmentalists who are primarily occupied with clean air and clean water or even with environmental health. All these assume that what technology has created in the form of waste, technology can clean up, and if completely closed-loop recycling systems are possible in the treatment of technological waste, there is no need to be concerned with the scale of resource throughout.[12] A concern for a wide range of amenities on the other hand has the possibility of raising the question of limits as a forceful element of human perspective. If quality of life is a major goal, then it pervades a wide range of decisions—from the number of children one has to the personal enjoyment of a clean, quiet, and natural environment. As we shall see later on, the role of space in environmental quality values, and especially the problem of land use, raises questions of limits of growth far more forcefully than do problems of technological waste.

III

Basic to the new concerns for environmental quality and the limits to growth are changes in human values and preferences that have come over the American people since World War II. And basic to these changes in values is the enormous productivity of the American economy, which has permitted a significant proportion of the population to think in terms of and choose amenities. Rapid economic growth after World War II led to sharply rising incomes, rapid vertical mobility, and increased levels of education. Fully half of Americans by 1970 were white-collar workers and more than that had completed a high school education; median family income by 1972 had reached well over $10,000; and 25 percent of Americans were upper-middle class individuals with some years of college education. While income and economic conditions remained unequally distributed, an increasing proportion of American families in the upper half of the income scale could and did think beyond the material comforts of life to amenities. Education was an especially important factor in changing the values of Americans and developing an interest in matters termed "quality of life." Individuals began to allocate their personal resources differently because they had more to allocate and the American economy as a whole could allocate an increasing share of its resources to those amenities.

It is relatively tempting to think of all this in terms of economic aggregates, of changes in overall allocation of resources in response to changing wants. Yet to understand it fully we must focus on the human situation and human circumstance. It is the way in which individuals think, prefer, and choose that add up to the total sum of actions. Consider one major aspect of value change involving amenities—

family size. Family size has undergone a long-run decline over many decades since long before World War II. That change reflects new ideas about quality of life. This has gone through several stages. Urbanized people in the nineteenth century most probably had relatively small families, while rural family size remained much higher, and immigrants, mainly from rural origins, persistently injected large families into the urban social order and kept the overall family size quite large.[13] However, with each generation modern values had a major impact on newcomers and by the mid-twentieth century there were few influences left toward large family size. By this time the family size of eastern European migrants of the late nineteenth and early twentieth centuries had declined markedly, and that of Mexicans and blacks, recently rural with rural preferences for larger families, were equally and markedly affected. Current data indicate that almost no ethnocultural group is free from the inverse correlation between educational level and family size.[14]

This indicates changing value preferences within the family, which add up to marked social changes. The desire to have fewer children is a decision about the allocation of family resources and a reorientation from quantity to quality. Wants and aspirations by children and parents for themselves go far beyond keeping body and soul together. They escalate, and a decision is made to allocate more and more real income among fewer and fewer people.

Modern birth-control methods are significant within this context of changing wants. There are two phases. In the past the main thrust of birth control has been to bring the actual number of births into line with the desired number of children.[15] The gap between the two had been quite large and, due to birth control, it has been narrowed. The wider use of abortion permits closure of the gap even more completely. But a second process also seems underway, involving changing views as to the appropriate family size. There has been a marked decline from the post-World War II level of three or four children to approximately two. Very few today believe that one child is desirable but the number who prefer no children at all is increasing very slightly. If the latter were to continue it would indicate even more strikingly the persistence of a historical tendency toward quality-of-life emphases. Adults would increasingly prefer to spend their income on themselves and not on children at all or to limit their own income to levels that reduce time spent at earning a living and increase time spent in consuming goods and services with quality-of-living objectives.

Change in family size is only one of the more readily identifiable indexes of change in value preferences that reflect a concern for quality of life and experience rather than quantity of goods and services. As the emphasis on consumption beyond necessities increased, Americans first began to consume more material goods to make life in the home more pleasant and to reduce physical labor—thus, the expansion of the durable-goods sector of the economy in the 1920s and beyond. After this came an emphasis on services and especially so as leisure time activities began to loom larger and larger. These changes were accompanied by an emphasis on the quality of external surroundings. Moves to the suburbs constituted a search for more space within the home and more open area outside it to making living more comfortable.

The values behind this are reflected in studies indicating that far more people today wish to live in less congested areas than can do so; the desire can be fulfilled only partially.[16] The move to the suburbs has been with us for over a century and a quarter, from the first stages of rapid urban growth in the mid-nineteenth century. Formerly only a fraction of urban dwellers could participate in it; more recently a larger proportion can and does. The large-scale suburbanization of the 1920s and beyond is one of the first major expressions of the search for environmental amenities, for less congested surroundings, clean air, and less noise. It was but a small step from this to the desire to bring those features of environmental quality to the city itself. Thus the values implicit in the search for quality of surroundings in suburbanization were brought back into the city. Even beyond that, the outward thrust from the city, as we shall see in more detail, led to the use of the wider countryside and remaining wildlands, the enjoyment of the environmental quality of even less congested and less environmentally degraded area.[17] This use was usually confined to nonoccupational times of one's life, either vacations or in retirement years, but it gave even more extensive expression to the search for clean, quiet, less developed, and more natural surroundings.

These changes in values that lie behind the focus on amenities can safely be predicted to grow, for the conditions that lead to them are increasing. Only a very small segment of society had these values and could realize them in the nineteenth century; only a few then, for example, moved to the suburbs to live or used the open countryside for vacations. The data are imprecise and not yet developed, but we might well speculate roughly that in mid-nineteenth century America less than 3 percent of families expressed these values while today far more than 50 percent do.[18] Incomes rose, levels of education rose, mobility and the possibility of escaping environmental degradation increased, and with all this came a more intensive interest in the quality of the surrounding environment as an aspect of a higher standard of living. The search for environmental quality has been transformed from an elitist to a broadly mass movement.[19]

There are, of course, conflicts between the continuing interest in a higher material standard of living and the search for greater environmental quality. Automobiles are one example. People wish the mobility advantages of the car and will not give it up as readily as they have reduced the size of their families. Many changes in style of life that seem socially desirable to enhance environmental quality do not come easily and, if they come, will probably involve efforts to persuade people to change preferences. Those responsible for environmental degradation and who attack the drive for environmental quality love to focus on these paradoxes and to belittle thereby the search for environmental quality as temporary and transient. Yet the paradox will not be resolved that quickly. The search for environmental quality is as fundamental as the search for a higher material standard of living: in fact the former is an outgrowth of a further development of the latter. We can look forward to a politics of conflict and paradox between the two.

IV

A second long-run secular development has provided a setting that closely relates to the search for environmental quality. This is the new capacity for environmental transformation or environmental degradation. We have learned ways and means of effecting environmental change far more powerful and far more extensive than ever before. Some of these are technological, involving new earth-moving and resource-moving capacities or new physical and chemical processes producing waste products in far greater diversity and extent than before. Others are organizational—the vastly increased scale in the capacity to organize and direct a technology from a central source of decision making, the increased size and scale of both private corporate enterprise and public governmental administrative systems. In both technology and organization larger scale has replaced smaller, and with it the capacity to destroy the human environment has been greatly enhanced. Just as people have become consciously concerned about enhancing the quality of their environment, we have also been engaged in the practice of destroying it more fully and completely. The two tendencies are closely related.

Let us sketch briefly the rise of three of these: resource-moving and -transforming equipment, production of waste, and generation of electric power. Three issues that have become important in the current environmental conservation movement are strip mining, clear-cutting, and highway construction.[20] All involve land use and all involve modern capabilities to modify the land surface extensively. Behind each is a technology that has developed in its present form since World War II. The giant drag lines and shovels used in strip mining, with their multiton loads, seem like massive vultures moving over the countryside, defacing and destroying, representing in fact and in symbol man's arrogant capacity to transform his physical environment at will. Clear-cutting is a practice that seems more justified by forest technology than by silviculture, by the cost of removing and regenerating trees than by multiple-purpose management of wildlands; it is peculiarly adapted to the large-scale machinery of modern logging, machinery that is incapable of selecting trees for cutting and requires that all growth be consumed in one giant, sweeping operation. And the ribbons of interstate, multilane highways cutting across the countryside are more massive, leaving larger scars, and disrupting wider areas than any highway construction did ever before. The reaction against all three of these is in the degree to which they themselves represent the capability of massive land transformation.

Our waste-producing capacities have also escalated beyond anything known in previous years.[21] The traditional practice of using air, water, and land for disposing of waste seems no longer feasible because of our enormously increased capacity for producing waste. It is one of those questions of finite environmental limits and exponentially increasing human pressure. There is only so much air, land, and water in which to dump waste, but the amount of waste produced by modern technology has escalated. New chemical processes have developed in industrial technology (for example, textile production) in such a way as to expand waste output and alter dramatically its character. Solid waste, in new forms of packaging, has grown apace without much attention to what is to be done with it. Larger and larger technical processes have produced greater outputs of pollution into the air as well. All this comes from the size and scale of modern technology and production, their capability of throwing a load of material into the environment that we have not before experienced. In the face of an increasing concern for environmental quality, the capability is, to say the least, not appreciated.

Finally, the generation of electric power seems to have focused many aspects of the impact of large-scale technology into one major enterprise.[22] The scale of electric power plants has increased enormously and the scale of distribution systems has grown similarly. The capacity for air pollution is well known, as the large plants in the Plains and mountain West testify; the capacity for thermal pollution is equally great; the occupation of land for production and distribution is more extensive than ever before. Nuclear energy is an even greater example of the problem, for it involves a massive scale of production with massive uses of water and resulting thermal pollution and massive production of a new and, to many people, fearful kind of waste. The environmentally transforming capacities of modern electric generation are undoubtedly the source of much of the attack upon it by environmental conservationists.

Note two aspects of this accelerating capacity for environmental transformation. One is that the very forces that constituted the conservation movement of the early twentieth century now have come to be the source of environmental damage. That early twentieth-century movement asserted the possibilities of a glowing resource future through large-scale, efficient management. In doing so it was only one factor among many preparing the way for large-scale, efficient, resource transformation and degradation. It is no wonder that the logical extensions of the early twentieth-century movement—large-scale, multiple-purpose river development and large-scale timber technology—should have been transformed from earlier conservation triumphs to later environmental disasters. The resource processes involved in this have continued to develop in the same direction; it is the human preferences and values that have changed course. Those preferences have displayed considerable flexibility and modification; but technology has remained rigid, moving ahead in the same direction as before toward larger and more massive environmental modification and somewhat removed from changing human wants and values. What is especially striking is the failure to develop decentralized technology and decentralized autonomous management that might well be more responsive to growing preferences for environmental quality.

A second implication is more significant. These capabilities represent two quite different developments. Massive waste production can, for the most part, be dealt with effectively by massive amounts of technology. That is what the new clean water, clean air, and solid disposal drives are all about. There are major issues over recycling versus diffusion of air and water waste and over recycling versus reduction in waste production at the source. But much of the modern environmental movement is an attempt to apply technology and scale to the redirection of waste products away from our finite land, air, and water, which have been used in the past as waste receptacles. It is thus possible to deal with the problem of finite resources and growing human pressure on them in the field of waste by redirecting waste with technology.

But there are other uses of finite air, land, and water that are not so easily solved. These resources are used directly as space for human activities, both permanent habitation and temporary enjoyment, activities for which there are no possibilities whereby a redirected technology can reduce their impact. It would be possible to change human values and persuade people to want to live in more congested areas. But the desire for open space seems not so easily changed; so long as it is a major element of the drive for a "better" standard of living, it constitutes an exponentially increasing pressure upon finite air, land, and water resources.[23] It is for this reason that the land-transforming processes implicit in highway construction, strip mining, clear-cutting, and second-home development become so crucial. It is for this reason that the word "conservation," which traditionally has been associated with land problems, remains with us, not wholly replaced by the word "environment" and leading to a more appropriate phrase, "environmental conservation."[24] It is for this reason that the new interest in land use will raise issues far more intense than issues of pollution and waste. For while there is a way out of the conflict between resource limits and exponential increases in waste, there is no way out of the conflict between resource limits and exponential increases in direct human occupation of land and its surrounding air and water. Finite resources will not expand, and if the value placed upon open space continues, the only solution is to reduce the pressure upon the land. As we shall argue later, this version of the experience of finite resources and increasing human pressure is one of the most significant sources of the concern about the limits to growth.

V

There are very different thrusts within the environmental conservation movement, and the concern for the limits to growth has deeper and stronger roots in some of them than in others.[25] Consider, for example, the dynamics of the recent wave of concern for air pollution. For the most part this is an urban-based political drive. People living in and around cities have reacted against the increasing use of urban air as a dumping ground for urban wastes, and urban-based organizations have raised an outcry for cleaner air. This impulse seems relatively divorced from concerns about limits of growth. The experience is one of an undesirable manmade urban environment; values and political strategies are worked out in terms of cleaning up that immediate environment. There is little in the primary urban experience to turn one's thoughts to relationships to the wider world, such as the environmental load that the city places upon the countryside. Matters of air pollution are experienced and worked out within a more confined urban experience, an environment that can be manipulated for improvement as well as for degradation.

Waste water problems develop within a slightly different context of experience. Water pollution concerns stem from a wider range of people, beyond cities, as well as from those within, for streams flow through wider reaches of territory, cutting across both rural and urban areas. Historically it has been those who use streams in this larger fashion, such as fishermen, who have been the major force behind clean water. But in recent years they have been joined by urban people who want to clean up the Cuyahoga, the Ohio, Lake Erie, the Savannah, and a host of other rivers and lakes. Out of this has come a movement to dispose of waste before it reaches streams and lakes, control at the source rather than diffusion, an affirmation that the traditional use of rivers as a waste receptacle is no longer acceptable. We are now in the midst of a new mode of thought, of divorcing liquid-waste disposal from rivers by means of closed-loop systems or land recycling. It is symbolized by the goal of "zero discharge." The possibilities of these innovations have divorced the movement to reduce water pollution from problems of limits.

Solid-waste disposal displays similar political perspectives. For the most part cities, which produce the vast share of solid waste, seek only to transfer the wastes elsewhere, and their interest lies primarily in the cost of transfer. "Out there," in the surrounding countryside, land is to be had—current waste land, abandoned strip mines—which could just as easily be a source of land for solid waste disposal. The problem is the cost of getting the waste to it. [26] Where such possibilities do not exist, such as in the more congested East, there is more serious thought about a large-scale system involving more genuine recycling—thus the inauguration of a statewide waste recovery program recently in Connecticut. For the most part a consciousness of limits to growth does not arise naturally from the experience of urbanites coping with the mountains of solid waste they produce.

In all these aspects of the rapid growth of technological waste there is always the temptation to feel that space is available elsewhere for waste disposal; there is little inclination on the part of most urbanites to view the problem from the vantage point of the wider countryside, which is a potential dumping ground for waste. From this point of view, for example, the crucial question in air pollution is "air degradation," the process whereby cleaner air in the open countryside is permitted to become dirtier. [27] Those who would permit air degradation argue that urban air can be cleaned up only if urban pollution sources move to areas where air is cleaner. The Four Corners energy generation projects, for example, simply transferred pollution from electric power production from Los Angeles to the less settled Southwest. This is another version of a "diffusion solution" rather than control at the source. It is significant that the drive to apply and enforce effectively the nondegradation clause of the Clean Air Act of 1970 has come not from the urban-based air pollution citizen groups but from the Sierra Club, concerned primarily with natural beauty and the environmental quality of the wider countryside as well as the city.[28] True, some cities and many urban states joined in the effort as friends of the court, but they had to be drawn into it and did not jump spontaneously to the enforcement. In similar fashion this is one section of the act that the Environmental Protection Administration has tried and continues to try to wriggle out of and around; its perspective, too, is dominated by the problems of the city, and it looks to the transfer of pollution to the countryside as a major answer to the urban problem.

The transfer of water-quality standards from the city to the countryside is a different matter. In this case the fishermen users constitute a political force within the countryside itself. Moreover, polluted water in the countryside can have serious consequences for down-river cities, and in this fashion the cities become more interested in their wider environment. It is significant, therefore, that the same principle involved in the hotly debated air nondegradation concept—that areas cleaner than acceptable standards not be allowed to get dirtier—has long been taken as a working principle in matters of water quality. In a number of states rivers are classified in terms of degrees of water quality, and differential standards are adopted in which rivers of a higher quality level are not permitted to be reduced to a lower quality level. This is a simple nondegradation policy applied to water, a response to a force within the countryside that demands that the waste-producing influences of economic growth, arising largely from urbanization, not degrade this aspect of their environment.[29]

With solid waste disposal the political setting is more complex. New standards of disposal, especially the establishment of sanitary landfills, are being brought rapidly to the countryside. However, this comes not from forces indigenous to the countryside or from the cities directly, but from public health concepts that are urban based in their origins and that have broad political support, that are generalized outward through the state from state public health administrations. Yet even here the relative cheapness of land for solid waste disposal renders this approach far more readily acceptable to the rural community than does a secondary treatment sewage system, which is a more costly proposition. As of yet there is relatively less thought that there are limits to the growth of solid waste because there is still land "out there" for its ready disposal.

Two aspects of this brief overview of the politics of technological waste disposal should be stressed. First, the political movement involved does not readily produce a concern for the limits of growth; we must look for the roots of that concern elsewhere. For the most part those who generate waste feel that there are abundant opportunities for disposal, and those who are concerned with cleaning up have similar views. Few thrusts in the environmental movement assume that we must stop producing waste because there are finite limits to our waste receptacles of land, air, and water. That lurks in the background, and such cases as the reuse of bottles are exceptions,[30] but the more widespread experience is that there are alternatives far short of such limits and that technology can clean up waste with pollution controls and recycling.

Second, the city and the urban experience are, for the most part, self-contained and do not give rise readily to a more extensive vision concerning the impact of the city on the wider world. The city is the source of the increasing pressure on the environment, a "growth machine" as one economist has called it.[31] Here the forces making for increasing human loads on our finite resources are generated in the first place, the bulk of the increasing waste is produced, and the demand for more resources, including use of space, is created. Yet urban people do not experience directly the impact of their pressures. They live within the manmade environment of the city and their most active political impulses are confined to modifying that environment as a living and working space. Their secondary environment, that beyond the city which they use in greater intensity as time passes, is one they use occasionally, temporarily, or at remote distances and which is, therefore, beyond their immediate and sustained political interest. Consequently, urban people who are confined within the primary urban experience do not for the most part spontaneously develop a concern for the limits of growth. Their main concern in the environmental movement is air pollution and waste disposal, a set of problems that generate only limited perspectives and experiences restricted for the most part to the manmade walls and corridors of the city.

VI

There are other forces in the environmental conservation movement, rooted in different experiences, generating different definitions of environmental quality, that do give rise, far more readily, to a concern for the limits to growth. They are concerned with air, water, and land as living space rather than as receptacles for waste or as commodities for throughput. Let us examine these forces in more detail, distinguish them from other forces, and relate them to the past.

One of these focuses on metropolitan open space and arises out of the relatively open atmosphere of the metropolitan suburb. Its main experience is that of an expanding metropolitan system—people, highways, buildings, stores, "development"—closing in on a previously more open environment, on limited air, land, and water.[32] The choice to live away from the congested center of the city constitutes a search for more physical openness, more open space, less congested air, land, and water, less noise, in short for "amenities." When it is discovered that environmentally degrading influences are being transplanted to the new community, a severe shock ensues and gives rise to the drive to protect these amenities, to exercise some "control" over development. This generates the formation of a host of groups, often dispersed and local, frequently focused on the residential community, geared to controlling the pace and shape of development in their neighborhoods. The examples, especially dramatic on the East and West coasts, are legion. These groups are by no means uninterested in pollution problems; in fact they are extremely active in attempts to cope with them. But they have a larger perspective—the entire physical environment of their communities, and especially open space. Their experience leads them directly to a basic concern for land-use planning, a phase of environmental conservation rather remote from the activities of clean air and clean water organizations. They are concerned primarily with the use, present and future, of the land and streams of their immediate environment. To them the concept of open space is crucial; their basic concern is to retain and increase that open space. Is land more valuable in open space than in more traditional types of development? Such a question is frequently raised. Far more typical of the expertise closely allied with their views is the landscape architect. And rather than relying on Barry Commoner's *The Closing Circle* for inspiration, they prefer Ian McHarg's *Design with Nature*.[33]

Because of the concern for quality of space, the metropolitan open-space perspective is drawn steadily into the whole realm of amenity questions. This tendency stands in sharp contrast with a technological waste vantage point, which is often at odds with larger amenity issues. The two perspectives differ strikingly. While the concern for pollution focuses on environmental repair, the open-space perspective seeks to prevent environmental damage in the first place. It finds common ground, therefore, with many other groups that seek preventive rather than ameliorative action, that are concerned with wilderness and natural space, with air and water nondegradation, with pastoral landscapes, and with population and consumption problems.[34] Its concerns are more versatile, more extensive, and run deeper into the entire environmental conservation movement than are those whose primary interests focus on technological waste.

Dovetailing with metropolitan open space impulses are the drives to maintain the natural quality of an even larger space, the wilder and less developed rural and forested areas. Here a dramatic historical process has been taking place since World War II. Up to that time rural and forested areas had experienced a persistent decline in population and occupancy for many decades, roughly from the 1880s onward. Post-World War II economic growth reversed this trend and gave rise to a vigorous increase in the number of urban people seeking to use the countryside for second homes, for recreation at reservoirs and ski areas, for tourism, for highways, for fishing and hiking and backpacking, for off-road vehicle recreation, for a wide variety of purposes geared to the needs of urban inhabitants. Because of the material advantage these activities bring—such as higher land values—many rural areas were and are vulnerable to participation in this process of urban-induced change. But many others fear such an impact and have moved to protect their amenities against urban-generated environmental degradation. At the same time, some urban users of the countryside seek to protect the amenities they already enjoy from prospective overuse by others. All this might well be considered a phase of the metropolitan open-space movement writ larger.

Reaction against urban penetration of the countryside has been expressed in a number of ways. States have established preferential tax programs intended to reduce the turnover of open rural land to other uses, which is often brought about by taxing land at its potential value rather than its actual use.[35] The pressure of urban-based activities upon hunting land generates among sportsmen a concern for the preservation of wildlife habitat.[36] Hiking trail clubs, accustomed to enjoying the solitude of a natural setting for hiking, have faced

encroachment on the disruption of their right-of-way by residential
and economic development.[37] And those who have been in the van-
guard of establishing permanent or temporary homes in a wildland
setting because of its amenities resist the onrush of newcomers whose
desire to do the same thing destroys the environmental quality of open
space. From many sources come the concrete and adverse experience
of population pressure upon areas less developed. Such experience
gives form and substance to the view that levels of population and
consumption have gone too far.

All this has several major implications. First, interest in the problem
of the limits of growth arises most readily from a concern about space,
the space of air, land, and water, and the search for space in more
natural surroundings, which are uncongested and free from urban
noise. One does not read about matters of population and limitation of
consumption in magazines devoted to problems of technological
waste. The best source of information about the limits-of-growth
movement, in fact, consists of publications from Zero Population
Growth.[38] Even more suggestive is the organizational base of some
state activities. The first state group to focus sharply on population
growth was the Michigan Population Council.[39] It was inaugurated by
the Michigan branch of the American Association of University
Women, which was joined by the Michigan umbrella organization of
ZPG, the Mackinac Chapter of the Sierra Club, and the Michigan
organization of sportsmen, the Michigan United Conservation Clubs.
This range of interests leans more heavily toward the perspective of
amenities as goals than the more limited view of a clean environment.

Second, it may be that the primary urban environment cannot
readily give rise to a concern for the pressure of population growth and
consumption upon the larger region and the nation. Urban people
confine their definition of reality to the city and not far beyond.
Extraurban and extratechnological experience of some sort seems
essential to generate a basic concern for the limits of development.
Many urban people seek out these experiences, using the countryside
for their recreational activities, and it is from some of these that a
concern for the limits of growth seems most likely to arise. Such a
wider view is currently most rooted in people who in their own
experience and activities face directly the adverse effect of the urban
load and urban-rooted growth on the larger world.

VII

Several types of primary experience generate and sustain the view
that there are limits to the growth of our population, our level of living,
and our economy. Some of these involve a scarcity of commodities that
we consider essential for a satisfactory material level of living. The
shortage of petroleum for heating and fuel is the most dramatic current
example. Usually material shortages do not translate themselves
directly into perceived restrictions on human activities; they are more
often than not obscured by their indirect effects. But heating and fuel
shortages bear directly upon the daily lives of individuals and generate
a sharp consciousness of limitation. The connection between the larger
limits of resources and the limits of personal daily activities is close and
well understood.

The impact of the energy shortage on popular thinking, however, is
not at all clear yet. The public is not yet convinced that an energy
shortage is really upon us and is inclined to believe that it is contrived,
if not wholly at least in part, and that the limitations upon human
activities it imposes are not permanent. Establishment experts argue
that the shortage is only temporary and that several decades of intensive research and development will resolve it. In very few quarters is
there held the view that the problem presents a permanent crisis of
consumption and that we must scale down the pressure of our energy
demands upon finite resources. Only a few environmental organizations seem to be willing to argue that serious attention should be given
to the task of reducing energy demands. And few have been willing to
give special attention to those facets of the economy that constitute
highly intensive energy consumption such as air, automobile, and
truck passenger travel and freight, so as to guide research and development into far less intensive modes of transport. This generates the
notion that our level of energy consumption can keep on growing, or
that there is some fat in consumption patterns that can make possible
the necessary adjustments without many sacrifices and provide for
selective energy growth.

Another type of experience that gives rise to notions about the limits
to growth comes from the adverse environmental consequences of
technology. This problem is the main thrust of the "environmental
impact" statements. Although it is often easy to justify environmental

degradation in these analyses on the grounds that the economic benefits outweigh the environmental costs, there are an increasing number of cases in which this is clearly not the case. Land and water manipulation in Florida has endangered the fresh water aquifer and thereby the water supplies of east coast Florida cities; engineering works to control sand dunes and offshore islands along the south Atlantic coast have become so expensive that the National Park Service has decided to let nature take its course and to adjust human activities to the limits of geological forces; flood plain occupancy, it is now realized, produces social costs far greater than the social benefits and, from a simple cost vantage point, must be restricted.

All these involve human occupancy and settlement and their impact on resources in such a way that the consequences, both immediate and more remote, are detrimental to society. In many cases these detrimental consequences are experienced solely in terms of general, unfocused, and indirect social costs, that is, general adverse consequences that render an environment undesirable. But in other cases a specific and focused social cost results, such as in the cases previously mentioned, in which one can balance direct costs with direct benefits. Thus, one can determine the relative cost over benefit of flood plain occupancy when the taxpayer is called upon to provide funds for flood victims for relief and reconstruction. When this is the case the issue becomes sharp and the environmental limits to human activities become clear. Most analyses of the environmental consequences of development, however, are not so striking and do not generate a sense of environmental limits.

At this point the most significant experience that generates a sense of the limits to growth comes from the development of new amenity values rather than from a desire for more material production and is closely connected with quality of space. The experience is rooted peculiarly among those individuals who prize quality of space. This can be observed historically as the concern for efficient development gave way to an interest in environmental amenities. The change is due partly to the desire to enjoy experiences beyond material goods, a change fostered particularly by the wider range of perspectives implicit in more years of education and by higher incomes that enable many Americans to go beyond material wants and purchase qualitative experiences.

The process of residential suburbanization and the search for leisure and recreational experiences in more natural surroundings reflect the desire to seek a higher quality of space, where natural forces are more in evidence than in the developed and congested areas of settlement. In both cases the initial search for quality of space soon becomes threatened by others who seek the same amenities. At some point the experience of "too many" begins to take shape, and the concept of the carrying capacity of the land, air, and water begins to form. This generates the belief that overuse can destroy the resource that one wishes to enjoy and leads to a sense of limits. While technology can expand material goods by extracting material resources from all quarters of the globe and deliver them to the consumer, it cannot expand the space of air, land, or water. If space is encroached upon by development there is less space as natural environment. At this point the serious question takes shape: what shall be the balance between developed and natural environment? If acceptable levels of the latter are to be maintained, then the former must be restricted. There are limits to growth.

The tendencies that lead to a concern for the limits to growth are long run and not temporary. They have arisen out of changing values and changing technological capacities for environmental manipulation, and they arise especially from increasing pressures and claims for use of the finite space of land, air, and water, pressures that do not diminish but grow more intense with time. The predominant pollution issues of the past decade have not yet brought this into focus. The upcoming preoccupation with land and land use are likely to raise these questions of competition for space far more sharply and to bring the question of the limits to growth to our attention more dramatically.

NOTES

1. The initial statement in the discussion was Donella H. Meadows, Dennis L. Meadows, Jorgen Randers, and William W. Behrens, III, *The Limits to Growth* (New York: Universe Books, 1972).

2. For elaboration of this argument see Samuel P. Hays, *Conservation and the Gospel of Efficiency: The Progressive Conservation Movement, 1890-1920* (Cambridge: Harvard University Press, 1959).

3. Ibid., 189-198.

138

4. For an account of the establishment and early history of the national parks, see Robert Shankland, *Steve Mather of the National Parks* (New York: Alfred A. Knopf, 1951).

5. State fish and wildlife programs can best be followed in doctoral dissertations—for example, John Henry Reeves, Jr., "The History and Development of Wildlife Conservation in Virginia: A Critical Review" (Virginia Polytechnic Institute, 1960), and Larry Maring Rymon, "A Critical Analysis of Wildlife Conservation in Oregon" (Oregon State University, 1969). Some account of federal wildlife policy in the 1920s is in Donald C. Swain, *Federal Conservation Policy, 1921-1933* (Berkeley and Los Angeles: University of California Press, 1963).

6. The historical development of these activities can best be followed in the publications of such groups as the Potomac Appalachian Trail Club, the Appalachian Trailways Conference, the Appalachian Mountain Club, and the Federation of Western Outdoor Clubs. Some historical material on one well-known aspect of hiking activities is included in Ann and Myron Sutton, *The Appalachian Trail* (Philadelphia: Lippincott, 1967).

7. Two examples of the impact of the amenity focus in forest management are Richard M. Alston, "Forest—Goals and Decision-making in the Forest Service," United States Department of Agriculture, Forest Service Research Paper Int-128, 1972, and West Virginia Forest Management Practices Commission, "Report on Forest Management Practices on National Forest Lands in West Virginia," mimeo., West Virginia Legislature, August 1970. An excellent blend of the new with the old focuses is Leon S. Minckler, *Woodland Ecology: Environmental Forestry for the Small Owner* (Syracuse: Syracuse University Press, 1975).

8. Two books in this vein are Richard L. Berkman and W. Kip Viscusi, *Damming the West* (New York: Grossman Publishers, 1973), and Robert H. Boyle, John Graves, and T. H. Watkins, *The Water Hustlers* (San Francisco, New York: Sierra Club, 1971). The continuing criticism of impoundments can be followed best in the regular publications of the American Rivers Conservation Council in Washington, D.C.

9. A major attack on clear-cutting is Nancy Wood, *Clearcut, the Deforestation of America* (New York, San Francisco: Sierra Club, 1971); a defense is in Eleanor C. J. Horwitz, *Clearcutting: A View from the Top* (Washington, D.C., Acropolis Books Ltd., 1974).

10. For examples of this view, see The Conservation Foundation, *National Parks for the Future* (Washington, D.C.: The Conservation Foundation, 1972), and F. Fraser Darling and Noel D. Eichhorn, *Man and Nature in the National Parks,* 2d ed. (Washington, D.C.: The Conservation Foundation, 1969). Continuing evaluation of the national parks from this point of view can be followed in *National Parks and Conservation Magazine, The Environ-*

mental Journal, published by the National Parks and Conservation Association, Washington, D.C.

11. This conclusion is based on a review of a number of environmental impact statements. See also an elaborate example of this perspective for the U.S. Forest Service in United States Department of Agriculture, Forest Service, General Technical Report NE-2, "The Pinchot Institute System for Environmental Forestry Studies," 1973, which emphasizes exclusively "environmental effects" and excludes consideration of "environmental goals."

12. An excellent publication in the field of pollution control technology that generates this limited perspective is *Environmental Science and Technology,* published monthly by the American Chemical Society.

13. Some sense of this process can be obtained from a comparison of different nativity groups with respect to children ever born per 1,000 women in 1910, as reported in U.S. Department of Commerce, Bureau of Census, *Current Population Reports,* Series P-20, No. 226 (November 1971), p. 28. The data were: for native whites, 3,251; for foreign born, 4,102; for native blacks and other races, 4,247. For foreign born the data included: England and Wales, 3,269; Ireland, 3,341; Russia, 5,349; Italy, 5,454; and Poland, 5,868. Precise time series to determine these comparative patterns depend upon future accumulation of historical data. By 1960 the data had converged considerably.

14. Ibid., p. 20.

15. The problem of unwanted births and its statistical significance is focused on in Larry Bumpass and Charles F. Westoff, "Unwanted Births and U.S. Population Growth," in Daniel Callahan, ed., *The American Population Debate* (Garden City, N.Y.: Doubleday, 1971), 267-273.

16. See James J. Zuiches and Glenn V. Fugitt, "Residential Preferences: Implications for Population Redistribution in Nonmetropolitan Areas," paper read before the 138th meeting of the American Association for the Advancement of Science," Philadelphia, Pennsylvania, December 1971, in William K. Reilly, ed., *The Use of Land: A Citizens' Policy Guide to Urban Growth* (New York: T. Y. Crowell, 1973), 86.

17. See Elizabeth R. Gilette, *Action for Wilderness* (New York and San Francisco: Sierra Club, 1973) and Michael Frome, *Battle for the Wilderness* (New York: Praeger, 1974).

18. This is a pure estimate visualized by comparing the very small percentage of the American people who in the mid-nineteenth century had access to outdoor amenities such as spas and watering places, as contrasted with the very large number today who have access to state and national parks.

19. The old argument that wilderness hiking and camping was "elitist" now has a hollow ring to it in the face of the increasing numbers of people, well into several millions, who use such areas.

20. For several examples of books in this vein popular among environmentalists, see Wood, *Clearcut;* John F. Stacks, *Stripping: The Surface Mining of America* (San Francisco and New York: Sierra Club, 1972); Helen Leavitt, *Superhighway—Superhoax* (New York: Ballantine, 1970).

21. An excellent account of the problems inherent in positive correlations between industrial output and pollution production is Julian McCaull, "The Tide of Industrial Waste," *Environment* 14 (December 1972): 30-39.

22. One recent expression of this is Louise B. Young, *Power over People* (New York: Oxford University Press, 1973).

23. An analysis of the social costs of this pressure in suburban areas is Council on Environmental Quality, *The Costs of Sprawl, Environmental and Economic Costs of Alternative Residential Development Patterns at the Urban Fringe* (Washington, D.C.: Council on Environmental Quality, 1974).

24. The use of terms to describe state agencies is instructive. New York is distinctive in that its agency is called the Department of Environmental Conservation, reflecting a strong combination of its long-standing involvement in land questions in connection with the Adirondacks and its more recent concern with environmental pollution.

25. The following conclusions are based upon reading a wide range of materials from national organizations such as the Wilderness Society, the National Wildlife Federation, the Sierra Club, the Environmental Policy Center, and the National Clean Air Coalition; general publications such as *Environmental Science and Technology, High Country News,* and *Science;* state general groups such as the Oregon Environmental Council, the Colorado Open Space Council, the Virginia Conservation Council, or the Pennsylvania Environmental Council; and more specialized groups such as the Michigan United Conservation Clubs, California Coastal Alliance, the West Virginia Highlands Conservancy, and the Pittsburgh Group Against Smog and Pollution.

26. A recent example is the effort by Philadelphia to secure disposal sites in northeastern, southwestern, and south central Pennsylvania, each one of which has aroused considerable local opposition.

27. An excellent introduction to the problem of air nondegradation is in *High Country News* 4,20 (September 29, 1972): 1, 4-6.

28. See Laurence I. Moss, "How to Prevent Significant Deterioration of Air Quality in Any Portion of Any State," mimeo., statement before the Environmental Protection Agency, Hearings on Significant Deterioration, Washington, D.C., August 27, 1973; and Moss, "Sierra Club Responds to EPA's Four Clean Air Alternatives," mimeo., statement before the Subcommittee on Air and Water Pollution, Committee on Public Works, U.S. Senate, July 24, 1973.

29. The stream classification system of Pennsylvania is a good example. For a description of it and its application, see Pennsylvania Department of Environ-

mental Resources, Bureau of Water Quality Management, "Final Report of the Pennsylvania Sanitary Water Board, 1923-1971," Publication Number 29, 1971. For an account of the political forces involved and in applying nondegradation concepts, see "Summary of Hearing and Comments" pertaining to stream reclassifications based upon water quality standards, hearings 13-18, January-March 1973, conducted by the Pennsylvania Department of Environmental Resources, available in mimeographed form from the department.

30. The most widely discussed example of a reusable container law is that of Oregon. See Don Waggoner, "Oregon's 'Bottle Bill,'" Oregon Environmental Council, n.d., mimeo.; Waggoner, "Oregon's 'Bottle Bill'—One Year Later," Oregon Environmental Council, 1973, mimeo.; Charles M. Gudger and Jack C. Bailes, "The Economic Impact of Oregon's 'Bottle Bill,'" School of Business and Technology, Oregon State University, 1973.

31. Harvey Molotch, "The City as a Growth Machine," mimeo., University of California, Santa Barbara, July 1973.

32.. There is a wide variety of literature concerning open spaces, which embodies directly and indirectly this sense. Several examples are William K. Reilly, ed., *The Use of Land* (New York: Crowell, 1973); Charles E. Little, *Challenge of the Land; Open Space Preservation at the Local Level* (New York: Pergamon Press, 1968); Richard E. Galantowicz, "The Process of Environmental Assessment," in five parts issued separately, North Jersey Conservation Foundation (Morristown, New Jersey, 1972-1973), and Susan Redlich, ed., *Guiding Growth; A Handbook for New Hampshire Townspeople* (New Hampshire: Society for the Protection of New Hampshire Forests, Concord, 1974).

33. Barry Commoner, *The Closing Circle* (New York: Alfred A. Knopf, 1971); Ian McHarg, *Design with Nature* (Garden City, New York: Doubleday, 1969). For a more recent model in the McHarg mold see the so-called Medford study, Narenda Juneja, "Medford; Performance Requirements for the Maintenance of Social Values Represented by the Natural Environment of Medford Township, New Jersey," Center for Ecological Research in Planning and Design, Department of Landscape Architecture and Regional Planning, University of Pennsylvania, Philadelphia, Pa., 1974.

34. These conclusions are based on a variety of organizational materials from such groups as the Virginia Conservation Council, the North Carolina Conservation Council, the New York State Environmental Lobby, the Oregon Environmental Council, the Colorado Open Space Council, and the Society for the Protection of New Hampshire Forests.

35. The preferential assessment programs of two states are evaluated in John Kolesar and Jaye Scholl, *Misplaced Hopes, Misspent Millions: Report on Farmland Assessments in New Jersey* (The Center for Analysis of Public Issues, Princeton: 1972), and Jerald W. Hunter, "Preserving Rural Land

Resources: The California Westside," *Ecology Law Quarterly* 1, 2 (Spring 1971): 330-373.

36. A good statement of the concern for habitat is Nathaniel P. Reed, "Environmental Concern and Wildlife—a Humane Approach," speech given before the American Humane Association, reprinted in *Pennsylvania Game News* 6, 44 (June 1973): 15-20.

37. This problem can be followed in the publications of such groups as the Appalachian Trailway Conference and the Potomac Appalachian Trail Club.

38. The activities of Zero Population Growth can be followed in its monthly, *National Reporter,* and its quarterly, *Equilibrium.*

39. The activities of the Michigan Population Council recounted here are derived from correspondence with it and its releases.

Daniel Aaron

HARVARD UNIVERSITY

9
Reflections on Growth and Literature in America

I

My thesis on the subject of growth can be summarized in the following assertion: Although a belief in the goodness and inevitability of growth has been an essential part of the official credo of the United States, American writers and intellectuals have given only a qualified allegiance to (or denied the validity of) the concept of growth as a good in itself.

The burden of the first part of this statement seems to me explicit or implicit in generations of speeches and orations, in manifestoes and declarations, in sermons, poems, plays, and fiction. Certainly the concept of growth pervades the terms and expressions historians have employed in chronicling the rise of the Republic: manifest destiny, expansionism, promotion, boosterism, progress, success, prosperity, and the like.

For a society that started, so to speak, de novo, growth was tantamount to survival. To stagnate or to retrograde was to die. Even a people who rated the spirit higher than the flesh obeyed God's injunction to convert wilderness into garden, to increase and multiply. Long before independence, North Americans were measuring the advance of civilization in quantitative terms, and men like Nathaniel Ames and Benjamin Franklin were envisioning an America transformed by the arts and sciences into Eden. A people had contracted with Providence to adhere to a set of divine edicts. In turn, God promised to reward

them. America's incubation lasted to 1776. Rhetoricians in the early
national period likened the young Republic to an infant rapidly out-
growing its swaddling clothes. By the 1830s and 1840s national growth
had become a subject of national gratulation, a proof of America's
manifest destiny, a justification for the boasting and fondness for
hyperbole foreign observers regarded as characteristically American.

II

If growth from this country's inception had provoked considerable
comment and reflection, the years between 1815 and 1929 were those
during which the gospel of growth received its most articulate formulation and the language of growth flowered most profusely. And it was
during this time as well that the approval of growth for growth's sake
was most freely given. Neither in the seventeenth century, when the
Old World concepts of space and time anchored the imagination and
the possibilities of expansion were limited, nor in the eighteenth
century when classic or neoclassic aesthetic theories inhibited romantic speculation, was growth celebrated as a good in itself—the dreams
of a future America notwithstanding. Even the first attempts after
independence to create a literature commensurate with the new
nation's aspirations resulted in stiff and static productions more retrospective in spirit than future minded. The God of the Puritans still
continued to ride herd on the unsanctified imagination.

Neoclassical criteria—decorum, measure, limitation, clarity—were
by no means abandoned at the beginning of the so-called Romantic
period, but the accelerating tempo of life between the second war with
England and the Civil War affected American self-assurance and
thereby national and verbal literary expression. These were the years
of oratory and steam power, of untrammeled speculation (both the
intellectual and economic varieties). The metaphor of life as a race
derived from the facts of American experience: presidential races,
steamboat races, the race to civilize the West, the race between cities,
the race to succeed—with every young American guaranteed an equal
chance to win the prize. Daniel Boorstin characterized this period as
the "democracy of haste" based upon the "technology of haste," a time
of "mushrooming systems of transportation." Boorstin's Americans

indulge in "booster talk" or "the language of anticipation." This is the language of infinitude, a language disdaining limits. The revealing words in the literature of the period are "boundless," "endless," "inexhaustible." Prairies are oceanic in their immensity. The manifest destiny of the United States is to grow and expand, and the celebrated American confidence is inextricably linked with the expectation of a perpetual land boom. If the concept of growth in the eighteenth century can be epitomized by the word "plenitude" (suggesting slow and organic development) in the Faustian nineteenth century the word is "dynamism."

The Civil War released new sources of energy. It was followed by an unprecedented growth that in less than a century brought the United States to the apogee of its power. Sustained by enormous resources and by a centralized coordination of the economy, the nation withstood disastrous economic setbacks and confounded the minority of pessimists. To be sure, the chief beneficiaries of the industrial takeoff were the large corporations rather than the underlying population, and the postwar prosperity was accompanied by a good deal of internal disorder; but the majority of Americans shared in the bonanza and trusted the stewardship of the capitalist managers and subscribed to the ideology of big business. By all the conventional economic measurements, the nation was in competent hands. Laissez-faire capitalism had its critics, but even they had to admit that it worked, at least until 1929; that year marked the end of the business man as the articulator of American values. Never thereafter would he be listened to so uncritically as the national oracle.

III

Symbolic of the general disenchantment following the crash was an episode F. Scott Fitzgerald recounts in *The Crack-Up.* Soon after his return to the United States, he climbed to the top of the Empire State building (an emblem for him as well as for some of his literary contemporaries of vaunting American pride and ambition) and discovered that New York City was "not an endless succession of canyons" he had always supposed but that *"it had limits,"* that it was "a city after all and not a universe."

This "awful revelation" must not be taken very seriously. Back in the 1920s Fitzgerald had suspected that America's power was not unlimited, and he dramatized his presentiments in stories of disaster. He was by no means the first to do so. Throughout the nineteenth and twentieth centuries (and no less so in the most expansive periods), American literature is filled with expressions of fear about the social and spiritual consequences of believing in growth for growth's sake. It is difficult to find any writer of consequence who is unreservedly optative, who does not reveal some apprehension that the gospel of growth and the glorification of progress and wealth might play down more important beliefs and values. In cautionary tales, in novels, essays, and poems, the acquisitive impulse and single-minded devotion to those material things by which growth is measured chill the hearts of the mercenary undertakers and insulate them from the "magnetic chain of being." Uncontrolled technological growth dislocates and disrupts because the social and cultural changes it precipitates proceed too rapidly and too convulsively for the human mind to adjust to.

American literature, it seems to me, betrays a latent conservatism even when it celebrates the bounty of the land and the go-ahead spirit of the American people. What separates our writers from their literal-minded and unreflective contemporaries is their uneasy attitude toward the instruments and symbols of growth. Machines liberate and enslave. The imagery employed by its apostles, as Leo Marx has shown, associates "technology with the destructive and repulsive." In essays, poems, and fiction, the vehicles of locomotion (steamboats, railroad trains, automobiles, airplanes) often get out of hand and blow up. Solitary and alienated men on the move or in transit—incarnations of the entrepreneurial spirit—come to a bad end.

It was not growth itself so much as an unregulated and mindless growth that repelled some of our representative writers; not wealth per se but the creatures made arrogant and rude by wealth; not machines themselves but machines that ran amok, desecrated nature, and reduced their tenders to automatons; not the new and innovative but newness contemptuous of the traditional, ignorant of the past, and riveted to the present.

Suspicion of uncoordinated and unplanned expansion was implanted in the New England consciousness from the earliest times. The Puritans in the seventeenth century moved into the frontier as communities replete with churches and schools. This policy was dictated, to be sure, by considerations of safety, but even if the Indians had not threatened security, the Yankee theocracy feared the "Indianizing" of persons and families living in primitive seclusion.

Perhaps the most dramatic clash between the forces of regulated growth and uncontrolled expansion occurred in the late 1820s and early 1830s when the anachronistic son of the Puritans, John Quincy Adams, lost out to a man whose elevation to the presidency legitimized the pillaging of the public domain. According to his grandson, Brooks Adams, John Quincy Adams had planned a vast consolidated American community. Its components were to have been an industrialized South (in which slavery had ceased to pay), government-sponsored communication projects, and a national university. But the opening of public lands (the source of national energy and plenty) deepened the slavery issue and ultimately caused the Civil War.

John Quincy Adams, Brooks Adams wrote, started with eighteenth-century assumptions. Science in the hands of rational men, he believed, would ensure the kind of progress a beneficent God delighted to contemplate. For President Adams democratic equality and education were mutually dependent. Too late he realized his mistake. Science produced wars, speculation, jobbery. Education stimulated the desire for wealth and "the disease of wealth rested on applied science." He discovered belatedly that "to conserve" was contrary to the instinct of greed pervading the democratic mind. His dream of a society led by the qualified and best and managed according to scientific principles was doomed at the start. And the democratic principles he advocated prepared the ideal climate for the unregulated economic forces that fragmented society. The American in the United States of Adams's grandsons was no longer the master of his fate. He was the "pure automaton . . . moved along the paths of least resistance" by forces he could not control.

Premonitions of the social penalties of growth are evident even in the decades when the agrarian dream of independent masterless men was in the ascendent. Washington Irving poeticized the boundless prairies and at times resorted to the language of infinitude, but raucous pushing democrats repelled him, and his most characteristic works indicate a preference for order and tradition, for old buildings and old servants and old lands. No one responded more exultingly to the magnificence of the American landscape than James Fenimore

Cooper, and no one tried harder to mediate between the centrifugal
and centripetal tendencies in American life. Natty Bumppo, in flight
from the contaminations of civilization yet equally averse to brutish
primitivism, would seem to represent Cooper's commitment to
orderly growth.

Although the booster in Emerson took satisfaction in his country's
material advancement, he complained of the tyranny of "things" and
subordinated the activities of the caucus and the marketplace to the
affairs of the mind. Thoreau, in the perverse way he had of attributing
opposite meanings to familiar words, employed entrepreneurial terms
to undercut the ritual of business and to explain his own brand of
transcendental economics. The "westering" he wrote about had
nothing to do with the forty-niners, and the agencies of "progress"
(banks, real estate, railroads) did not enter into his private explora-
tions. Melville warned his countrymen as early as the 1850s that the
land boom that thus far had enabled the United States to escape the
blights afflicting the Old World could not last, that limits to American
progress were already discernible. Industrial growth, he warned,
would be obtained at the expense of personal freedom, and he made
the machine process (as Thoreau did) a symbol of nemesis or fate (that
which limits). After the Civil War, if not before, this insight had
become a cliché.

IV

From mid-nineteenth century on, American writers and intellectuals continued to regard the uninterrupted and seemingly inevitable
growth of their country with mixed feelings, impressed by the size and
wealth of the United States yet fearful lest the nation be poisoned by
its own power. How they expressed these feelings depended upon
their age, regional origins, culture, and class affiliations as well as
sundry other loyalties. The following groups or categories might be
considered as a rough and inexact breakdown of writers (along with
some other members of the intelligentsia) from 1865 through World
War II.

1. Those coming of age shortly before the Civil War uncomfortably

straddled two ages—the decentralized antebellum society with its agrarian ideals and the new technological and plutocratic society, at once marvelous and appalling. Two examples would be Mark Twain, the pessimistic celebrator of these times, and Walt Whitman of "Democratic Vistas" and "The Passage to India."[1]

2. A number of writers in the second half of the nineteenth century were shocked by the disparities between progress and poverty and by the excessive social costs of industrial growth. They were not Luddites and appreciated the improvements in living standards made possible by science. But they challenged the methods and policies—not to mention the philosophy itself—of the capitalist managers and suggested the possibility of a more civil and humane society than the one Herbert Spencer prescribed. Theirs might be called the utopian response to unregulated growth. They wanted to conserve, to keep the social fabric intact, to prevent the polarizing of American society that might lead to revolution and tyranny. Henry George, Edward Bellamy, and W. D. Howells belong to this group.

3. None of the writers thus far falls neatly into a single literary configuration, and the same is true of writers who might be labeled elitist or mugwump. In their eyes, the apostles of growth for growth's sake had created a society dominated by cultural barbarians who exploited and manipulated a mongrelized population. These writers upheld the genteel tradition, reflected the loyalties and prejudices of old-stock Americans, and espoused both liberal and illiberal political causes. They were likely to oppose both open immigration and military expansion. They supported conservation. Collectively they make up a mixed bag: Francis Parkman, T. B. Aldrich, J. R. Lowell, Henry and Brooks Adams, to name only a few.

4. The writers in this group are related to those in the previous category, but they were less civic minded and less comfortable with the everyday realities of their society. They might loosely be defined as the aesthetes. They regarded America's sprawling development with distaste and sought refuge in more finished and culturally mature civilizations. Some of them became expatriates or spent considerable portions of their lives outside of the raw republic. Henry James is too large a figure to be confined to this constellation, but writers like F. M. Crawford and some of the twentieth-century expatriates might serve as examples.

5. Included here are writers critical of the official ethos of growth as

a measure of national greatness (and representing a broad spectrum of
political opinion) who nonetheless entered fully into American life,
were not overly disturbed by its discords, relished its vulgarity and
vast dimensions, and felt some kind of identity with the people and
practices they condemned and satirized. Among them are Mark
Twain, Frank Norris, Theodore Dreiser, Sherwood Anderson, Sinclair
Lewis, Carl Sandburg, and Thomas Wolfe.

V

On notable occasions before the Great Depression, political and
economic crises had momentarily halted the course of "triumphant
democracy" without seriously affecting popular faith in America's
capacity to grow and improve. The national preservation usually
turned out to be the seemingly inexhaustible bounty of the continent.
Technically, the "frontier" was "gone at last" (to use Frank Norris's
phrase) by 1900 but not the fertility of the land or timber reserves or oil
and mineral deposits. Nor had these redemptive resources disap-
peared by 1929.

The economic debacle in the next decade weakened confidence in
America Unlimited even among the Menckenians who had been
debunking boosterism and the paltriness of American culture but who
had never seriously questioned the ability of the capitalists to keep the
machines running. The literary radicals of the 1930s did not criticize
the principle of growth itself so much as the failure to spread equitably
the largesse of farm and factory. Writers who had never been
enchanted by production figures of the United States discovered a
kind of poetry in Soviet statistics (most of them highly unreliable) as if
reported annual increases in electric power kilowatts or hectares under
cultivation or tractors manufactured beatified the politburo. No
American poet or novelist wrote with comparable enthusiasm about
the TVA or Boulder Dam, although a brief section in *The Grapes of
Wrath* describing a government-managed migrant camp might be
classified a New Deal idyll.

Steinbeck is the first contemporary author I know of who gave a
sociological meaning to what had heretofore been almost exclusively a
biological term. He wrote of organisms (including the human)

destroyed by natural or manmade dislocations of the environment. Much of his fiction and nonfiction are fables on the penalties of man's impiety to nature. The disastrous dust storms that routed the Okies from their farms and started them on their lemminglike trek westward are partly a consequence of the philosophy of growth that sanctions the "conquest" and "exploitation" and "rape" of the land. Steinbeck is only one of a number of American writers from Cooper on who reported the ransacking of the continent or who showed how progress and growth had often been confused with superfluous accumulation. Emerson the functionalist condemned what he called "vicious ornamentation." "It is a rule in paleontology," Steinbeck wrote in *The Sea of Cortez* (1941), "that ornamentation precedes extinction."

In the last several decades, the hypertrophy of things has haunted the literary imagination with dreams of catastrophe. Of course the literature of disaster has a long history in America. In fiction (I do not count the premonitory parables of Poe, Hawthorne, and Melville), America's vaunted civilization has been destroyed by class war *(Caesar's Column,* 1891, and *The Iron Heel,* 1907) or threatened with holocausts unless the right economic path was taken *(Progress and Poverty,* 1879, and *Looking Backward,* 1888). Henry Adams took a ghoulish satisfaction in the implications of entropy and pinpointing the moment when the great machines would stop or people would blow themselves up. But the "fu-topian" mentality of the 1950s and 1960s touched up the nightmare. It pictured a mindless society managed by conmen and paranoids, and it did so through the medium of black comedy.

I have been suggesting that serious American literature has always been critical of the official credo and of the code of personal success embodied in the Alger myth. Indeed it has been largely an itemizing of the costs and penalties of success objectified in the careers of Ahab, Lapham, Cowperwood, Babbitt, Gatsby, Sutpen, and others. No comparable figures can be found in major current fiction. The "Mr. Bigs" lurking behind the scenes in Mailer's novels and detective fiction are criminal types,[2] not exemplars of the American dream. The authors of the most significant books written after World War II are probably more at odds with the official credo of American society than their counterparts in the past. They favor the antihero. They celebrate the unheroic. The antagonist is no longer the splendid villain, primordial nature, or demons erupting from the unconscious but what might be called the agency of organization (or in its pejorative forms—bureaucrats, totalitarians, manipulators, computerizers).

Armed with machines for registering, sorting, storing in memory banks, the organizers change people into integers, wipe out identity, convert men to things. And the agency of organization is really the by-product of growth. After a society reaches a certain size and complexity, it must operate efficiently or stifle. In the hands of wicked men, the machine turns oppressor, but in all mass societies, no matter how disinterestedly operated, freedom and the sense of personal identity are jeopardized. In the early nineteenth century when society in the United States was still open and flexible, Thoreau called the railroad (symbol of progress and organization) *Atropos*. The contemporary literary mind, here and elsewhere, is wary of bigness—big business, big cities, big armies, big universities, big churches, big countries. Perhaps the new antinomianism now pervading so much of our art and politics, the refusal of many people to accept the second-hand and the given, the emphasis on feeling, the impulse to establish a direct connection with assorted godheads are all responses to a society that has become unbearably large and impersonal.

VI

In sum, I should say that growth was and remains an important value in the United States, a sign of divine favor, historical tendency, a proof of the efficacy of democratic institutions. It can almost be said that growth is part of every American's birthright guaranteed by the preamble to the Constitution.

But from the start, writers interpreted its meaning and value in many different ways and from differing points of view. Size, growth, natural bounty—the zest of becoming—helped to make up for the paucity of culture and tradition. Deprived of an ancient history, the literary imagination could be quickened by Niagara Falls and limitless savannas and the prospects of cities springing up where the cry of wolves was recently heard.

Yet from the seventeenth century on, the preachers of lay or secular jeremiads feared what the phenomena of growth (wealth, progress, power) might do to unregenerate Americans. Had not this surfeit of success, this obsession with progress, induced them to connive with the devil in stealing land from Mexico, condoning slavery, cheating Indians, exploiting workers, tolerating slums?

In recent years the critique of growth has not altered much, although it has taken a different tack. American literature is full of statements rating quality over quantity, and at no time have American writers been more suspicious of the official claims for growth or the magical properties of the GNP. The sheer size of the United States ("the mightiest power in the world") is no longer so intoxicating as it once was; the rapid exhaustion of natural fuels and the current power crisis recall the dire predictions of Henry Adams and may be the objective correlatives of an inner power crisis. Most important of all, I suspect, for writers and artists is the identification of size and growth with pollution in all of its forms—economic, political, moral. Contemporary writers, to my knowledge, have not invented any new values to supersede old ones. When they reject growth it is because they feel more precious values are being sacrificed to obtain it. They seem to be saying, in short, that growth that warps and stultifies the minds and lives of its alleged beneficiaries is not true growth at all.

NOTES

1. The ambivalence of the first can best be illustrated in his *Life on the Mississippi,* at once a castigation of southern backwardness and a nostalgic glance at the brave and unharnessed prewar society. His expressed satisfaction at the industrial development of the river towns is undercut by sardonic comments on the chicanery of business types he encounters. In *A Connecticut Yankee* progress is even more clearly associated with disaster. Whitman, too, in his darker moments contrasted New World democracy's "materialistic success" with its social and cultural failure.

2. I do not count the anarchistic titans in Ayn Rand's novels who are forced by herd men into illegal acts.

John Wilmerding
DARTMOUTH COLLEGE

10
The End of Growth
as an American Value?
A View Through the Arts

I

In many areas of American life—intellectual, geographical, political—
growth as both a value and a reality appears to have reached a limit.
The power of the American presence abroad, whether the dollar,
military engagement, or political idealism, seems blunted or devalued
at every turn. At home an environmental and ecological crisis is at
hand, one that derives from the fact that physical space has run out
within the continental limits, at least for the kind of expansion that has
existed in American history up to the present. The concerns of
retrenchment, preservation, and conservation have come into sharp
focus in the 1970s. There are two facts about these constraints that are
significant: First, they are primarily *physical* or material (rather than
philosophical) in nature. Second, whatever the occasional precedents
in previous decades, this awareness of limitation, and even its transformation into an idealism of restraint, have emerged decisively only in
the 1970s.

Questions arise as to whether Americans are, willing or not, being
forced to give up their long-held values of growth and its corollary,
progress. If so, how is such a shift reflected in the arts; further, what
other values might emerge in compensation? The concept of growth is
evident in the earliest visions of America as defined by the first

explorers and settlers, and it gathers perhaps greatest momentum, finds fullest expression, during the expansive years of the first half of the nineteenth century. Although strongly tempered by the shocks of the Civil War and the subsequent insecurities of American life in the later years of the century, the idea of betterment, enlargement, aggrandizement has managed to survive as an emblem of the American character into the twentieth century. In large measure this sensibility has been tied to the continuing acquisition and possession of physical space or landscape. The celebration of discovery and the experience of the new have captured the American mind from the explorers of the sixteenth century on the edge of the New World to the adventurers of the nineteenth moving into the American West, the Arctic, and South America, to those who today venture to the moon and into space.

Consequently, with land and other natural resources physically running out and overpopulation threatening, with America unable to win a war for the first time in its history, with its assumptions of moral rightness and supremacy often successfully questioned, the national identity is facing an unprecedented challenge to one of its fundamental values. While growth and progress may have been stunted periodically before, the apparent totality of their limitation, both imposed and espoused, is uniquely new to the present situation. If this proves to be true, the nation faces a period of uncertain duration in which it will have to redefine its aspirations in order to regain its self-image and even self-acceptance.

It is significant that the first major artistic movement of the 1970s is conceptual art, indicating a withdrawal away from the physical and material world. As the outer world becomes too crowded (and pollution in its various forms is a type of density or crowding), the artist has eschewed the making of commodities or objects that fill up space further, whether by sale or exhibition, in favor of retreating to the world of thought and imagination. He stresses process over product. The very term "conceptual" refers to an introspection and inwardness that have been possibly the central responses to limits imposed on physical growth.

Conceptual art has been a widespread movement in recent years, taken up by a variety of artists across the United States and to some degree as well by individuals in other industrialized countries. Its primary forms of expression have been in two related areas: the environment (earth art) and the human being (body art). Rather than using up physical resources and materials to fabricate traditional paintings and sculptures, conceptual artists strive to make use of existing situations. They make their artistic statements by commenting on, drawing attention to, occasionally modifying the actions of their bodies or the presence of the landscape—but without damaging or polluting either if possible. Thus, they place primary emphasis on thought and idea, asserting that aesthetic achievement lies as much, if not more so, in the conceiving as in the making of a work of art.

They wish to force us to recognize that the artistic process exists not only in the finished result, but perhaps even more in the initial act of imagination. In addition, body art reflects some aspiration for renewed humanity in a technological world, while earth art has spoken equally to the still existing beauty in an increasingly ravaged environment. As with all avant-garde art forms when they first emerge, conceptual art in its various forms was perplexing to many when it first emerged at the beginning of the 1970s. But as time has passed, we have increasingly come to recognize how poignantly and tellingly these artists have been the seers of a new age.

One can also find in the terminology of other recent art movements a language of reduction: pop, op, minimal, systemic. The terms are clipped, abbreviated, and tight. In short, by the 1960s there was already a sense of pulling in. The excesses of America after World War II may well prove to have been the final flourishes in the nation's long experience of expansion. That the contemporary artist now seems more interested in idea than fact is at once a response to the limits of growth and a possible indicator of the transformation coming to the national consciousness.

To support the above arguments best I will examine more fully periods in American history that are representative of both the flourishing and inhibition of growth as an ideal. Many characteristics of the American vision are first stated in the images of the early explorers, and their fulfillment is exemplified in Jacksonian America. Correspondingly, the disruption of the Civil War initiates a period of tempering seriousness, which culminates in the dislocations and unsureness of the end of the century. The earlier phase of idealism should help us to understand the American value of growth; the later phase of realism may illustrate where these values were temporarily fragmented or restrained. Together they should put into some perspective the questions of the present moment.

II

The very term "New World" indicates that the condition of newness was from the beginning to be associated with the land that would ultimately be called America. To Europeans crossing the Atlantic there was always a horizon before them, and later a frontier. Truly, the first images of America are maps, both in the ordinary sense of explicit drawings of islands and coastlines and in the metaphoric sense of sketches recording local flora and inhabitants. The drawings and watercolors of the first settlers, John White, Thomas Hariot, Jacques Le Moyne in the sixteenth century, are in effect catalogs, visual records or measurements of experience. In them is an implicit wonder at both the scale and plenitude of the New World. Mapmaking, then, is a language of discovery, and so set in motion from the start was a process of exploration beyond the edges of the known, to possess by clarification further stretches of land.

The discovery and exploration of America were, of course, the result of many factors: the emergent Enlightenment and scientific inquisitiveness of the Renaissance mind, the transformation of late medieval superstitions about the perfection of paradise in the golden west, an escapism born of religious persecution and commercial adventurism, and conceivably the extension of ideas of progress, perfectability, and expansion held by Europeans who were then feeling some restraints on growth at home. Whatever the explanation, the image of the New World was already formed in European eyes before the acts of discovery and settlement.[1] Once they reached the shores of North America, explorers continued to experience the awesome and threatening facts of the unknown, the seeming infinity, the raw beauty and power of both landscape and natives. Tests between man and man, as well as between man and nature, became constant and inevitable. Furthermore, the geography invited, even confirmed, the need to maintain exploration and settlement.

The physical facts of scale also played a role. The sheer extent of the coastline, at first dropping off the edges of the earliest maps as literal and metaphoric reminders of the unknown, and later the vast expanses of the plains or the towering rises of the Rockies, persisted in the consciousness of each generation of pioneers. Direct or indirect awareness of this scale recurs frequently in the history of American painting, from John White's maps and later the Hudson River school landscapes of Albert Bierstadt or Frederic Church to the panoramic abstractions of Jackson Pollock and the environmental allusions of pop art.[2] Surely critical for America in the last third of the twentieth century is that the reality of almost unlimited geography is at last seen to be finite. The consequent dislocation in national self-confidence is manifest throughout contemporary American life and conduct.

If national values were gradually formed in such a context of expanse and power, then the country's citizens were summoned to respond with endurance and ingenuity. Repeatedly Americans have celebrated the virtues of self-reliance, independence, and pragmatism in their affairs. The image makers reflect these qualities in the self-assured, forthright faces of Puritan worthies; in the very fact that portraiture (with its insistence on individuals) was the primary mode of artistic expression in the colonial period; in the assertive functionalism of early American architecture and gravestones; and in the stress on craftsmanship or artisanship before aesthetics.

With the great period of national expansion in the decades between the War of 1812 and the Civil War, however, one comes to the exemplary period of growth in national life and its expression in the arts. Formally, the Republic had been founded and national institutions established. The American colonies were literally transformed into the United States, which in turn were to increase in number throughout this period. By mid-century the continental idea of the country was clear (though it is pertinent to note that new states were still being added to the union in the middle of the twentieth century). Perhaps the most vivid political expression of this so-called national period was the idea of manifest destiny, with all its moral rightness and implications of unending possessiveness.[3]

In architecture no less than the revival of pure Greek forms was called upon to embody the grand aspirations of a new democratic order. Heroic landscape called forth heroic architecture. Above all, the Greek temple reflected a clarity that all (democratically) could understand, as well as an appropriate rationalism and purity.[4] More than borrowing from the past, this was reincarnation, again referring to America's will for newness, especially in comparison to the corruptions endemic to the aged civilizations of Europe.

But most of all landscape painting during the first half of the nineteenth century came ta incorporate Americans' fundamental beliefs about history and morality. Nature philosophers like Emerson and Thoreau, writers like Cooper and Bryant, painters like Thomas Cole and Asher Durand, all shared the sense of nature's divinity and man's harmonious place in it. Cole and Durand were leaders of the first native landscape school, centered at first in the Hudson River valley and later in the mountains of upstate New York and New England. For them and others the painting of the American wilderness came to symbolize the potency of the national vision. A site like Niagara Falls alone emerged as a foremost icon of the country's unlimited power and breathtaking beauty. During these decades countless known and unknown painters made their way there to paint the natural wonder, emphasizing its grandeur and force. What distinguished the American landscape was both its vastness and its virginity.

The painter developed an inconography suitable to these sentiments. Cole consistently stressed the presence of a blasted tree trunk in the foreground of his pictures, set off against flourishing foliage nearby to indicate nature's regenerative power. Durand favored sweeping woodland vistas, with man harmoniously present, and serenely optimistic conditions of light. Frederic Church emphasized strong lateral expanses or deep panoramic thrusts of space, and he often included cleansing storms crossing his landscapes. Although many of these canvases were derived from firsthand observations and experience, the philosophical overtones and moral content were equally clear to the public. Possibly the best example of this mode is Church's summary painting *Niagara* (1857). With a sweeping format he places the spectator at the lip of the falls, the water rushing by his feet. The power of its turbulence seems to pulse across the canvas virtually uncontained by the edges of the composition. The eye pushes across this metaphor of energy, so actively described in the foreground, to the distant horizon, where billowing clouds seem to rise from beyond the limits of sight itself. In every way Church has delineated an imag e of raw, expansive force. The implication is that we are standing at only the edge of a magnificent continent that extends beyond what we see to what we might envision.

An equally telling image is Albert Bierstadt's *Last of the Buffalo* of about the same period. There across a spacious plain a massive herd of buffalo trails off into the distance, while the foreground is the setting for the brutal confrontation of Indian and animal locked in a life and death battle. Bierstadt intentionally juxtaposes the serenity and openness of the landscape beyond with the raw conflict nearby. Strewn

AVDONNIERVS ET REX ATHORE ANTE COLVMNAM A PRÆFECTO PRIMA NAVIGATIONE LOCATAM QVAMQVE VENERANTVR FLORIDENSES
Jacobus Le Moyne de Morgues ad vivum pinxit

Jacques Le Moyne, *The Natives of Florida Worship the Column Erected by the Commander on His First Voyage*, 1565. (Courtesy of the New York Public Library.)

Thomas Cole, *Sunny Morning on the Hudson River*, ca. 1827. (Courtesy of the Museum of Fine Arts, Boston.)

Frederic E. Church, *Niagara Falls*, 1857.   (In the collection of the Corcoran
Gallery of Art, Washington, D.C.)

Albert Bierstadt, *The Last of the Buffalo*, ca. 1889.   (In the collection of the
Corcoran Gallery of Art.)

William Sidney Mount, *Cider Making*, 1841. (Courtesy of the Metropolitan Museum of Art, purchase, 1966, Charles Allen Munn Bequest.)

Thomas Cole, *The Voyage of Life: Youth*, 1842. (Courtesy of the National Gallery.)

Winslow Homer, *Fishwives*, 1883. (Courtesy of the Currier Gallery of Art.)

Thomas Eakins, *Mrs. Edith Mahon*, 1904. (Courtesy of Smith College Museum of Art.)

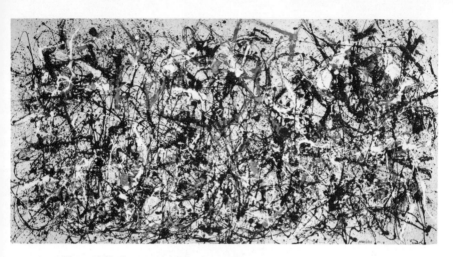

Jackson Pollock, *Autumn Rhythm*, 1950. (Courtesy of the Metropolitan Museum of Art, George A. Hearn Fund, 1957.)

Andy Warhol, *Campbell's Soup*, 1965. (Collection, The Museum of Modern Art, New York.)

Robert Smithson, *Spiral Jetty*, 1970, Great Salt Lake, Utah. (Photo by Gianfranco Gorgoni; courtesy of the John Weber Gallery.)

Christo, *Valley Curtain*, 1972, Rifle Gap, Colorado. (Photo by Harry Shunk; courtesy of Harry N. Abrams, Inc.)

Vito Acconi, *Hand and Mouth*, 1970, super 8 film. (Photo courtesy of Sonnabend Gallery, Inc. and *Avalanche* magazine.)

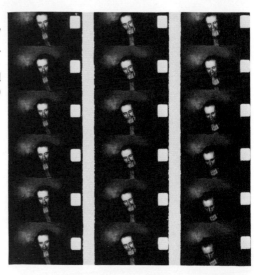

Bruce Nauman, *Self Portrait as a Fountain*, 1966. (Collection of the Whitney Museum of Art.)

about are the skulls of earlier deaths, thus completing the cycle depicted here of the various stages of life and death. The painting retains a documentary character while also conveying a larger, perhaps more unconscious image of indiscriminate slaughter in a landscape of overwhelming plenitude. The final irony of the image is apparent only when one considers contemporary attitudes to the environment and to killing.

Other subjects painted by American artists prior to the Civil War reflect in parallel ways the belief in continued enrichment, the unchecked optimism of perfectability, the assumptions of endless resources. Genre painting, for example, emerged in the 1820s as another mirror of American experience. Telling the stories of ordinary people in everyday situations, scenes of farming, electioneering, simple pastimes, and games showed the goodness of life in America. Collectively, artists like William Sidney Mount, George Caleb Bingham, J. G. Brown, James Clonney, and Jerome Thompson depicted a portrait of national well-being and fulfillment. Men and women were shown to be industrious, the landscape productive, the seasons mellow, the light and atmosphere glowing with promise. American still-life painting by mid-century presented effulgent arrangements of fruits, food, and flowers, always a cornucopia of crowded and rich forms. The characteristic compositions of John F. Francis or Severin Roesen exude a fitting sense of ripeness and fruition. But of all the images from this period, Cole's *Youth* in the series *Voyage of Life* (1840) stands out as an eloquent vision of the American belief in possibility. The concept, of course, implied growth or progress beyond immediate boundaries, and in those years everything seemed possible.

III

The wider disruptions of the Civil War were symbolic of the first substantial constraints put on American aspirations at mid-century. What before seemed always possible, even inevitable, now was subordinated to a new pragmatism. The major advances in technology and transportation in America were creating an increasing sense of regionalism and fragmentation in national life. The expansion of the union geographically continued unabated to the West Coast, although the gold rush of the 1850s was a signal that the ideals of growth embodied in the westward frontier were about to turn to exploitation and false hope. The hardships that followed were indicative of the first limits placed on growth in America.

The latter half of the nineteenth century suggests none of the moral absolutism, the uniform idealism, or the naive self-confidence of the first half. Europe appealed anew to American artists and writers, as many succumbed to a new period of insecurity. Though the exclamatory character of the Hudson River painters continued to survive in Church, Bierstadt, and some of their younger contemporaries, their pictures tended to become more bombastic and finally hollow. These artists who were in touch with the changing mood and realities sensed the need for a different style, one more down to earth, more realistic and serious.[5] The neutrality of photography proved to possess an objectivity and starkness that seemed needed for the shock and gravity of these later decades. This must account partially for its emergence as such a powerful form of expression in the Civil War.

Where the founding vision of the nation had for so long celebrated promise and fulfillment, now Americans had to face failure, discord, and suffering. Even Reconstruction was given up after a time. One can find the corresponding shift in artistic style in a number of painters working through this period. Winslow Homer began his career in the 1850s drawing anecdotal genre scenes in the carefree manner of Mount and Bingham. Sent to the front by *Harper's* magazine, he saw (like Whitman) the inhumanity and drama of the war years close up. By the end of the 1860s and during the 1870s he increasingly turned to a manner of severity. His subjects take on a new isolation and thoughtfulness. Carefree youths give way to serious adults preoccupied with survival.

American society and institutions were buffeted periodically through the latter decades of the century. The triumphs of technology were on the threshold of producing disquieting ugliness. If the Corliss engine was a romantic wonder at the Philadelphia centennial exhibition, Henry Adams' dynamo was a deeply disturbing intimation of coming chaos by the beginning of the twentieth century. In fact, well before then a variety of contradictory forms had begun to appear in all of the arts. The single-mindedness of the earlier national vision was now dispersed into eclecticism, competing styles, and fragmented expressions. In architecture the skyscraper and the marble palace served different aims. Sculpture vacillated between the lingering classicism of Augustus Saint-Gaudens, the highly subjective expressionism of William Rimmer, and the mass-produced plasters of John Rogers.

Among the painters, some went abroad virtually for good: James A. M. Whistler, Mary Cassatt, John Singer Sargent. Others withdrew into themselves: Albert P. Ryder, Thomas Eakins, and Homer. Realism, impressionism, trompe l'oeil, and romanticism continued to have exponents simultaneously. If art reflected a certain disequilibrium or disarray, the unease was in the air nationally and internationally. The sense of fin-de-siecle genuinely forebode the immanence of a new age. It is revealing to find a feeling of melancholy, introspection, or elegaic reverie pervading much of the painting at the end of the nineteenth century. An air of mystery and contemplativeness informs the late portraits of Eastman Johnson and Thomas Eakins, the haunting marines of Ryder and the wistful landscapes of Thomas Dewing, the brooding Adams memorial by Saint-Gaudens, and the tattered fragments of Peto's still lifes. The sense of loss appears to be shared in common, and it would seem a significant precedent that artists together turned inward in response.

Today's sense of loss is also deep and widespread. It is manifested in various reactions ranging from frustration to withdrawal. The new elements in today's limitations to growth are the decisiveness and near totality of confinement. It is more than accidental that the reductions of conceptual art should coincide with the frustrations pressing American military, economic, and political power at the beginning of the 1970s. The art of the preceding decade is filled with the many cross-purposes that surfaced in American life. The dynamic energies of abstract expressionism continued to reflect the tensions and violence of industrial and urban life, while pop art declared the massive impact of consumerism and conspicuous consumption in contemporary experience. At the same time movements like op, minimal, and systemic art reflected another desire in the 1960s for order, even if sometimes inhuman, along with an effort to reduce artistic expression to a fundamental language of pure form. (Possible parallels exist in concrete poetry and music.)

The current limits to growth most frequently called to the public's attention are ecological, and therefore to the heart of the American dream. Recently Ketchum, Idaho, banned for an indeterminate period new building within the town. A few years ago the state of Oregon encouraged tourists to visit but not to stay; now the governor wants to curb growth of both development and tourism.[6] A federal task force has recently recommended that the future development of private property be regarded as a public or communal concern.[7] The report of the task force did not go so far as to urge no growth, but it did stress severe restriction and regulation. In California the idea of the end of progress is being seriously discussed.[8] The idea of progress as a goal first gained momentum in the eighteenth century when the United States was founded with phrases like "the pursuit of happiness." Due to the increasing acceleration in the rate of change since then, the notion of pursuit has now reached a condition of satiation. In California meditation and withdrawal have become familiar practice.

Conceptual art of the 1970s also stresses these same values: "The world is full of objects, more or less interesting; I do not wish to add any more" (Douglas Huebler).[9] "Under attack is the rationalistic notion that art is a form of work that results in a finished product" (Robert Morris).[10] "I do not mind objects, but I do not care to make them" (Lawrence Weiner).[11] These artists reject the creation of commodities in favor of defining situations. Experience, information, process become valuable in their own right. Thus, the elements of repetition, variety, and timing assume new importance. Where sculptural form heretofore might have been the vehicle of meaning, now the more documentary media, such as photographs and books, play a major role (e.g., Edward Ruscha). Earth art or earth-works (Dennis Oppenheim, Robert Smithson, and Christo) at once illustrate the concern for the environment along with the idea of making art through the "overlay of an art context, an art framework, or simply an art awareness . . . on existing situations."[12] Body art (Vito Acconci and Bruce Nauman), too, calls attention to what already exists and how that information or situation can be transformed or modified, however briefly.

Whether in dealing with the environment around one or with oneself, the idea of transformation is more important than its completion. Sometimes the activity of these artists is absurd, gratuitous, unexpected, or whimsical, but in the words of Michael Kirby, "I consider my work to be basically contemplative."[13] We may resent or be baffled by their gestures, yet ultimately theirs is an art of thought, of human and individual assertion, and of the primacy of creative activity. Clearly this movement partially mirrors the larger limits to growth now impinging on the American experience. Remarkably and paradoxically, conceptual art is not an expression of negation or frustration but points the way toward other American values, notably self-reliance, ingenuity, pragmatism.

We might conclude by considering one of the central images of this period: the American space rocket.[14] Just like a piece of sculpture, its scale, materials, technology, and power all typify the national imagination. Even more significantly, this embodiment of tremendous wealth is consumed in a single venture. Perhaps growth in terms of the American desire for newness, for continually expanding frontiers fraught equally with beauty and danger, will not cease after all. The push into space will be a human and a national urge. Even so the earth from which we launch these vehicles of aspiration will have to submit to a new and rigorous process of ordering. But since we are also traditionally practical as well as adventurous, we may now summon these other characteristics to the fore.

NOTES

1. See Howard Mumford Jones, *O Strange New World, American Culture: The Formative Years* (New York, 1864), especially Chapters I, "The Image of the New World," and II. "The Anti-Image."

2. John McCoubrey, *American Tradition in Painting* (New York, 1963).

3. See David C. Huntington, *The Landscapes of Frederic Edwin Church, Vision of an American Era* (New York, 1966).

4. See William Pierson, *American Buildings and the Architects, The Colonial and Neo-Classical Styles* (New York, 1970), especially Chapter X, "American Neo-Classicism, The National Phase: The Greek Revival."

5. See Howard Mumford Jones. *The Age of Energy, Varieties of American Experience 1865-1915* (New York, 1971).

6. "Gov. McCall Seeks to Curb Oregon's Growth," *New York Times* (May 7, 1973).

7. *New York Times* (May 19, 1973).

8. See Michael Davie, *California, The Vanishing Dream* (New York, 1972), especially Chapter 10, "Things to Come."

9. Quoted in Ursula Meyer, *Conceptual Art* (New York, 1972), p. 137.

10. Ibid., 184.

11. Ibid., 217.

12. Lucy Lippard, *Six Years: The Dematerialization of the Art Object from 1966 to 1972* (New York, 1973), 5.

13. Ibid., 143.

14. See Meyer, *Conceptual Art,* p. xvi.

Part IV

Growth as a
Factor in
America's Future

Robert H. Walker

WOODROW WILSON INTERNATIONAL
CENTER FOR SCHOLARS

11
"The Eagle When He Moults Is Sickly"

I

It is possible that some new Edison will show us how to convert smog into energy; that the forest and meadows will reclaim the slag heaps and parking lots; that Jesus or Gautama will come once more to electrify us with a word. But there is no sign. There is, on the other hand, abundant evidence that the United States in the last ten years has been experiencing a special kind of transition; and, as Thomas Carlyle admitted during the last similar occasion,

> Such transitions are ever full of pain;
> thus the Eagle when he moults is sickly;
> and, to attain his new beak, must harshly
> dash-off the old one upon the rocks.[1]

To recognize this unhappy condition may not bring joy, but the recognition can serve in a number of ways. It can save us from the extremes of either false hopes or exaggerated despair. It can guard against partial and insufficient solutions by helping identify the true level of change and the true center of opposition. To be aware of the process of transition as a paradigmatic experience may itself be useful as we take those lonely and uncomfortable steps away from the comforts of

175

traditional values toward an undefined future. It has happened before.

Only five or six years ago it was common to use the term "revolution" to describe an obvious shift in cultural attitudes. Now, particularly with the passing of a crisis in the civil-rights movement and the tailing off of American involvement in Southeast Asia, the issues are much less two-sided. There is no substantial opposition to the principle of minority rights or equal pay. No sane person wants to escalate to nuclear warfare. No one favors pollution. The "revolution" has come to resemble more the turning of a wheel than the opposition of armed camps.

Yet the wheel has not completed its turn. Assessments of the state of the nation are predominantly negative—even more than usually so. With all the public positions "against," there are very few positive alternatives. Furthermore, this negative inventory is by no means confined to a single area of national behavior but stretches from urban life to education, from politics to foreign policy. No one act in any of these areas—even the "resignation" of President Nixon—can respond to more than a small segment of the complaint. The present condition is transitional because it is nonconfrontational and incomplete; it is a special kind of transition because it is sweeping and profound.

II

The culture seems to be moving away from a set of modes and values acquired some 150 years ago in another era of rejection, transition, and conversion. Central to that conversion was a new definition of growth; this new definition has been so vital to the national character and is now so central in the process of transition that it becomes an essential place to begin.

Probably all cultures at all times have valued some form of growth, progress, expansion, fulfillment—or whatever term might have been used to distinguish these overlapping concepts. The Bible called on man to go forth and multiply and fructify the earth. The philosophers of the Enlightenment saw progress in terms of an increasing under-standing of natural law. Given the choice between more or less, most bodies—nations, corporations, churches—have striven to grow. But the kind of growth that concerns us now is not the kind of growth that can be found with only contextural differences around the world and throughout history. It is something different. In the first place, it is not limited to natural or inevitable growth. It is not confined to one special area—territorial expansion, for example. It does not shy away from the consequences of the growth of growth, that is, acceleration; or, to put it another way, the restraints on growth are so minimal that the growth rate will almost inevitably become exponential. Although often considered as a means to an end, growth in truth becomes an end in itself.

This kind of growth is so different from what is often meant by this word—both conceptually and consequentially—that a different word is called for. In the history of ideas it has been referred to as "dynamism." But it may be easier and more helpful to use still another but more common word, "pace." Since this word too has more than one meaning, a capital letter will equate Pace with the attitude toward growth described in the paragraph above. The use of this particular word will keep in the forefront of this discussion a fact so obvious it is often forgotten: our problems today stem not from growth itself but from comparative rates of growth, that is, from the relative pace at which social and technical mechanisms evolve.

At its base, the transition of the 1960s and 1970s is a movement away from a complex philosophy that introduced a new definition of growth to the literate citizens of the early nineteenth century. Understanding of social direction today can begin with the identification of Pace, historically and philosophically.

III

The view of the universe that was to transform growth to Pace first appeared in the ruminations of a group of German philosophers who were actually trying to defend a highly structured, rationalistic philosophy. These men—Leibnitz, the Schlegels, Schleiermacher, and most importantly Immanuel Kant—ended by redefining the universe in a historically original way. God, to this time, had been depicted as either a vengeful, mysterious judge whose inscrutable mercies we all awaited or a kind of benign watchmaker who had set things to working according to fixed natural laws and then withdrew to observe the outcome. In the new view God became the concept of the world creating itself. Perfection was only an ideal; imperfection was the law of life with novelty and innovation occurring constantly. Change and growth were the only constants. Everything and everyone was seen as importantly different. The parts of the universe were interrelated like the parts of a living tree, not like the parts of a manufactured watch. In its briefest form, this philosophy can be summarized as a belief that the universe is dynamic, organic, and diversitarian.

This radically new philosophy came into American consciousness via certain English men of letters—Coleridge, Carlyle, Wordsworth—and was most fully expressed on native soil by Ralph Waldo Emerson and his fellow transcendentalists. It entered and was expressed in other ways as well, but the important thing was its timing.

Although much debate has been lavished on the cause-and-effect relationship between ideas and events, it is safe to say that neither one causes the other. It is equally safe to assume that they are capable of conflicting with and diminishing one another or of combining with and reinforcing one another. If so, it is hard to imagine in history two events as importantly interrelated as the development of philosophical romanticism—which is what this new view of the universe is most accurately called—and the birth of a new nation under emigrated European leadership on the Atlantic coast of North America. Without this reinforcing coincidence it would be easy to imagine at least four nations existing where the United States now stands—just to cite one of the most obvious consequences.

This philosophy suited the circumstances and aims of the new nation remarkably. In underlining change and innovation it devalued tradition and authority, thus justifying a revolution against the English monarchy in particular and the European tradition in general. Similarly it endorsed the search for new philosophies and religions in place of obedience to a single established religion. Against a whole static, mechanistic system of thought represented as Enlightenment, the new philosophy gave dignity to what might otherwise have been considered but an unwashed miscellany. Its greatest impact rested on five features: four of them concurring with social directions in the new nation and one in opposition.

1. Most obvious was the timeliness of the concept of Pace on a sparsely populated community, effectively protected from European

interference from the east and facing apparently unlimited frontiers for expansion to the west. There seemed no reason for restraining any kind of increase whether in population, in commerce, in extractive or manufacturing industry. In fact, in the very commitment to a more rapid growth rate than Europe's lay, according to literature of the times, one source of pride to which the young Americans could point in rebuttal to Europe's existing achievements.

2. At least as important, and very closely related, was the idea that America should define itself in terms of *processes* rather than fixed standards. If God was himself a process of creation, the new nation could invoke the highest sanction for devoting itself to the process of growth, to the democratic process of self-government, and to the slower but equally vital process of approaching social justice. Another term for philosophic romanticism would be "philosophy of process," the elevation of "becoming" to an end in itself. What more fitting ideological underpinnings for a land of opportunity where the act of achieving became the central meaning of the culture?

3. Affecting both Pace and process was the inclination, under the new world view, to replace fixed standards with relative, quantitative measures. If the essential truth about the universe is its dynamic growth, then the most appropriate activity for the individual or society is to expand the areas of achievement and perception. So, in this philosophic sense, quantity of experience had intrinsic merit. It is but a short—if troublesome—leap to the application of quantitative criteria in place of subjective or traditional standards. Democracy itself is in some ways a resort to quantitative decision making, as Tocqueville long ago pointed out in his alarm at the potential tyranny of the majority. In many other areas, numbers were readily applied to demonstrate achievement: in miles of rivers and canals made navigable, in tons of ores extracted, in dollar value of commerce conducted, and in all areas of behavior where quantitative data were available. Not only did cities and banks boast of their population and deposits but churches seemed willing to be judged on membership, authors on their sales, and painters even on the size of their canvases. Interest in numbers has been by no means confined to this nation or this era, but it flourished there and then, encouraged by the implications of the new world view.

4. More special to America has been the wide and lasting commitment to pluralism and individualism. This characteristic, too, gained

strong endorsement from the new view, for, as Arthur O. Lovejoy explained, diversitarianism made it "the first duty of an individual or a people to cherish and intensify the differentness, idiosyncrasy . . . with which nature has endowed him or it."[2] To place such strong value on extreme individualism is to produce conflict with other values. Some of the conflict came from a tension between newer and older world views; some was intrinsic to romanticism as it expanded from an academic to a social philosophy. The realization of this conceptual tension—as between democracy and individualism—gave considerable force to much American expression throughout the nineteenth century, particularly the work of Walt Whitman.

5. If the transcendentalists transmitted romanticism in a way that was reasonably faithful to its German sources and its English elaborators, they simultaneously came to represent a breach between one of this philosophy's fundamental tenets and the direction of the new nation. At issue was the concept of organicism through which the Romantics explained the structure of the universe. Pace, process, and change were meaningful only insofar as the experience they produced was organizable in organic terms, that is, interrelated in the way that nature had provided in the metaphor of the tree. Organic perceptions were to replace the flat, one-dimensional, rationalistic thought of the previous century. It was one of the great negative coincidences of this era that, while accepting the other tenets and implications of romanticism, Western civilization attached itself tenaciously and unequivocally to technology.

It is possible, from an exalted view, to perceive the proliferating manifestations of invention and manufacture as a grand organic evolution out of nature, but it has not seemed so to most observers. To the worker in the mill, his machine has trapped him in a mechanistic, push-pull world of limited horizons and little dynamism. To the writer and thinker, the products of technology intruded so violently on his organizing metaphor that the manmade secondary environment has been increasingly blamed for denying the act of growth the positive consequences it was supposed to produce. The force of this irony can nowhere be seen more dramatically than in an 1829 essay, "Signs of the Times," in which Thomas Carlyle expressed his hopes for the new order as opposed to the old:

This deep, paralyzed subjection to physical objects comes not from Nature, but from our own unwise mode of *viewing* Nature. . . . If Mechanism, like some glass bell, encircles and imprisons us, if the soul looks forth on a fair heavenly country which it cannot reach, and pines, and in its scanty atmosphere is ready to perish,—yet the bell is but of glass; "one bold stroke to break the bell to pieces and thou art delivered!" . . . Indications we do see in other countries and in our own, signs infinitely cheering to us, that Mechanism is not always to be our hard taskmaster, but one day to be our pliant, all-ministering servant; that a new and brighter spiritual era is slowly evolving itself for all men. . . .[3]

In Carlyle's sense, the devotion to technology—which he linked with mechanistic philosophy—has kept society under the glass bell. Even that climactic act in theory so perfectly romantic—nuclear fission—has ended by adding to the sense of entrapment.

The history of the United States from early in the nineteenth century until very recently has been importantly influenced by romanticism: by the emergence of Pace as a condition and concept in a cluster of related values stressing process, quantitative measurement, and individualism. The impact of this philosophy has been importantly and ironically complicated by the fact that, whereas these ideas were theoretically united by a perception of organic interrelationships, they have in fact been expressed largely through a technology that has kept experience under the glass bell of materialistic mechanism. One way of viewing today's dilemma is to see it as the logical consequence of adopting an attitude of varied dynamic growth but substituting the insulation of the technological environment for the challenging exposure to organic perceptions.

IV

All American values did not come into the culture with romanticism. From older sources the society had acquired and kept the idea that America had a special mission among nations; that in material achievement there was some indication of spiritual grace; that in items of fundamental importance all men were indeed equal; that human behavior was sufficiently predictable so that a system for maintaining order and promoting progress could be devised; that education of as many citizens to the highest possible level was essential to social well-being; that in spite of the contributions of science and technology some kind of moral law was at least as important as natural law. With this rather cumbersome list of values—which, with time, tends to grow larger and more complexly interrelated—the American system has taken shape as a number of processes that have operated under the conditions of Pace with very little negative criticism for the last 150 years.

These processes included the increase of population and the assimilation of many of its elements into a dominant culture; the expansion of territorial sovereignty and world power; the taming of nature with technology; and the establishment of a consumption-oriented commercial economy. Social change has been based on the extension of participatory democracy coupled with subsidized education. The rise in general educational level has aimed not merely at an informed electorate but also at an augmented audience for high culture: literature, music, and art. All of these processes have been based on continuing growth rather than on any fixed standards. If achievements seemed sometimes less than satisfactory, there was always the reassurance of emulation and immigration pressure. Much of the world obviously admired the application of Pace to these processes. Indeed, the perspective from the far edge of this 150-year surge of physical, demographic, and social momentum reveals a set of achievements scarcely imaginable at the start, and an incredible degree of balance and poise on the crest of this explosively expansive, dynamic process, loaded as it was with all the runaway implications of Pace.

V

The kind of growth here labeled Pace is indeed a difficult force to contain. Signs of this difficulty have been apparent for a good many years to those who take the arts to be more than entertainment, and the insistence of the evidence has been itself increasing dramatically.

Films, the best medium for dealing with the machine in motion, have long alarmed their viewers with scenes in which the threatening motions of some piece of mechanical equipment went maddeningly and acceleratingly haywire. Runaway trains and automobiles have now far outdone the runaway horse of earlier days. Painters, sculptors, and photographers have forced us to look upon highway carnage as a kind of art form. Ishmael Reed's metaphor of a broken-down radio is but more direct than many other literary and dramatic treatments of a cultural dizziness produced by more and more things happening to more and more people at an indiscriminatingly meaningless and mindlessly zooming rate of speed.

Henry Adams was the first American writer to see this problem in its literal sense. Using the second law of thermodynamics and the law of acceleration, he pointed out that the faster energy was produced, the faster heat escaped the universe. His exponential curve led to a cold death of the earth after but four years of a "radium age." This hypothesis—so incredible when it appeared—looks fully believable today against the background of serious warnings against using up the planet, not to mention the dire crying of the inventors of the atom bomb. Modern writers mirror this intensity of concern in their unprecedented degree of concentration on violence, insanity, perversion, and other messages of cultural rejection. Here is a wildness that can be symbolized only by the hydraulic hum of the great gears under the insane asylum at night, the Stetson-hatted pilot riding his H-bomb toward Russian earth, of the "foundation-man" frantically pointing his brainwave transformer at all who come within range. (The allusions are to Ken Kesey's *One Flew over the Cuckoo's Nest,* the film *Dr. Strangelove,* and Walker Percy, *Love in the Ruins.)* Perhaps most fitting of all is the extended allegory of a motion picture run backward, particularly the one visualized by Kurt Vonnegut wherein the bombed city restores itself, the explosives arise toward the planes, which fly accurately backward to their takeoff point, whereas the bombs are unloaded, disassembled, and the ingredients returned to earth. The accurate modern metaphor of protest is the process reversed.

Pace resembles a jet engine in its demands for ever-greater speed in order to achieve ever-greater efficiency. Once a consumer-oriented society has been taught to expect a shiny new automobile every year or two, it can be easily sold a motorcycle, a second car, a power boat, a swimming pool, and so on at a rate of increasing wanting that outstrips even the advertising industry's ability to match the inflated desire for concrete objects. In an almost parallel manner, a deprived group within the population learns to expect not gradually improving conditions but concessions at an ever-growing pace until each accommodation produces two new objectives; the two granted, four more emerge. This kind of acceleration is easy to understand—to applaud—on grounds of social justice. It is difficult to fashion a society that can respond adequately over a period of time.

Once science and technology got really rolling in the early nineteenth century, breakthroughs in theory and practice followed one another with an exponential rush. The climax—at least to the popular awareness—came with nuclear fission, an achievement that should have been a grand moment unassociated with an act of slaughter. Instead, nuclear power has meant a threat to peace and to the very life of the planet. Even its peaceful use has caused problems because of the radioactive hazards of rare earths and of the environmental damage inflicted in heat-energy transfers at atomic power plants. Thus in science and technology, too, the unavoidability of Pace has produced an atmosphere in which problems seem to outweigh contributions.

Many of America's current frustrations are directly related to Pace and to the processes set in motion in the early national days. The growing antitechnological feeling, rational or not, is built into those objections to momentum, unthinking consumption, and violations of nature. For a culture that placed such weight on applied science that it was accused of promoting a "religion of technology," this rejection is—all by itself—an index of change of great magnitude.

At least as serious are the suspicions aroused by the observations of econometrists and social scientists attacking central domestic processes. If a system is to be exempt from judgment by arbitrary standards, it must continue to show a measure of advancement along the intended line of development. There are now reasons to doubt that progress toward economic and social democracy is continuing to result from existing political and educational machinery.

Education, the basic warranty for equality of opportunity and upward mobility, may not be equal to this task. Heredity and environment—in proportions that cause widespread disagreement—combine to limit what can be accomplished even with preschool programs, special head starts, and remedial programs of the most advanced pedagogical design. The question is not whether the nation has achieved a reasonable degree of social democracy, for, once wedded to a process, it is essential that the process continue and that it continue to give evidence of relative advance toward the preconceived end.

The political system was also designed for testing on economic grounds. Although textbooks often miss this point, it is clear that from the very first days of national existence political leaders sought some degree of economic equity as the payoff for political democracy. Extending the franchise and purifying the system was meant to create the popular power to destroy special privilege, to raise the floor for the disadvantaged, and to show an increasingly equitable distribution of wealth. During some periods the system seemed to be working; but since World War II the direction has been toward maldistribution of wealth and income. Historical evidence now seems to indicate that the present direction is representative of long-term expectations. If so, there is serious reason for disillusion with one basic process.

VI

These disillusions with fundamental processes and the symptomatic dizziness induced by accelerating Pace indicate a transition away from that cluster of values created by circumstance and reinforced by philosophy early in our national history. If this is true, then the nearest historical model must be extracted from the experience of the culture at the time it adopted those values, having itself rejected an earlier order and survived a period of transition. To a great extent this transition was shared by the West, particularly by Germany, England, and the young America. Its classic interpreter was Thomas Carlyle who read and understood the German philosophers as well as any other Englishman. As a devoted personal friend of Emerson and a favorite of other influential Americans, he was crucially responsible not only for the transfer of Romantic ideas but for depicting the experience of transition itself.

Carlyle's central work, *Sartor Resartus,* used the symbol of clothes to represent ideas and followed the wanderings of that unfrocked protagonist, Diogenes Teufelsdröck, from the casting off of his rationalistic ideas to the sensing of "organic filaments," which would bind together his new romantic beliefs. A much more familiar parable centering on the same experience, is Samuel Taylor Coleridge's *Rime of the Ancient Mariner* in which the old order was symbolized by the albatross treated as a pet and mascot by the ship's crew. Rejection of the old order comes as the mariner shoots the albatross; the period between convictions is the becalming with the eventual starvation and death of all the mariner's shipmates. Thus, like the central figures in all these allegories, the mariner is isolated, miserable, and wracked with self-doubt. The midpoint of rebellion occurs when he spies another ship on the horizon and moistens his throat to cry out by biting his arm and swallowing his own blood. He approaches conversion when, in the midst of visions and hallucinations, he unconsciously blesses the sea monsters and thus prepares himself for a full acceptance of the diverse and organic universe.

The nation, it could be argued, went through this kind of experience in its early days. The Enlightenment view had passed its prime in Europe and was patently unsuited to the temper of the young nation. In reluctantly rejecting the philosophy of the revered founding generation, however, the new Americans could arrive at no satisfactory counterview for some time. Federalism was only opposed with "anti-Federalism," and a kind of negative exercise was performed in which the disliked features of the old order were pilloried. This negative inventory went against Royalists, Tory sympathizers, the Church of England, and the state and national banks. The first political symbols in America were negative symbols taken from the costumes of the elite. After a generation of groping that must at times have seemed pointless and frustrating, a new direction and philosophy were put into effect with enthusiasm, if not without the usual amount of compromise.

Although a nation does not undergo conversion with the sequential neatness and dramatic timing evident in a literary parable, it is possible to hear Coleridgean echoes in the events of recent years. The 1964 presidential campaign of Barry Goldwater appears as a desperate attempt to revert to the stability and assurances of the old order; even the 1972 landslide victory for Richard Nixon had more than a little of that same feeling. Yet there are many signs that the old order is dead:

violent demonstrations against universities, agents of the law, political parties in convention; rejection of the sacred cow of technological advance: the supersonic transport and the megabudget space program; eloquent mistrust of Detroit, Madison Avenue, and Pennsylvania Avenue. In addition to protest there has been an unusual amount of quiet withdrawal and lonely dissociation.

One is tempted to find in the spectacular public self-torment of the Senate Select Committee hearings on the Watergate a parallel to the mariner's desperate biting of his own arm in order to cry out. One should no doubt beware of reaching for close parallels between history and literature, but the cumulative evidence is meant to depict the nation as fully engaged in the act of rejection and somewhere near midpassage in its transition toward a new synthesis. Defending actions in Southeast Asia, trying to support a sinking dollar, coping with an energy shortage, seeking to restore a supportable balance of trade— America as a nation has very much resembled Professor Teufelsdröck or the ancient mariner in midpassage: isolated, alienated and rejected, bewildered, and occupied with programs that are essentially negative or reactive.

Before abandoning the paradigm of rejection, doubt, and rebirth, it must be pointed out that nations—unlike individuals—rarely move in single coordinated steps. Even the ability to take ideas seriously is limited to a rather small—if influential—proportion of the population. Thus, as Lovejoy points out, the universe long recognized as limitless by scientists is still treated by most of us as though it had a fence around it. Similarly, although many influential people have been converted by the thoughts that stemmed from Kant, most of us often act as though the world operated more as depicted by Newton, Locke, and Adam Smith. It is therefore possible that, while some of the more articulate people who influence our social direction are rejecting the philosophy of Pace and process, many more of us at a less exalted level are expressing a discontent with the technological entrapment that Carlyle hoped we were escaping almost 150 years ago. This kind of concurrent negative revolution in values, operating in a somewhat contradictory way at different intellectual levels of society, would help explain why some signs of resentment are found so pervasively and why technology in particular has begun to bear such a conspicuous part of the resentment, being as it is, inimical to both viewpoints.

VII

To be midway through the conversion process is, by the very nature of this experience, to be unaware of the new order. Furthermore, an entire culture—unlike an individual on the way to rebirth—will not vibrate to a simultaneous unifying experience adumbrating the new arrangement of values. Yet by observing what society is agreeing to oppose and by referring to similar experiences in the past, one may at least weigh some probabilities.

To begin with, the fact that growth assumed a special kind of value here called Pace does not mean that its negative alternative can become a guiding process of equal force. No growth is an objection, not a new value. Even in their short lifespan the no-growth fanatics have revealed themselves as mindlessly undiscriminating as the most ardent growth advocates of the past. Already it can be seen that growth, although restrained in some areas, will be pursued with new fervor in others. The protection of the environment has already produced its own set of new growth industries. There is no rational evidence for closing the door on technological growth so long as the culture is willing to accept technological cures for ailments created by technology. Emotionally, however, the culture shows signs of finding this sequence increasingly difficult to accept. Even the American Association for the *Advancement* of Science recently sponsored a (very interesting) session on *antitechnology*, an act performed with no outward show of irony.

William James abhorred the destructiveness of war but recognized that the martial virtues are valuable and should be retained by the culture even if universal pacifism were achieved. Hence he speculated on a moral equivalent for combat experience and came up with something that reads like the rough-hewn offspring of a Peace Corps volunteer and a Girl Scout. It is doubtful that William James found a moral equivalent for war, although there are those who have seen a modern improvement on his proposal in professional sports.

If no moral equivalent for war has been discovered, is there hope for a moral or psychological equivalent to growth? Not likely; nor should there be. Growth and Pace are stimulating. It is much more invigorating—socially and intellectually—to enter a situation where the outcome is not preimagined and where even the forms of expression are malleable. Although Pace makes us nervous and although uninhibited growth will use up the planet, we would still—like William James—prefer to preserve the growth virtues while restraining growth itself. Senator Hubert H. Humphrey's "proposal for achieving balanced national growth and development," for example, allies itself with the spirit of progress while seeking a reduced net sum of growth activities. [4]

Those aspects of Pace that have become oppressive may be eliminated through planning and through discriminate growth. But as the culture moves away from Pace it is also moving away from process— that is, from those social mechanisms that justify themselves not by fixed standards but by relative progress along dynamic lines. With the deemphasis on Pace will necessarily come the increasing emphasis on fixed standards. Instead of hoping that we are moving toward better distribution of wealth, for example, we may have to go further in the direction of minimum and maximum wages and hours. Controls will inevitably strengthen in a more static situation. Something will have to come down for everything that goes up. We have had considerable experience in standard setting, particularly in economic matters— everything from interest rates to conditions of labor. But these standards have been set against a moving backdrop where renegotiation was always on the horizon. In the future these standards will have to be devised and applied with even greater care, since they will have to resist presures from all sides without the relief hitherto provided by a drastically expanded economy.

Another way to look at the current transition is to assume that because there have been but three major world views in Western history and because we are moving away from one of them, we are likely to return our principal allegiance to one of the other two. Yet this does not seem likely; there are no great signs of a return of dominant rationalism of the eighteenth century nor of the rise of a socially powerful religious view such as held the center of the seventeenth century stage. Furthermore, as Americans left these two world views, they did not reject them completely but kept from them values they found usable and durable: equality, the social compact, moral law, national mission. Nor should it be expected that the entire cluster of values that came in with Pace will be cast out. Among those values, the one that centers on the worth of individualism seems the most deeply imbedded in the national character; it is also the least dependent on the dynamics of Pace and process and therefore the one most likely to endure. It would not be unprecedented were we to return to an older world view; it is the evidence in the negative inventory that falls short of suggesting this. It would be unprecedented were the culture to reject the whole package of values that came in with philosophic romanticism.

The negative inventory suggests that some of the society's major institutions may be modified: institutions dealing with courtship, marriage, child rearing, education, job satisfaction, and the sense of community. Existing modes have been attacked in a sporadic and scattered way but with enough cumulative force to make a number of points: that people should not be so possessive of one another; that homemaking groups need not consist of one adult male and one adult female bound together for life; that physical love should be considered more a natural and less a social act; that schools should cease resembling monastic factories turning out mass-produced personalities in isolation from what is real in the contemporary world; that work is satisfying only when one is creating some object or situation that is useful and/or pleasing and when one can be involved in the whole process of making it; that neighborliness and interdependence can replace suspicion and locked doors if work is shared more wisely and if material goods are not possessed so proudly and exclusively; that all individuals and groups must maintain close contact with nature and draw what is needed from nature without violating it. Many of these attitudes have been expressed in urban settings but only in a necessarily limited way. It is difficult to grow an organic garden in mid-Manhattan.

When one stresses the opposition to mass production, consumption, competition, and materialism, one begins to think of William Morris and John Ruskin. When one looks for places where the greatest number of these new values have come together, he begins to search out the new communitarians who stem also from Oneida and New Harmony. Some of these communes have done well as examples of both ecological and social reform; like their predecessors, they seem to have done best when blessed with strong leadership and isolation. Even were they all unqualifiedly successful, though, they would be something less than a model for 200 million city-dominated Americans wakeful with the noise of commerce. As George Santayana wrote with eerie prescience in 1900:

Mid Uncle Sam's expanded acres
There's an old secluded glade
Where grey Puritans and Quakers
Still grow fervid in the shade . . .
Yet the smoke of trade and battle
Cannot quite be banished hence,
And the air-line to Seattle
Whizzes just behind the fence.[5]

The key to where we are going may lie behind a phrase heard more frequently every day: the quality of life. It peppers Senator Humphrey's proposal. It comes over the television in surprising ways. What does it mean? Not very much as yet, although at the outset it is logical to accept it as a first blow against the Pace-oriented habit of measuring everything in quantitative terms. The quality of life is surely not the quantity of life. One clue may lie in looking inward, in observing groups in the population who have become interested in experiencing a growth unrelated to external measurement. My friend and colleague Raja Rao, accustomed to coming back to America after intervals in France and India, marvels at the way the younger people have become less interested in objects—even sexual objects as very recent evidence has begun to show, less hurried, less acquisitive, less driven toward traditional success, and more contemplative. It has been theorized that the group that shows these characteristics is the group that can afford to because of their relatively affluent parents and that another group more upwardly motivated will replace them, enabling the cycle to continue. But there are others who think the situation is more special than cyclical.

Beyond just the young there is a two-pronged religious trend that lends substance to the idea of internalized growth. The great ecumenical middle of our religious structure, it has been observed, is losing its appeal. In its place there is a growing popularity of the fundamental sects at one end of the spectrum and the mystical persuasions at the other. Where the two extremes meet is on the common ground of internalization. The churches that are growing are those that advocate the denial of material and social indulgences. They ask for the renunciation of earthly pleasure and stimulations. Some demand tithing and strict church attendance. Some of them, like Christian Science and

Mormonism, retain features of mind control and spiritualism. They all stress prayer and meditation and hold out spiritual growth as the only meaningful form of growth. It is no great leap across the great middle to the disciples of Zen and Hinduism who restrict diet, develop the bodily controls of yoga, and work toward the aggrandizement of the inner life and the denial of material selfhood. There is no need to think that the whole United States is going either mystic or Baptist. It is possible to couple these observations with trends in existential philosophy, conceptual art, and expressionistic literature and to see a society that is in some ways increasingly prepared to accept growth on other than external, materialistic terms.

This is a good moment, if the evidence has been correctly read, to give our old order a hearty hail and farewell and to salute it for the heady trip it provided into a magic land of undreamed comfort, convenience, and physical achievement. It may also be a time to sense on the horizon an emerging set of values that will restore a more reasonable pace and a more natural balance in which to savor the days more calmly and profoundly with more nonmaterial richness. It would be human—it would be intensely American—to end on this note of hope and anticipation of a future that may be in some ways greater, if not grander. The truth is that there are both positive and negative signs; that for every indication of a new and acceptable value there is another sign of rejection of older values upon which crucial reliance has been placed in the past. It is as honest to hope as it is to fear; but the most intelligent thing we can do at the moment is to recognize transition when we see it and—most particularly—to see how very fundamental is this kind of rare transition from one set of national values to another. Neither gloom nor celebration is truly appropriate. We need sympathy from friends and patience with one another, for the eagle is truly sickly when he moults. We also need a broad, imaginative alertness attuned to signs of a new set of "organic filaments," as Carlyle called them, that will bind together and give workable coherence to the emerging set of modes and goals. If the culture is extremely lucky it will discover a fabric that will express as much achievement and unity as the "morality of growth" and its attendant values have supplied for the last century and a half.

ACKNOWLEDGMENTS

The words and ideas in this essay have come together over the last several months from a number of sources and in a number of circumstances. Responsive audiences from the Philippines, Australia, and New Zealand to Millersville and Hattiesburg will have heard most of them under such headings as "New Direction in American Values" or "The End of an American Era." Some were published as "Education and the *New* American Revolution" in *Academic Forum* 2 (Winter 1971-1972): 24-26.

An essay like this is meant to be speculative and suggestive rather then demonstrative. Some of the assertions are not susceptible to "proof"; others would require considerably more space than is here available for their documentation. If there is any originality here it is in the way separable concepts have been put together, not in the concepts themselves. Where the individual ideas came from I think I know, although I am by no means able to acknowledge all sources.

My debts begin with David Potter and Morse Peckham, both of whom I have had the privilege of knowing. Through Peckham, I accumulated my debts to the work of Lovejoy, Kant, Wordsworth, Coleridge, and Carlyle. Two of my friends—Kenneth S. Lynn and Arthur S. Miller—were good enough to read and criticize.

A large input has been derived from my status as Fellow at the Woodrow Wilson International Center for Scholars and from my colleagues there who contemplate "sustainable growth," particularly Chester Cooper, Raja Rao, Albert Meisel, Michael Lacy, and Kurt Spillman. The Center favored me with a most helpful research assistant, Ann Palumbo. It also allowed me to assemble a symposium of four scholars in the arts and humanities, each of whom explored the meaning of growth in his own subject: Daniel Aaron, Sidney Ahlstrom, Charles Powers, and John Wilmerding. Their papers were supportive and helpful.

NOTES

1. Thomas Carlyle, *Sartor Resartus* (Boston: Ginn, 1896), p. 146. The work first appeared serially in England from 1833 to 1834.

2. Arthur O. Lovejoy, "The Meaning of Romanticism for the Historian of Ideas," *Journal of the History of Ideas* 2 (June 1941): 277.

3. Thomas Carlyle, *Critical and Miscellaneous Essays* (Philadelphia: Carey & Hart, 1848), p. 195.

4. Hubert H. Humphrey, *A Proposal for Achieving Balanced National Growth and Development* (Washington, D.C.: GPO, 1973).

5. George Santayana, *Hermit of Carmel* (New York: Scribner, 1901), p. 204.

Franklin A. Long

CORNELL UNIVERSITY

12
Economic Growth, Technology, and the Quality of Life

I

This essay is concerned with prospects for an improved quality of life in the United States, with an economy that is characterized by zero (or low) industrial growth, although it is growing in other ways. The relationship of technology to this economy will be of particular concern. Will the attainment of a low or zero growth of industrialization lead to diminished utilization of and interest in technology? Or, as an extreme alternative, will enhanced utilization of technology be an essential characteristic? Because the odds are high that major changes in economic growth will be initiated or accompanied by large changes in social priorities and perhaps even political institutions, the prospective social and political aspects of a changed pattern of economic growth must be discussed, even if only briefly. The time scale of the analysis is long—three or four generations, or roughly a century—so the conclusions are decidedly speculative. Finally, the discussion in its principal aspects is restricted to the United States, a limitation that will ultimately become so embarrassing as to necessitate a final section relating the conclusions, however inadequately, to world problems of economic and population growth.

Restricting the discussion to the United States permits use of an important simplifying assumption: that in a fairly short time, perhaps thirty or forty years, the growth of the U.S. population will have slowed down to the point where the approximation of zero population growth will be essentially valid. As many scholars have pointed out, this plausible assumption is also a dangerous one since it implicitly assumes an understanding of the social aspects of human reproductive behavior that does not in fact exist. Nevertheless, the assumption is made.

Two important recent discussions on questions of zero growth, both in terms of population and economic growth, serve as a helpful background for the present analysis and indeed might constitute a superior guide to problems of growth. The first is the fall 1973 issue of *Daedalus,* entitled "The No-Growth Society," in which some fifteen of the best-known analysts of zero growth give their views, pro and con.[1] The second important background study is the stark and pessimistic essay, *An Inquiry into the Human Prospect,* by Robert Heilbroner, who, looking at world prospects for the next couple of centuries, concludes that "the outlook is for convulsive change . . . change forced upon us by external events rather than by conscious choice, by catastrophe rather than by calculation."[2]

In reaching the harsh conclusion that there is no hope for man "without the payment of a fearful price" Heilbroner identifies three immensely foreboding challenges that mankind must face: (1) the outlook for continued rapid population growth over the next century or so; (2) the continued likelihood of war, including the prospect of an obliterating nuclear war; (3) intolerable environmental disruption, caused principally by continued industrial growth. In Heilbroner's view, the social and political systems of the world are inadequate to meet these challenges, and science and technology, far from offering any amelioration, constitute a fierce driving force for the intensification of the threats.

Because I shall reach a decidedly more optimistic view than Heilbroner with regard to the prospects for the United States, it is incumbent on me to explain why I do not accept his somber conclusions. In some measure, the answer is that I am viewing only the United States, a nation whose position, vis à vis the future, is fortunate in many ways. It is already a rich, developed, and industrialized nation. Its mineral and agricultural resources are extensive. Its population density is fairly low, and most importantly, I am assuming that its rate of population growth will be roughly zero.[3] Finally, I am assuming—as Heilbroner also ultimately does—that the ultimate catastrophe, an all-out obliterating nuclear war, will not occur. This leaves us to consider for the United States only the problems of minimizing the deleterious consequences of economic growth and (the possibly much more difficult task) of avoiding catastrophic interactions with other parts of the world whose success in facing these challenges may be much less and whose political and social turbulence may consequently be disturbingly high.

II

Disagreement remains high on the feasibility, consequences, and desirability of zero economic growth. (In contrast, there appears to be broad agreement, at least in the developed parts of the world, on the desirability of a low or zero growth rate of population.) Much of the difficulty rises from the fact that a limitation of economic growth appears at best to be an imperfect instrument for alleviating the major social and environmental challenges that face us. There is general agreement on the character of these challenges, if not always on their relative importance: (1) the burgeoning global industrialization is using up the world's nonrenewable resources of fuel and minerals at a dangerously high rate; (2) air and water pollution has become a global problem; it is costly and unpleasant even now, and over the long term it carries the threat of irreversible climatic change and environmental deterioration; (3) as man increases his global energy consumption to the point where the waste heat approaches the amount deposited on the earth by the sun, the long-term danger arises that the earth's average temperature will increase to the point where catastrophic climatic and geophysical damage will result;[4] in the effort to supply food for an increasing world population, there is grave danger that the earth's renewable resources of land and ocean will be overworked so that long-term damage will result.

The ultimate threat from these challenges resides in the well-known "tyranny of the exponential," the effects of which were dramatically evoked in *The Limits to Growth*.[5] Take, for example, the effect of the world's climate of waste heat from energy utilization. Right now, the effect is negligible; mankind produces on earth perhaps one ten-thousandth of the heat deposited by the sun. But if energy usage increased steadily at a rate of 5 percent per year, it would only be about a century before man's contribution of heat would be 1 percent of that of the sun. If this same rate of increase then continued for only a few more decades, the effects would be catastrophic.[6] And so it will be with other environmental threats arising from growth *unless we do something.* More importantly, as many analysts have noted, well before these environmental insults cause major ecological or climatic damage, their impact will become evident in a deteriorating environment for human existence: smog, dirt, noise, poisoned rivers, polluted ocean beaches, and so on.

In facing these problems over the next decade or two, the United States is in an especially fortunate situation. Its citizenry is already aroused to the threat of a deteriorating environment. As a nation, it has the time, the space and the resources—physical, intellectual, and financial—to do something about it. But should a focus on zero economic or even zero industrial growth be a key component in the country's responses to the threats to the environment? The case is far from clear. Proponents of continued high economic growth for the United States, and there are many,[7] argue that only a steadily rising GNP (or NNP, net national product) will permit the United States to solve the serious problems of continuing poverty, urban decay, and environmental deterioration that plague us. Take, for example, the alleviation of poverty by measures of income redistribution. This is socially and politically far from easy, even in a growth economy when average income is increasing; it will surely be considerably more difficult if it is carried out during a period of constant average income. Furthermore, as a weapon to counter environmental deterioration— for example, urban decay or air pollution—a policy of no growth seems curiously indirect. Why not instead attack these problems frontally? This, incidentally, is the gist of arguments by Marc Roberts who calls for reform rather than elimination of economic growth.[8]

For the short term, reform measures seem a sensible prescription. Absent a revolution, one probably must start gradually, and why not focus first on direct measures to improve the quality of life? However, for a time scale of a century, the central problems will need to be faced. If economic growth and industrialization continue unabated and along their present trajectories, the threats of resource depletion, degradation of the environment, and irreversible harm to the land and the seas will become more pressing. It is these consequences that impel even the United States to continue to think seriously of a major reform of economic growth.

In considering why we need and want a major change in our economic and industrial style of life, it is simpler to think of the problems that face us in terms of only their physical aspects—resource depletion, environmental deterioration, and the like. However, the nonphysical aspects may ultimately be the more important. There are the problems of social justice, a humane society, and, more broadly, the quality of life. Problems of social justice enter in two levels: what we want for our own society and what we should do in fulfilling our obligations to the rest of the world. The specific goals are to eliminate poverty and its degrading consequences, to remove the subtler manifestations as well as the overt and legalized forms of racial segregation, and in other ways to work toward a more egalitarian and just society. Externally, the problems are really much the same, but they can usefully be put into different words. What, for example, in the name of social justice do we owe to the poorer half of the world? How long can a wealthy 6 percent of the world's people continue to use 30 percent to 40 percent of the world's fuel resources? What example do we want to set to the 2 billion people of the world whose chances ever to attain the current Western level of affluence look increasingly dim? Surely these problems suggest the need for a very different U.S. society from that of today. Hopefully, it will be a much more egalitarian society, where conservation will have replaced conspicuous consumption, and collaboration will seem more appropriate than competition. It will be a society where services loom much larger than goods, where the focus is more on education and the arts and less on striving for higher incomes; more on decent housing and transportation and less on keeping up with the Joneses. One strongly suspects that the attack on the physical aspects of the problem will be feasible only if there is this kind of shift in societal values and priorities. Equally, one suspects that effective attack on income distribution, racial equality, and other social problems subsumed under the phrase "social justice" will also require these shifts in societal values and social conscience. The summary phrase for all these implied changes is "a better quality of life," environmental, social, and intellectual. A more detailed tabulation of what is typically included under the term "quality of life" may be helpful, but in considering the following outline, note that there remain even here difficult problems of choice and priority.[9]

Aspects of Quality of Life

A satisfying personal life—
  Individual freedoms
  Intellectual stimulation
  Access to art, beauty, solitude

A sense of community—
  Social justice
  Mechanisms of mutual support
  Equality of opportunity
  Community decision making

Job satisfaction—
  Work conditions
  A sense of personal achievement

Internationalization of growth—
  Leisure and recreation
  Spiritual growth
  Alternatives to materialism

Fortunately, there are many signs that American society is even now prepared to move substantially in these directions. The growing concern for the environment, dissatisfaction with our urban society, and the new values of the younger generation are cases in point. Very probably Charles Reich's *The Greening of America* made these shifts in society's priorities appear too near and too easy, but the implied new directions may still be "right on."[10] The United States may well be ripe for change.

III

What specifically should be our long-term societal goal? In my belief, the objective ought to be what I shall call a quasistationary state of economic activity, a state in which the goal is no growth, even perhaps a decline, in our industrial, energy-consuming, goods-producing economic activities, combined with increased emphasis on a better quality of life with continuing growth in programs directed toward environmental improvement, better social amenities, and more social justice. There are several programs that can lead us toward these goals, and we shall look more closely at their technical, social, and political components. But first it is worth emphasizing that these new directions imply a greatly changed social ethic, and one must assume that the essential moral underpinnings for it exist or will be developed. (It probably exists; after all, is the old-fashioned Christian ethic so very different from what is needed?)

The new ethic should gain increased acceptance as the programs unfold. The initial steps for such a program are obvious enough—conservation, resource management, environmental improvement—and many of them are already being taken. Nevertheless, there is a basic doubt that must be resolved before too long: do Americans have the social will, which can in turn generate the political will, to go firmly and substantially down this road of reform and change? Do we not perhaps need more citizen understanding, with perhaps a sharper, more exhortative goal (or slogan) for us to rally around? The phrase "no-growth society" with its negative implications is no such goal or slogan. Would "quality of life" or "social justice" serve better?[11] But let us return to our projected quasistationary state.

An essential component of a projected quasistationary state is virtual elimination of growth in the utilization of energy. A second component is a considerable decrease in the utilization of minerals and other nonrenewable resources, including fossil fuels. These components imply a considerable redirection in the character as well as the outputs of our industrial activities. There will need to be, for example, extensive recycling of minerals and other materials, almost full utilization of so-called wastes, emphasis on conservation in all of its aspects, including longevity for consumer goods, low-energy agriculture, and more use of solar and geothermal energy. Because a parallel objective of this restructuring process is to improve the quality of life in the United

States, there will need to be much greater emphasis on minimizing the impact of industry on the environment. Also implied is a shift in the economy toward the service activities—education, recreation and the arts—and substantial growth of programs of urban improvement and mass transportation.

This brief list of the changed directions implied by our quasistationary state makes it evident that the society that develops it will in no sense be a static one, and it would be seriously misleading to call it a no-growth state. Indeed, one can argue that the attainment of no increase in energy use and in use of natural resources necessarily calls for substantial social and technological change, quite belying the adjective "static." Later we will discuss in detail the social and political acceptability of these new directions, but we must first ask, What about the *technical* and *economic* feasibility? To put it bluntly, are we discussing conceivable goals or indulging in utopian dreams?

The economic concerns are obvious: what are the possible impacts of these new directions on unemployment, on balance of trade, on inflation, and on other aspects of our economy, and how can ill effects be avoided? Economists are already addressing these questions and we can anticipate important further contributions from them. On the other hand, the wide range of economic systems that the world has used to address these problems—almost pure capitalism, almost pure statism, and various intermixes—suggests that a viable working economic system can be developed to fit almost any set of reasonable social objectives. There is, however, one aspect of the problem that is often cast in purely economic terms but whose significance is so central to our objectives as to require explicit discussion. This is the question of impact on our standard of living.

Typically a discussion of standard of living focuses first on the per capita value of the GNP, expressed in dollars and usually corrected for inflation and other changes in purchasing power. But it has long been argued that, even apart from questions of income distribution, the GNP is an ineffective measure of the set of desirables that most of us have in mind when we speak of standards of living. First, the GNP includes as positive values some expenditures—for example, those for national defense—that most of us consider either as irrelevant to our standard of living or as a negative component of it. More significantly, the GNP does not include a variety of positive goods that are difficult to measure as "products" but that all of us value in varying degrees: the salubrity of our environment, the time and opportunities for leisure and the arts and for doing whatever we want. Nor does the GNP include as negatives the clear deterioration of aspects of life that we value. In sum, we shall only be distracted from our principal objectives if we use the GNP as our dominant measuring device.

All of us like to assess criteria like standard of life as objectively as possible, preferably quantitatively. It is of interest, therefore, that at least one attempt has been made to establish a quantitative economic measure that attempts to redress some of the more obvious shortcomings of the GNP. This new scale is the Measure of Economic Welfare (MEW) formulated by Nordhaus and Tobin. [12] The MEW excludes certain "regrettable" expenditures such as funds for national defense; it also includes figures for important nonproduct items not in the GNP. Specifically, it includes figures for leisure time and for nonmarket activity. It also includes a modest negative correction for "disamenities," such as polluted waterways. This different measure, applied to economic data for the United States from the period 1929 to 1965, increases about half as rapidly as the GNP but still shows a significant per capita improvement, leading Nordhaus and Tobin to the conclusion that growth is *not* obsolete. A difficulty, as these authors would be the first to admit, is that the quantitative measures for leisure, for nonmarket activity, and for disamenities are woefully inadequate and hence the actual numbers are relatively unpersuasive. Doubtless, the procedures for arriving at specific figures could be improved and made more plausible, but the fundamental problem remains how to give numerical measures to items that are fundamentally nonquantitative. [13] Clearly a numerical evaluation of standard of living will remain uncertain and controversial. The development of a more useful measure than GNP would be a marked advance. One suspects, however, that the principal economic problems of the quasistationary state will be less involved with living standards per se and more involved with quality of life defined more broadly, including, for example, a more equal distribution of income, better housing, and broader programs of public health and medical care. But even assuming that we can understand and address the economic problems of a quasistationary state, there remains the question of whether it is technically feasible.

IV

As a preliminary to looking at new technological directions and individual technologies, we need first to ask whether by discussing a set of new technologies we are not already weighting our new objectives with a burden that will sink them—a commitment to continue development of technology. Numerous scholars, among them Roszak and Marcuse, have charged that science and technology are themselves principally to blame for our present precarious condition. The implication is that in projecting a new and better society, one should explicitly minimize the role and status of both science and technology. Consider, for example, Robert Heilbroner in *The Human Prospect*.[14] Early in his essay he comments, "Now I must identify an unmentioned challenge that lies behind and within all of the particular dangers we have singled out for examination. This is the presence of science and technology as the driving forces of our age." Later on, Heilbroner refers to "a command over natural processes and forces that far exceeds the reach of our present mechanisms of social control." He speaks even more harshly of the "runaway forces of science and technology." The point is clear that science and technology are the bête noire of our current difficulties. Not surprisingly, Heilbroner sees only a small role for science and technology in the society that he hopes will eventually emerge: "The long term solution requires nothing less than the gradual abandonment of the lethal techniques, the uncongenial ways of life and the dangerous mentalities of industrial civilization itself." And further, "It is likely that the ethos of 'science,' so intimately linked with industrial application, would play a markedly reduced role." And who is to argue with much of this? Who, after all, favors "lethal techniques," "uncongenial ways of life," and "dangerous mentalities"? Not I, for one. But are the ethos of science and the utilization of technology to play much reduced roles? This I seriously question. The *level* of scientific research may be diminished in the quasistationary state, giving way to other kinds of studies with a higher social priority. The *status* of scientists may be lower, to the degree that they really will become, in that fine British phrase, "on tap but not on top." But the ethos? Science is really two things: first, a methodology for studying the ways of the universe and, second, the accumulated knowledge from all the scientists of the past. The first of these is simply an organized response to a very basic human trait, the desire to understand. As such, it can hardly vanish even though society may reduce its scope. As to the knowledge itself, there it will be, all bound and indexed, accessible to the planner, the engineer, or whomever. Or would the antiscientists propose to burn the books?

Technology also is both knowledge and a methodology for devising new and modified technology. Harvey Brooks gives the following excellent definition:

> Technology is essentially a specifiable and reproducible way of doing things. It is not hardware but knowledge, including the knowledge not only of how to fabricate hardware to predetermined specification and functions, but also of how to design administrative processes and organizations to carry out specified functions, and to influence human behavior toward specified ends. The key element in all technology is the capacity to specify how to do something in the publicly communicable and reproducible way.[15]

Technology, in other words is essentially a tool for mankind. As with science, the social planner or politician of the future will have available all of the accumulated technology of the past and present, consisting of both knowledge and a sophisticated methodology, much of it science based, incidentally. Furthermore, he will badly need it and vigorously use it. All of the principal technical characteristics that we have suggested for the quasistationary state will require good, often new, technology. Actually, two rather different categories of new technology will be required,—physical technology and social technology.

The physical technologies that will be developed will, to a first approximation, link to those that we are familiar with—for example, mining, manufacturing, agriculture, communications. The new and modified technologies will, however, respond to the two essential characteristics of our projected quasistationary state. They will give very high emphasis to low energy utilization and to low utilization of nonrenewable resources. Equally, they will give high priority to minimizing impacts on the environment. A partial list of the required kinds of technologies might be the following:

- Technologies for effective recycling of major materials of

commerce, for example, aluminum, titanium, steel, copper, plastics, paper.
- Modified low energy processes for industrial manufacturing.
- Development of household and industrial appliances with long life and recyclability.
- Effective waste collection and utilization systems.
- Technologies for low energy agriculture.
- Processes for more effective use of solar and geothermal energy.
- Transportation systems with low energy demand and negligible air pollution.

Let me give an example to illustrate both the challenge and the opportunity. Currently one of the worst pollutants of our fresh water streams is the effluent from the manufacture of paper. The technology for paper manufacture is not especially sophisticated,[16] and one could imagine the development of a self-contained closed cycle process that would not release pollutants into the streams or the air. The problem is that this new technology might well be much more costly than the present technology. The challenge then is to develop a modified or new technology that will have negligible impact on the environment but that will be reasonably cost effective. As a second example, consider the question of technologies for harvesting solar energy. The opportunity here is immense, but current technologies are simply too awkward and expensive to be competitive with fossil fuels at their current prices. The technological challenge is clear: to get a far more effective and less costly set of technologies for solar energy.

The development of these new and modified physical technologies will be accompanied by a parallel development of new social technologies. Specification of the needed new social technologies is decidedly speculative. This is a less fully developed field than that of physical technology, and the background of fundamental knowledge in the social sciences is much less complete than the base that the natural sciences offer to physical technology. Even so, one can see the directions that these new social technologies will take. In the quasistationary state there will surely be much more concern about the behavior of social systems, implying that systems analysis and cybernetics will be the source of important new technologies. Questions of social planning and of choice and decision making will loom large, as will the management of social organizations. There will be much more explicit long-range planning, including analyses of policy alternatives and the new policies will in turn call for new or modified social technologies. One function of these social technologies, and of course one reason for their development, will be to modify and humanize the required physical technologies.

When one adds these projected new social technologies to the new or modified physical technologies that also will be called for, it is safe to conclude that the role of technology in the United States will continue to be a large one. It, of course, does not follow that the social significance (the "driving force," in Heilbroner's somewhat pejorative phrase) of technology will be all that large. This will depend upon the social priorities and life-styles that will be developed as part of the attainment of substantially modified social objectives and priorities. Here, too, a preliminary analysis seems required, even though it can only be speculative.

Even considering only the technological aspects, the projected quasistationary state implies a society considerably different from the current one. The emphasis on low energy consumption, resource recycling, and protection of the environment all imply more consensus on national objectives, greater social collaboration, and more planning and systems analysis than we have today. Also implied is a good deal more regulation, by license, laws, and taxation, of our social systems and of our individual lives than today. To the average citizen this translates into a continuing, intensive, and often intrusive presence of government agencies. Heilbroner put it well: "To a very great degree, the public must take precedence over the private—an aim to which it is easy to give lip service in the abstract, but difficult for someone who is used to the pleasures of political, social and intellectual freedom to accept in fact."[17]

The question is, will the American public tolerate these directions? Will it additionally accept self-denying measures so as to provide a larger fraction of the world's resources for the poorer nations in the immediate future and over the longer term, for the later generations of mankind? Speaking only of the United States, will the politically dominant middle and upper classes accede to the substantial redistribution of incomes that the elimination of poverty requires? Heilbroner is exceedingly pessimistic that nations will, in fact, have the political will and capabilities to carry forward the transformations that are required. Much of his pessimism comes from his belief that human nature will not alter to permit easy or spontaneous changes; thus, major and probably highly unpopular political initiatives will be required. In his words, "There seems no hope for rapid changes in human character traits that would have to be modified to bring about a peaceful, organized, reorientation of lifestyles."

If it were really true that the development of new life-styles required modified "human character traits," then Heilbroner's pessimism would, no doubt, be justified. But I strongly suspect that this requirement is greatly overstated. The real requirement, it seems to me, is a good deal more modest and more accessible; it is for a new set of human and social *priorities*, including a clearer understanding of what is really involved in an improved quality of life. The priorities that characterize our current industrial societies are not all that basic or hallowed or ancient. Numerous successful human societies have utilized very different social priorities and human objectives. Socially speaking, humanity is decidedly plastic and mutable.

What I suspect is needed now is not one grand program but a sensible mixture of social, ethical, political, and technical efforts, all of which will serve to help carry the United States toward a society in which the quasistationary state will fit naturally. Furthermore, the initial elements of this mixed program are already at hand: new technical efforts of energy conservation and environmental improvements; social programs for better housing and medical care; political programs for more responsive and more honest government; ethical concerns about elimination of poverty, equality of education, and evenhandedness of justice. It does not seem to me an insuperable task to build on these present initiatives and guide their successor efforts toward the modified society and the improved quality of life that the quasistationary state implies.

V

This vista of a greatly modified society may sound fairly engaging, if necessarily somewhat vague. The key problem, however, remains: we still have to get from here to there and the path is uncharted But assuming we do get there, will life *as judged by current standards* be all that pleasant? The answer is very probably, no. But that, of course, is not the point. The modified society and the new life-styles must necessarily go hand in hand. Our grandchildren's values will very probably not be our values, but we can hope and assume that they will be appropriate to the time, the place, and the circumstances. If the outcome is as fortunate as this implies, we can hope that our great-great-grandchildren will enjoy improved social justice and a satisfying life in a society that industrially and energetically has attained a steady state and that in most other ways may be very different indeed from the one we live in.

This brings me to a final, troublesome point. What about the rest of the world, especially the poor and underdeveloped nations? The essentially optimistic prophecy that I have outlined for the United States builds on the very favorable position the country now enjoys: wealth, an educated people, an industrial base, low population density, a good supply of natural resources. By leaving the rest of the world out of consideration, there is an unhappy implication of "fortress America" since only a few other nations are as fortunate as the United States. For the poorer two-thirds of the world, essentially Africa and South Asia, the prospects for the next century must, as a minimum, be labeled grim. Most of the nations involved are now plagued by poverty, illiteracy, inadequate industrialization, and a precarious food supply. Growth rate of population is invariably high, 2 percent to 3 percent per year, and success in lowering the growth rate has so far been slight. Heilbroner goes so far as to suggest that a hundred years from now the current population of 2.5 billion for these areas may have increased to 40 billion.[18] Even if this is too high by a factor of two or three, the prospect is terrifying. In a world with diminished supplies of fossil fuels and minerals resources, where will the food, the housing, the education come from? Where will the nations involved find the flexibility to modify their societies? One must conclude that for many of the people of these areas, the likely prospect may not be an improved quality of life but instead a grim struggle to survive against heavy odds.

Can the United States stand by, while other peoples suffer, and concentrate only on its own new society? It hardly seems possible. If, under pressure of the increasing challenges, the United States succumbs to political tyranny and government by dictatorship, an inwardly oriented fortress America may be the outcome. But if the

United States does manage to build a better, more humane, more just society, the ethical precepts that will undergird it cannot stop at the ocean's edge. It must and (in my belief surely will) be impelled to give major help to the rest of the world. Food will be an obvious contribution and so will be technology. The new U.S. technology that we picture for our own quasistationary state, with its emphasis on conversion, product longevity, and low energy utilization, will be appropriate to the less developed countries in a way that our current "affluent" technology is not. Technology transfer will really make sense.

The skeptic can ask, Where will the money come from, given our projected low growth society with its increased emphasis on nonmonetary satisfactions? One source comes immediately to mind—the obscenely large and relatively unproductive military expenditures of the United States and the U.S.S.R., which are now approaching $200 billion per year. (This in a world presumably to be characterized as a "generation of peace.") If the notion of a better society means anything at all, it means that the current obsession with military programs for "national security" will subside and that other more ethically acceptable paths to security will be increasingly turned to. Major assistance to the poorer parts of the world should be one such path.[19]

But even for the United States, will it all come out this way? Will we really be able to develop our quasistationary state? So many other less happy outcomes are conceivable, even plausible. Among the grimmer ones are: all-out nuclear war, fortress America, a divisive class struggle culminating in a dictatorship. Perhaps we cannot avoid one of these unhappy outcomes. Conceivably the late twentieth century will be enviously looked back on by the people of later centruies as the golden age. But if we *are* to avoid the worst of these outcomes and have a modest prospect for a better life, we had better start now in identifying our objectives and taking the first steps.

NOTES

1. *Daedalus* 102 (Fall 1973).
2. Robert L. Heilbroner, *An Inquiry into the Human Prospect* (New York: W. W. Norton, 1974); see also the special supplement of the *New York Review of Books,* January 24, 1974.

3. There is an important policy problem for the United States implicit in this assumption. The internal rate of growth of the U.S. population may soon approach zero, but the pressures for immigration, which now account for about 20 percent of the population increase, will remain high. Will the United States move to restrict immigration still further?

4. Although with continued growth in man-generated heat the long-term danger is assuredly a too-hot earth, the character of the shorter-term climatic trends is much less clear. Since we are now still in a period where natural climatic variations dominate, it is entirely possible that for the next two or three decades the greater concern will be that of a too-cool world, with shortened growing seasons and lower food production in many regions. Even the initial climatic impacts of industrialization are uncertain: particulates in the atmosphere could result in a cooler earth; the "greenhouse effect" from increased carbon dioxide could result in a warmer earth.

5. Donnella H. Meadows, Dennis L. Meadows, Jorgen Randers, and William W. Behrens III, *The Limits to Growth* (New York: Universe Books, 1972).

6. For details, see Robert V. Ayres and Allen V. Kneese, "Economic and Ecological Effects of a Stationary State", *Annual Review of Ecology and Systematics*, 2 (1971), Annual Reviews, Inc., Palo Alto, California.

7. Several of the authors of essays in *Daedalus* 102 (Fall 1973) make elements of the positive case for economic growth. See especially R. Zeckhauser, "The Risks of Growth," 103-108, M. J. Roberts, "On Reforming Economic Growth," 119-137, and W. R. Johnson, "Should the Poor Buy No Growth?" 165-190.

8. Roberts, "On Reforming Economic Growth."

9. My thanks to Professor Robert Walker of George Washington University for suggesting this listing and contributing to it.

10. Charles Reich, *The Greening of America* (New York: Random House, 1970).

11. The proposals outlined here are similar to those of Roberts, "On Reforming Economic Growth," 119-137, to which they owe a great deal. The fact that a professional economist finds it possible to urge the implied major economic reforms is greatly supportive to a noneconomist. R. N. McKean, "Growth vs. No Growth: An Evaluation," pp. 207-227, also points to the "imprecise linkage between a no-growth economic policy and the elimination of undesirable 'externalities.' " He argues instead for direct attacks utilizing taxation and regulation.

12. William Nordhaus and James Tobin, "Is Growth Obsolete?" pp. 1-80, Fiftieth Anniversary Colloquium (fifth speece), San Francisco, 1970. *Economic Growth* (New York: National Bureau of Economic Research, 1972), National Bureau of Economic Research, General Series 96, "Economic Research: Retrospect and Prospect," vol. 5.

13. The following summary of the Nordhaus and Tobin preferred calculation (see "Is Growth Obsolete?" Table 1) of MEW for 1929 and 1965 identifies principal terms and illustrates the areas of uncertainty.

MEW in Billions of Dollars, 1958 Prices

		1929	1965
1.	Personal consumption, national income a products accounts	139.6	397.7
2-4.	Durable goods purchases, etc.	–33.5	–121.9
5.	Services of consumer capital imputation	24.9	62.3
6.	Imputation for leisure	339.5	626.9
7.	Imputation for nonmarket activities	85.7	295.4
8.	Disamenity correction	–12.5	–34.6
9-10.	Other	5.1	17.8
11.	MEW, total	548.8	1243.6
15.	Per capita MEW, in 1958 dollars	4506.0	6391.0
	Ratio of 15 relative to 1929	1.0	1.42

14. Heilbroner, *An Inquiry.*

15. Harvey Brooks, "The Technology of Zero Growth," *Daedalus* 102 (Fall 1973): 139-152.

16. For a broad discussion, see F. Keith Hall, "Wood Pulp," *Scientific American* 230 (April 1974): 52.

17. Heilbroner, *An Inquiry.*

18. Ibid.

19. Heilbroner, ibid., suggests that nuclear blackmail may be used by developing nations "to force the developed world to transfer large amounts of wealth to the poverty stricken world." I find this scenario pretty implausible. A century hence, unless their population growth decreases considerably and unless the developed world freely helps, most of the poorer nations are far more likely to be overwhelmed by social disorder and starvation than to be organized enough to wage what Heilbroner calls "wars of redistribution."

Chester L. Cooper

WOODROW WILSON INTERNATIONAL
CENTER FOR SCHOLARS

13
Growth in America:
An Epilogue

I

It is one thing to invite a group of scholars representing many disciplines to attend a series of seminars entitled "Growth and American Values"; the intellectual mix and the subject itself are bound to result in lively discussion. But it is another matter to bring together, for the benefit of a wider audience, the various essays that provided the central core of the oral exchange; such an enterprise is hostage to accidental and purposeful differences between a "chapter" in a tightly knit book and a "contribution" to a collection of papers. But when all is said—when the philosopher and the economist, the historian and the scientist have addressed this intellectually untidy subject—are there some common themes that can be perceived? Or do the dozen efforts to examine growth in America evoke the tale of the blind men and the elephant?

These essays do not proceed in an ordered and stately way from problem definition to policy prescription; it would be astonishing if they did. But neither do they comprise a haphazard collection of unrelated propositions; there are many common threads that tie them together to form an intellectually manageable fabric of ideas and insights.

There would seem to be no argument, for example, with the theme developed by Professors Aaron and Wilmerding that growth and

expansion (economic, institutional, spatial) are deeply rooted in the
American ethic. Abundant natural resources, a temperate climate, and
a virtually boundless continent provided a congenial setting for wave
after wave of immigrants who came to America in search of what they
were denied at home: economic opportunity, religious freedom, social
mobility. For Americans during the early days of the Republic and for
a century after, "Growth," as Daniel Aaron suggests, "was tantamount
to survival." And the "assumption that the land of destiny was limitless," as Professor Powers observes, "gave unspecified 'growth' the
context it needed, and the promised destiny gave it purpose." In due
course, "growth" and "progress" became synonymous.

The growth concept has become so dominant an American value that
the no-growth option, whatever its merits or demerits, would be a
difficult course for Americans to follow. On the other hand, as virtually
all the contributors acknowledge, pell-mell economic and population
growth has produced disamenities and risks as well as advantages.
There have, of course, always been groups of Americans who have
been left behind or shunted aside as the nation moved from hardship
to comfort to affluence. But now a vast number of our countrymen
sense for the first time that congestion rather than spaciousness,
scarcity rather than abundance, clutter rather than variety, characterize their present estate and will comprise the legacy they are
destined to pass on. And so there is little disagreement among the
contributors on the need to address the problem of channelling or
influencing growth in ways that will preserve the best and mitigate the
worst of its effects. Thus, Rostow: "The challenge of seeing what kind
of organized life man can build in the wake of high mass consumption
will continue to engage most men and women." And Skolnikoff: "The
current challenge to a growth ethic is not so much for rejection of
growth as a rediscovery and reemphasis of other objectives. . . . The
public wants economic growth to serve these other objectives relatively more than simple economic prosperity."

The contributors view the past and the present, at least, with a
remarkable degree of agreement. Despite their divergent backgrounds and intellectual perspectives, they all have one important
characteristic in common: they are perceptive analysts living in the
United States in the early 1970s. It should come as no surprise, then,
that they all sense that America is passing through a period of great
transition.

II

This period of transition is intimately related to the unwieldy bundle of issues and considerations we have labeled "Growth." Intellectually or viscerally, an increasing number of Americans are coming to the realization that the central proposition put forward by the Club of Rome and the authors of *The Limits to Growth* cannot be simply shrugged off. Certainly most of the contributors to this volume would subscribe to Professor Long's list of principal concerns: "Burgeoning global industrialization is using up the world's nonrenewable resources of fuel and minerals at a dangerously high rate; air and water pollution has become a global problem; as man increases his global energy consumption . . . the long-term danger arises that the earth's average temperature will increase to the point where catastrophic climatic and geophysical damage will result; in the effort to supply food for an increasing world population, there is grave danger that the earth's renewable resources of land and ocean will be overworked so that long-term damage will result."

And most would agree with Professor Hays: "The tendencies that lead to a concern for the limits to growth. . . . have arisen out of changing values and changing technological capacities for environmental manipulation, and they arise especially from increasing pressures and claims for use of the finite space of land, air, and water."

But the issue of growth versus no growth is obviously more subtle and complex than may be implied by quoting snatches of a few essays. Moreover, the ominous risks noted by Long and Hays (and by several other contributors, too), are too long run, too Wagnerian, to weigh heavily on most of us as we proceed with our day-to-day affairs. The clamor for "more" has by no means been stilled; economic growth itself has its own dynamic and inspires expectations of yet a bigger slice of a bigger pie. "The inhabitants of the lower (income) brackets," notes Wallich, "are continually exposed to a demonstration effect from above. They know how they would spend their money if they had twice as much of it or four times as much." The father of modern economics said much the same about his contemporaries two centuries ago: "The desire of food is limited in every man by the narrow capacity of the human stomach; but the desire of the conveniences and ornaments of building, dress, equipage, and household furniture, seems to have no limit or certain boundary." Adam Smith was a better seer than he could have known.

But there is yet another sound to be heard—perhaps not in the decibel range of a clamor but audible nonetheless. And this provides additional, albeit less dramatic, evidence that America is in a state of transition. It takes the form of an articulation of boredom, of impatience, of frustration—boredom on the assembly lines and in the classrooms, impatience in stacked-up airports and in jammed-up city streets, frustration with a wide range of contemporary phenomena from feckless governmental services to shoddy home appliances.

This still-fluid amalgam of restiveness may produce a crystallization of a new version of the American dream. What we sense could be a groping for a new national goal. Despite the current recession and the desire to scramble back on the growth path, the quest for more may yet have to make way for the quest for quality. Thus, America and several other industrially advanced countries as well may be on the threshold of a great societal decision: we have enough; now we want better. Efficient new hospitals do not necessarily produce compassionate (or even efficient) medical care; shiny new schools do not automatically provide good education; the expansion of the federal and state bureaucracies does not inevitably produce better social services.

Rostow would subscribe to this: "In the past, it has sufficed in Western societies for the government to provide the roads and the suburban infrastructure required to permit high mass-consumption to proceed. But that has changed and is changing as some societies move beyond high-mass consumption to a stage I call the search for quality." And so would Walker: "Many of us . . . are expressing a discontent with the technological entrapment that Carlyle hoped we were escaping almost 150 years ago."

This pervasive, albeit as yet inchoate, sense of unfulfillment has created a receptive audience for the advocates of limits to growth. It is not without significance that, at a time when traditional organized religions complain about mass backsliding, the nonmaterial aspects (good and bad) of economic growth have seized so many with so much fervor. The arguments, dealing as they do with man's obligations to nature and with his responsibilities to generations yet unborn, have, as Professor Ahlstrom reminds us, deep roots in the Judeo-Christian tradition. Indeed, says Ahlstrom, "the great debate on the limits to growth is fundamentally religious."

III

But if the debate has profound spiritual overtones, the prescriptions for achieving a state of grace (whether defined as continued, albeit tempered, growth, or as zero growth) tend to be highly pragmatic. They address such mundane issues as mineral reserves, alternatives to conventional energy sources, environmental impacts, technological breakthroughs, and resource substitutions. In our examination of the past and our assessment of the present, there is, as we have observed, considerable agreement. Looking around him or glancing back over his shoulder, each—whether humanist or scientist—sees much the same as his fellows, although shapes, shadings, and contours may vary according to the perspective of a particular discipline. But in peering ahead for a view through the murk, and especially in selecting a course to reach the desired goal, significant differences arise.

It is not unexpected that in the realm of future strategies as opposed to current or historical perceptions, the economists, technologists, and model builders crowd the humanists from center stage. And yet, the two scientists among our contributors have a surprise in store: Long and Holdren present a jaundiced view of the possibilities of technology to lead America in general into the promised land, especially if non-material as well as material ingredients of quality of life are factored in. And both favor substantial constraints on the growth process through tamping down the use of energy.

Long takes as his analytical time scale the period of a century. From this perspective, he is ready to accept short-term modifications or improvements in the growth process, providing that America assigns to itself, indeed works toward, a "quasistationary state" over the longer haul (scientist Long, like humanist Walker, feels that "no growth" is a slogan rather than an objective). He believes that a society adopting such a goal would "in no sense be a static one. Indeed . . . the attainment of no-growth in energy use and in use of natural resources necessarily calls for substantial social and technological change."

Holdren's views are in the same vein as Long's, although he is somewhat more pessimistic about the prospects in avoiding what the Meadows refer to as "overshoot and collapse." He is even less sanguine than Long that technology can provide a path that will skirt disaster. His prescription is a national strategy of no-growth to be taken on a timetable considerably shorter than Long's.

On the other hand, economists Wallich and Rostow do not subscribe to either Long's goal of a quasistationary state or Holdren's objective of no growth. To them, the pressures for continued growth in a society such as ours seem inescapable if not desirable; the challenge is to shape and influence economic growth in beneficial directions. Several other contributors (in particular, ethicist Powers) appear to subscribe explicitly or implicitly to this view.

But even if the goals to be sought were sharply etched on the horizon and even if there were general agreement among all contributors as to the compass sighting, there would still be some divergence of opinion as to how to get from here to there. In most forums where this question is raised, the argument quickly reduces itself to one of the free market versus planning. Although the here-to-there issue was not the focus of this series of essays, it inevitably intruded into many of the papers. The spectrum of views ranged widely.

Wallich would put considerable faith in the free-market system. Congressman Brown (see Appendix B), on the other hand, is concerned about "the predominant influence of controlled, or bargained, prices and wages in some of the most important sectors of the U.S. market and the invulnerability of the multinational corporations to either market or other controls in much of their operations." Brown, in short, advocates more effective national planning to deal with many of the problems the contributors addressed. Skolnikoff's position appears to lie in between. He recognizes the advantage of improving available "self-regulating mechanisms." To the extent the market "can be made more sophisticated and sensitive to presently nonquantitative, noneconomic signals, the greater relief there will be on the political process." But there is "the need to develop planning and dispute settling mechanisms able to function more rapidly and with more authority at as local a level as a dispute allows."

It seems clear to this observer that unless our leaders and our society as a whole are prepared to regard the zigs and zags, the lurches and lunges of laissez-faire, pell-mell growth as a spectator sport (none of the contributors, incidentally, seem prepared to do this), a greater degree of planning at all levels of government is necessary. The problems that plague us and that have been alluded to in virtually every essay require long-term solutions, are related one to the other, cut horizontally across disciplinary (and therefore departmental) lines, and spill over from national to local jurisdictions and from governmental to private sectors.

We can ignore all but today's most urgent crisis, of course, and, like Mr. Micawber, wake each morn in the hope that something will "turn up" to alleviate our chronic distress. But perhaps more than any other time in our history, there is now an apparent inclination to take tomorrow more seriously, to apply a smaller discount to the interests of future generations. For better or worse, the recession of the mid-1970s has forced many Americans to brood not only about getting the machine going again but also about the destination and the route to be taken once it gets started. The time has come to plan.

IV

"Planning" has long been a dirty word when applied to the federal government. Yet the thoughtful man who "plans" his own course is universally admired, and the farsighted corporation that engages in "planning" is more likely to obtain a higher Dun and Bradstreet rating than the one that does not. Popular hostility toward government planning has deep roots. In the era of American history characterized by a strong spirit of individualism—the period of the pioneers, the Yankee clippers, the railroads, the small farms the development and multiplication of factories and mills—"Washington" was regarded as a necessary evil. Those who made up the federal bureaucracy were scorned as the failures and the dropouts in a system dominated by a scramble for individual success. The less they interfered with the system, the better. This changed during World War I because of the need to rally the resources of the country for military purposes and, again, in the Great Depression, because of the need to marshal national resources to fight the battle of economic survival. By World War II, there was little question of Washington's taking charge. In each of these crises, of course, it was implicitly understood by both the planners and the public that once the crisis had passed the country would return to normal. "Normal" meant that the national planning efforts would be dissolved.

It is not difficult to account for the cynicism and suspicion that characterizes the popular American attitude toward government planning. Images of ration tickets, ubiquitous bureaucrats, and red tape are easily evoked. But the most telling obstacle to an acceptance of planning is an almost automatic popular transference between proposals for a national planning effort in the United States and the cumbersome, all-embracing central planning of socialist countries. No wonder those who favor government planning have such a hard row to hoe.

Despite all the caricatures and red herrings that are invoked, the planning process need not cover a multitude of sins. Indeed, the process that most advocates now envision involves an array of constructive, nonoppressive functions that have little to do with ration stamps, five-year plans, and red tape. Rather, it is designed to transform the business of policy making from one of crisis management and damage limitation to one that can more rationally cope with the long-run problems we confront. It involves such actions as goal setting, forecasting, early warning, analysis of available options, and monitoring of performance.

We can accept the propositions advanced by Long and Holdren that, in effect, will lead to a dampening down of the growth process in America. Or we can subscribe to the views of several other essayists that imply a need for continued growth but in directions that will mitigate the worst of the social, environmental, and physical by-products of rapid growth and promote the best. In either case, however, a heavier federal hand will be more necessary in the future than it has been in the past. None of the essayists, with the possible exception of Wallich, appear to favor a laissez-faire approach. A few, at least, seem ready to agree with Brown. "We need," the congressman emphasizes, "comprehensive national goals and priorities, and national planning to achieve them . . . national planning which can only be carried out by the national government."

V

Americans will certainly face their third century with much less ebullience, pride, and confidence than their great-grandfathers did their second. But perhaps the current mood has deeper roots in our history than we, in our present state of malaise, may credit. The

America of two centuries ago faced problems that in the eyes of our forefathers must have seemed as formidable as we perceive our own to be. There was little experience in governance, the national cupboard was bare, disunity and disillusionment were rife, corruption—grand and petty—was all too common. Then, as now, the nation was stepping across a historic threshold—and what lay on the other side appeared unfamiliar, even uncongenial. Within a few decades of the nation's birth, the issue of growth was to become a matter of debate and concern. "This invasion of Nature by Trade with its money, its credit, its steam, its railroad," wrote Emerson in 1839, "threatens to upset the balance of man, and establish a new, universal Monarchy more tyrannical than Babylon or Rome."

There are important differences, of course. One, a critical one, is the matter of elbow room—time and space to maneuver. America is infinitely richer and more powerful now, but the very forces that have blessed us with wealth and power—economic growth and population growth—have also increased the complexity and interdependence of our society and economy. We are now virtually imprisoned by our physical infrastructure, institutional rigidities, and standard of living. Turnaround opportunities are fewer and more costly, corrections of "mistakes" and reversals of policy decisions take much more time to put in effect.

America approaches its bicentennial decade, confronted with the need to clear away the debris, social as well as physical, that two hundred years of growth have left behind, and with a hearty residual appetite for yet more of the material goods and personal services that growth can deliver. But there are, as we have seen, some other, less tangible, but no less vexing requirements; those who lead us into the third century will have to reckon with these. Among them are escalating expectation for government services in a quantity and of a quality that no democratic national government has, thus far at least, been able to provide. "You expect more and you get more," is a Madison Avenue slogan that may have credence when touted by the manufacturers of a few consumer durable goods; it is not necessarily a valid promise in connection with the provision of social services. And accumulating, unfulfilled expectations bode ill for democratic societies.

No society would voluntarily choose to arrest a healthy growth pattern in mid-flight merely to take stock of its goals and its directions.

But, for better or worse, the recession that has afflicted virtually every industrially advanced country in the mid-1970s presents just such an opportunity. Here in the United States, circa 1976, we have a special reason to deliberate our future course. This series of essays dealing with growth in America should provide some contribution to these deliberations.

Arthur Kantrowitz

AVCO EVERETT RESEARCH LABORATORY, INC.

APPENDIX A
Controlling Technology
Democratically

I

Two strongly contrasting doctrines can be set forth for the control of our nearly infinitely powerful technology. The first is the doctrine of the moral responsibility of scientists, which calls for scientists to take full responsibility for the consequences of science. It holds that they should do their best to anticipate whether the knowledge they are discovering and the understanding of nature that they are creating will be used for good or for evil.

According to this doctrine, their duty is to develop knowledge they perceive to be good and to act to prevent the development of fields of knowledge they perceive will be harmful. It is argued that scientists who are engaged in opening up a new field of knowledge have a deeper opportunity and more time to think about its moral and political consequences that does the general public. This superior opportunity demands that they act to prevent any harmful consequences they foresee.

It goes without saying that the individual scientist has a personal responsibility for his own work. But his right to make personal moral choices about what he will work on is a separate issue from his responsibility to render scientific evaluations to the government or to society. As will be seen, this distinction must be most sharply drawn when the evaluation of scientific facts contributes to the making of large-scale decisions that control the development of technology.

In considering the consequences of governance of technology under the doctrine of the moral responsibility of scientists, it must first be recognized that much of our society already depends on what we do with advanced technology and still more will depend on our choice of which technologies to develop for the future.

Second the employment of the prestige of science to advance political and moral views raises very serious questions. It is, for example, unthinkable in a democratic society that scientists would actually be endowed with the authority necessary to assume full moral responsibility for the social impact of science.

This view was expressed eloquently by Harold Laski in his Fabian Tract No. 235, *The Limitations of the Expert:*

> . . . it is one thing to urge the need for expert consultation at every stage in making policy; it is another thing, and a very different thing, to insist that the expert's judgment must be final. For special knowledge and the highly trained mind produce their own limitations which, in the realm of statesmanship, are of decisive importance. Expertise, it may be argued, sacrifices the insight of common sense to intensity of experience. It breeds an inability to accept new views from the very depth of its preoccupation with its own conclusions. It too often fails to see round its subject. It sees results out of perspective by making them the center of relevance to which all other results must be related. Too often, also, it lacks humility; and this breeds in its possessors a failure in proportion which makes them fail to see the obvious which is before their very noses. It has, also, a certain caste-spirit about it, so that experts tend to neglect all evidence which does not come from those who belong to their own ranks. Above all, perhaps, and this most urgently where human problems are concerned, the expert fails to see that every judgment he makes not purely factual in nature brings with it a scheme of values which has no special validity about it. He tends to confuse the importance of his facts with the importance of what he proposes to do about them.

The implications of this doctrine of the moral responsibility of scientists have lead Theodore Roszak to say in *The Making of a Counter Culture*:

The key problem we have to deal woth is the paternalism of expertise within a socioeconomic system which is so organized that it is inextricably beholden to expertise. And, moreover, to an expertise which has learned a thousand ways to manipulate our acquiescence with an imperceptible subtlety.

Roszak sees no solution to this key problem and concludes that technology is uncontrollable. He therefore advocates the return to what he calls "non-intellective thinking."

If fully applied, the doctrine of the moral responsibility of scientists leads to a kind of a paternalistic control of society by a technological elite who will determine what is good for "the people." It amounts to a modern version of governance by noblesse oblige.

II

The second doctrine is one that I call democratic control of technology. Its essential feature is that decisions concerning which technology is good and which technology is evil are decided by the democratic process that gives each person one vote.

It is difficult in today's America to retain any illusion that democratic process guarantees good government. However, I do not propose to discuss alternatives to democratic process, being personally persuaded of the wisdom of Churchill's aphorism that "democracy is the worst form of government, except all the others." My purpose simply is to discuss the methodology of democratic control of technology. The essential problem is to find truth among the conflicting claims made by sophisticated advocates when there is serious controversy within the technological community.

How can the people or their elected representatives be helped to make informed decisions in the presence of such controversy? The need for a formal procedure was well illustrated by one of the debates in 1971 over whether to continue the development of the SST. In the last few weeks before the Senate vote, experts came forward with the claim that the operation of a fleet of SST's would deplete the ozone in the upper atmosphere, allowing more ultraviolet radiation to reach the earth, which in turn would result in an increase in the incidence of skin cancer. This possibility was denied by equally competent experts, and one hundred senators found themselves faced with the necessity for deciding their vote in part on the basis of an extremely complicated set of scientific claims, which were being vigorously disputed among the experts. To the extent that their decision was swayed by this issue, no one in the Senate was really equipped to make a reasoned judgment.

Another example of a difficult decision involving new technology as well as value judgments is the question of how rapidly to reduce automobile pollution. Implementation of the Clean Air Act of 1970 called for reducing automobile emissions by about a factor of ten by 1976. The costs of this reduction using current (or really hopefully available) technology have been estimated to be tens of billions of dollars per year, but many technical questions about feasibility and the health benefits that might result continue to give rise to controversy.

Decisions of this sort, which are frequently faced by our government, I will call "mixed decisions." Mixed decisions all involve extrapolation of known scientific fact or currently available technology and are of sufficient political or moral importance so that divergences of opinion are bound to appear.

The essential input from the scientific community to decision making in the United States is via the scientific advisory committee. Without going into detail about this process, I would like to make several points. In evaluating scientific advice on questions of great social importance, we must first recognize that the moral responsibility that many scientists feel very deeply can easily affect their judgment as to the state of scientific fact when the pertinent scientific facts are not yet crystal clear. Second, it should be noted that the selection of scientific committees has always been beset by the dilemma that one must choose between those who have gone deeply into the subjects under discussion and who, accordingly, have preconceived ideas about what the outcome should be and those who are perhaps unprejudiced but also relatively uninformed on the subjects under discussion.

As Warren Weaver put it,

A common procedure is to set up a special committee of experts on X in order to find out whether X is a good idea. This committee is, characteristically, national or even international in scope, is formed of external experts of recognized standing (external as regards the Agency in question but most emphatically internal as regards X), and always contains a comforting proportion of what might be called right names. These are men intensively interested in X, often with lifelong dedication to X, and sometimes with a recognizably fanatic concentration of interest on X. Quite clearly, they are just the lads to ask if you want to know whether X is a good idea.[1]

Finally, the fact that scientific advisory committees have, in many cases, played an influential role in decision making without taking public responsibility for their judgments warrants serious concern. In the making of mixed decision, the validity of the scientific input has frequently been brought under question.

III

I have three recommendations directed toward institutionalizing the scientific advisory function with a view toward increasing the presumptive validity of the scientific input on which democratic decision making can be based.

1. *Separate the scientific from the political and moral components of a mixed decision.* It has occasionally been maintained that scientific and nonscientific components of a mixed decision are generally inseparable. It is, of course, true that a final political decision cannot be separated from scientific information on which it must be based. The reverse is not true; a scientific question that logically can be phrased as anticipating the results of an experiment can always be separated from any political considerations. Thus, the question, Should we build a hydrogen bomb? is not a purely scientific question. A related scientific question, Can we build a hydrogen bomb? could in principle be answered by an experiment.

It is almost inevitable that scientists who have been engaged in research relevant to the scientific side of great mixed decisions should have deeply held political and moral positions on the relationship of their work to society. Scientific objectivity, a precious component of wise mixed decisions, is thus very difficult to achieve. I personally do not believe it is possible for scientists to have deeply held moral and political views about a question and simultaneously maintain complete objectivity concerning its scientific components.

In the past, moreover, scientific advisory committees have frequently developed close relationships with the officials who have final decisions to make. They have frequently advised political figures about what final decisions they should reach, not only about the scientific components of a decision but about the moral and political implications as well. Although the close relationship may be valuable, it does point up a need for an alternative source of scientific judgment that will forego taking any moral or political stands and will seek to optimize objectivity.

This proposition—the separation of scientific from nonscientific components of a mixed decision—is the key proposition that I have to make. It is the old issue of the separation of facts from values, and I submit that this separation can always be made. In order to maintain democratic control of mixed decisions, it is essential that great care be taken to avoid the invasion of objectivity by strongly held moral or political views.

2. *Separate the judge and advocate.* To my mind, there is no other solution to the problem discussed earlier of combining the highest level of expertise with lack of prejudice except the solution arrived at centuries ago in the similar legal problem. If one insists only on expertise in the advocates and expects them to marshal the arguments for one side of a scientific question, one can call on the services of people who have delved most deeply into a particular subject and who have in the course of this work arrived at a point of view. Such advocates, in addition to presenting their side of the case, can be very useful in criticizing the cases opposing advocates make.

The requirement of the judges on the other hand is simply that they must clearly understand the rules of scientific evidence, have no intellectual or other commitments regarding matters before them, and possess the mature judgment needed to weigh the evidence presented. Thus it is almost inevitable that a scientific judge would have earned his distinction in areas other than those in which he could qualify as unprejudiced.

It has occasionally been suggested that the advocates should present their points of view directly to political leaders who have decisions to make. This procedure suffers from the grave difficulty that political leaders are unable to spend the time necessary to understand scientific debates in sufficient depth to distinguish the relative validity of positions taken by sophisticated advocates. The scientific judge would differ from the political leader sitting in judgment on scientific questions in that his scientific background should more quickly enable him to assess the evidence presented by opposing advocates and to participate in something analogous to a cross-examination procedure. He would, on the other hand, not be expected to have the deep acquaintance with the field required of the advocates.

Scientists are traditionally advocates, and judicial functions, in smallscale science, have never had an importance comparable with that of advocacy. An experiment can always overturn anyone's judgment on a scientific question. However, the judicial function becomes important in large-scale science and technology when we must anticipate the results of experiments that cannot be performed without the expenditure of great amounts of money or time. This increase in the importance of the judicial function requires the development of a group of distinguished people who will devote themselves to scientific judgment.

The point has frequently been made that a scientist must stay actively engaged in creative work in order to maintain his expertise. I submit, however, that if a mature scientist is deeply involved in finding the truth between the claims and counterclaims of sophisticated advocates, his education will be continuously improved by the advocates, and he will be continuously mentally stretched in the effort to reach wise judgments. Communication between the judges and the scientific community and the public would also contribute to maintain their expertise and reputation.

The selection of people to serve as judges and advocates would, of course, be the most crucial and difficult matter in reaching wise decisions under this scheme, as under any other. It would be very important that everything possible be done to elevate the positions of advocates, and especially of judges, in order to attract people whose wisdom will match the importance of the judgments they must make.

When Congress recognizes the need for a mixed decision, leadership on both sides quickly becomes identifiable; for example, congressional leadership of the pro- and anti-SST forces was clearly evident. From the mixed issue, questions of scientific fact that would not require any value judgments would be separated; for example, how large is the danger that a fleet of SST's would produce an increase in the incidence of skin cancer?

If there were agreement that scientific judgment was needed, the leaders of opposing sides would be asked to name scientific advocates who would support their respective positions. These advocates would participate in the selection of scientific judges from a panel, each having the right to challenge judges for evidence of prejudice. The advocates, in addition to presenting their side of the question, would participate in a cross-examination procedure intended to exhibit weakness in the opposing case.

3. *Publish the scientific judgments.* In many instances, the findings of scientific advisory commitees have not been made available to the public for reasons other than national security. The existence of such privileged information makes it very difficult for the public to assess the degree to which a mixed decision is based on political grounds.

I would propose that the opinions of scientific judges, reached after hearing opposing advocates, should be published, within the limits of national security. The publication of these judgments would serve two purposes. First, it would provide the whole political community with a statement of scientific facts as currently seen by unbiased judges after a process in which opposing points of view have been heard and subjected to cross-examination. Hopefully, these opinions would acquire sufficient presumptive validity to provide an improved base on which political decisions could be reached through democratic process. Second, the publication of opinions reached by scientific judges would inevitably increase their personal involvement and also would encourage distinguished scientists to participate in the decision-making process.

One serious potential difficulty lies in the traditional conservatism of scientists, even those who have exhibited great imagination and daring in their own work. I have no formula to offer to overcome this bias other than an insistence that the advocates of novel approaches be heard. It is important that they be cross-examined by skeptical experts and that the judges feel a responsibility not to render negative judgments on inadequate evidence. It is, of course, very difficult to offer rigorous proof that something cannot be done, and usually the most that can be said is, "I cannot see how to do it." Scientific judges whose opinions would be published should be more accountable for errors in judgment. It is very important that the institutional procedure not be allowed to interfere with the small-scale creative science, which must precede any major decision making. This work flourishes best in a climate of wide opportunity for individual initiative—a kind of private enterprise, laissez-faire system in which I firmly believe.

When large-scale funding is requried, the number of technological approaches that are pursued must be restricted. Hence the question might be raised whether the formalization of institutions for scientific judgment would result in harmful restrictions on initiative. However, the scientific advisory procedures that now exist have also been guilty in this respect, and greater formalization of these procedures might include designing a system to control the narrowing of the number of alternatives pursued simultaneously as a project grows in size.

IV

Congressional review of important scientific programs requires an independent source of scientific judgment. It would be valuable if the Congress could acquire that judgment in a manner different from the procedures that have been developed in the executive branch. I propose that the Congress create, on an experimental basis, an institution for scientific judgment. The scientific questions referred to the institution by the Congress should relate directly to forthcoming major congressional decisions.

The future of such an institution would depend on the degree to which political and scientific communities would accept its initial judgments in comparison with the judgments reached by existing procedures. It seems possible that with a relatively modest start, an institution could be developed that, in the course of time, would achieve a much higher level of presumptive validity than now exists in communication between the scientific community and Congress. Such an institution could be invaluable in providing an improved scientific basis for future mixed decisions of the Congress.

It has occasionally been suggested that adversary proceedings are very cumbersome. By contrast, present committee procedures seek to get all sides together and achieve a unanimous position, assuming that sweet reason will prevail. But in the highly controversial issues raised today, sweet reason is likely to prevail only when a committee is selected with foreknowledge about what "reasonable" men think about the questions at hand. I believe that any attempt to reach such decisions in the absence of an adversary procedure is a delusion.

The issue of the applicability of adversary procedures to the settlement of technological questions has been addressed in depth and with great wisdom in the divided opinion of the U.S. Court of Appeals, District of Columbia, in the case of an appeal (February 10, 1973) by various automobile companies for release from a decision of the then administrator of the EPA, William D. Ruckelshaus. He had ruled that the companies were not entitled to an extension of time because the technology for meeting the Clean Air Act of 1970 was judged available. In remanding the case for further proceedings, the majority of the court, who held that the sixty days available for the administrator to make his decision was insufficient time for adversary proceedings, commented: "We see no principled manner in which firm time limits can be scheduled for cross examination consistent with its unique potential as an 'engine of truth'—the capacity given a diligent and resourceful counsel to expose subdued premises, to pursue evasive witnesses, to 'explore' the whole witness, often traveling unexpected avenues."

The majority also said, "We revert to our observation that a right of cross-examination, consistent with time limitations, might well extend to particular cases of need, on critical points where the general procedure proved inadequate to probe 'soft' and sensitive subjects and witnesses. No such circumscribed and justified requests were made in this proceeding."

Chief Judge Bazelon, in a separate opinion, while concurring in the result, made a strong plea for the use of adversary proceedings to establish technological facts in the presence of controversy. Thus he wrote: "These complex questions should be resolved in the crucible of debate through the clash of informed but opposing scientific and technological viewpoints."

V

I have been suggesting this kind of an institution for almost a decade. Gradually I have come to understand the source of opposition and at last to appreciate why such an institution has not been created in spite of the fact it seems so necessary. The need has often seemed obvious to many of the people in groups to whom I have spoken on this issue. However, it is a political rule that any existing process has a power structure and that any disturbance of that power structure will displace vested interests. When you propose to displace vested interests, you must expect opposition.

What are these vested interests? One of my first efforts was to propose this plan at a Senate subcommittee hearing.[2] In the course of that hearing and many other contacts with the Congress, I discovered that there are not many legislators who would voluntarily give up the flexibility they gain from being able to hide political motivations behind a smoke screen of scientific confusion. It is most useful for a political figure to be able to say that his scientific advisors have provided him with the "facts," which clearly support the position that is politically convenient for him anyway. Political figures would lose a great deal of flexibility by the creation of an institution whose judgments would have presumptive validity high enough so that they could not easily assemble their own group of scientists with enough authority to challenge that judgment.

Then there is the role of the Washington scientific advisor. Many people have made a career of providing scientific advice in high places. Some have tried to be objective but most have been quite ready to offer advice not only on scientific matters but also on related moral and political questions. They have acquired a political influence far greater than they would have if they merely stated the facts. Exactly as in the case of the politicians, they are reluctant to give up the power provided them by the existing relationship between science and politics. In an institution for scientific judgment, it would be incumbent upon scientists to disqualify themselves whenever their political and moral opinions might interfere with scientific objectivity. Thus, this group would also lose flexibility.

Obviously, neither side of the science-government relationship would enthusiastically welcome the establishment of a new institution that would limit their freedom. Considerable public support for a proposal to institutionalize scientific judgment would therefore be needed to overcome the resistance of these vested interests.

In summary, an institution for scientific judgment appears to offer a solution to what Roszak called the key problem, the paternalism of expertise. If the making of mixed decisions is meticulously separated into scientific and nonscientific parts, then a system can be devised by which the experts can make objective judgments regarding the scientific parts of the question, leaving the determination of what is good and what is evil to the democratic process. I see no other way in which our extremely powerful and vigorously growing technology can be controlled democratically.

NOTES

1. *Science* 130 (November 20, 1959).

2. U.S., Congress, Senate, Committee on Government Operations, Subcommittee on Government Research, *Research in the Service of Man,* 90th Cong., 1st sess., 1967.

George E. Brown, Jr.
CONGRESSMAN

APPENDIX B
The Problems of Implementing Technology Assessments: The Congressional Context

I

Technology assessment has been defined as "the process of identifying and studying consequences of the application of science."[1] The emergence of technology assessment as a separate area of concern within the scientific and technical community, as well as within the executive and legislative branches of government, is well described by Richard Carpenter and by David Keifer in an article in *Chemical and Engineering News*.[2] Additional background material is found in a statement by Congressman Emilio Daddario when he was chairman of the Subcommittee on Science, Research and Development of the House Committee on Science and Astronautics[3] (now the Committee of Science and Technology) and in the report to accompany HR 18469, "Establishing the Office of Technology Assessment and Amending the National Science Foundation Act of 1950."[4]

There seems little question that the continually increasing rate of accumulation of scientific knowledge and the decreasing time interval between invention and dissemination of new technology will force new techniques and mechanisms for technology assessment by both the Congress and the executive branch, as well as by institutions in the private sector. I have not been so much concerned that the Congress would be unable to establish an adequate mechanism for securing the information it requires to assess the import of specific technological developments on society. As Carpenter points out, the Congress certainly does not lack information.[5] If the problem is of sufficient importance, the Congress will find a way to secure the expert advice it needs. Congress showed that it was well aware of the technology assessment problem by passing legislation to establish the Office of Technology Assessment in 1972 (PL 92-484, the Technology Assessment Act of 1972).

I am more concerned, however, about what Congress will do with its technology assessment input now that it is beginning to obtain it. I would, therefore, like to devote this essay largely to raising questions about how Congress makes its decisions, develops its programs, and sets its goals and priorities.

II

As a background to raising these kinds of questions, I must first point out that the historical development of technology as the fruit of knowledge raises vitally important philosophic questions that every scientist, engineer, and technician should be concerned about. Technology was with man before there was science—in the sense we now know science. The discovery of fire, copper, lead, and iron, the invention of the lever and fulcrum and the wheel, the development of language and writing, were all triumphs of technology. Each led to major changes in the human condition and new paths toward additional technology. As man learned to record, transmit, and retrieve his hard-won store of knowledge and then to organize his methods of achieving and expanding on that knowledge, we began to have what we now call "science."

The earliest technologies made possible the beginnings of civilization and its institutions. It produced the surpluses that made possible the first cities, law and government, and religion, art, architecture, and philosophy. But even from the beginning, it produced results not always benign. It created extremes of poverty and wealth, class divisions, bureaucracies, the ability to maintain large standing armies and to conduct protracted wars.

The moral and ethical questions presented to us today, while far more urgent than before, are not in essence different from those presented man 5,000 years ago as he emerged into civilization. At their simplest and sharpest, these questions relate to man's nature and purpose. Is he a creature primarily seeking awareness of himself and the universe he finds himself in, an expansion of his individual and collective consciousness; or is he a creature seeking more domination of the material environment and more consumption of the resources of that environment? Is technology to be the servant of the liberated man, or is man to be the serf of uncontrolled technology?

No one concerned about technology assessment should be unaware of the significance and importance of these questions. They remain the subject of much scholarship and debate. The rationalization of production resulting from technology has been bleakly described by Juenger in the following words: "There can be no talk of riches produced by technology. What really happens is rather a steady, forever growing consumption. It is a ruthless destruction, the like of which the earth has never before seen. A more and more ruthless destruction of resources is the characteristic of our technology."[6]

For those who feel that the prewar writings of this German scientist-philosopher have little relevance to the technological situation of today, I commend the contemporary remarks of M. King Hubbert of the U.S. Geological Survey:

Because of the impossibility of sustaining rates of industrial growth such as those which prevailed during the last century and a half, it is inevitable that before very much longer such growth must cease, and some kind of stability be achieved. . . . The future period of stability could be characterized either by a continuation of a technological culture with a high level of energy consumption, or by a cultural decline to a primitive low energy level of existence.

Regardless of which of these possible courses may actually be followed, it is clear that the episode in industrial exponential growth can only be a transitory epoch of about three centuries duration in the totality of human history. It represents but a brief transitional epoch between two very much longer periods, each characterized by rates of change so slow as to be regarded essentially as periods of non-growth. Although the forthcoming period poses no insuperable physical or biological difficulties, it can hardly fail to force a major revision of those aspects of our current economic and social thinking which stems from the assumption that the growth rates that have characterized this temporary period can somehow be made permanent.[7]

At a further point, Juenger states, "We are approaching a point— here and there we have already reached it—where technological rationalism in production is more important than the profit produced. In other words, technological improvement must go on even if it spells financial loss."[8] It is interesting that nearly thirty years later Galbraith makes much the same point about the modern corporation, pointing out that the enlargement of its sphere of planning and control has become a more important goal than maximizing its profits.[9]

The literature critical of technology, or at least of a blind subservience to technological progress as a goal in itself, is growing rapidly. This is true both in the developed industrial societies and in the underdeveloped world. Radical thinkers such as Ivan Illich[10] and others question whether industrialization and the resulting urbanization should be considered practical goals for the poorer countries of the world. Gandhi, of course, raised this same question with regard to India forty years ago, preferring to think in terms of strengthening village life, cottage industry, and small farming. In an article that I wrote several years ago, I projected a fantasy in which the entire world reached our standards of technological development one hundred years from now.[11] The result, of course, was the complete exhaustion of the earth's supply of nonreplenishable resources. While many scientists feel that technology will provide a "technological fix" for these problems before they become catastrophic,[12] there is every reason for a healthy dose of skepticism in our attitude toward the blessings of unfettered technology.

The point I wish to stress to all would-be technology assessors, whether in Congress or the executive branch or outside of government, is that man—not the machine, not the rationalized mechanized system—must be at the center of our concern. Perhaps even more important is the nature of that man—man the seeker, not man the consumer or man the destroyer.

III

Technology assessment, if used by the Congress and the executive branch as part of a comprehensive approach to national program planning and policy execution, will be extremely valuable. However, and this is a very large however, the major weakness of Congress today is its lack of a coordinated national program planning capability. The executive branch is only slightly better with regard to its overall planning capability, although its information and analysis resources are greatly superior to those of the Congress. We must begin our exploration of the problems of implementing technology assessments as far as the Congress is involved with this point clearly in mind.

The Congress is highly fragmented in its operations. As a principle, organization fragmentation, or dividing up into a multitude of committees in order to approach a multitude of problems, is not necessarily bad. It becomes bad when there is a lack of organizing principle, of rational framework, of ability to coordinate the whole of a problem, as a result of the fragmentation. That is the general condition in the U.S. Congress today.

A few examples will illustrate this point. Until 1974 Congress did not prepare a national budget of its own, or a coordinated economic plan of any sort, although it had the constitutional responsibility for raising revenues and appropriating monies. Its handling of the nation's finances over the past several years has been increasingly chaotic. The passing of the Budget Act (The Budget and Impoundment Act of 1974, PL 93-344), in which the responsibility for an overall view of the total expenditures authorized and appropriated by the many individual committees was finally vested in a single budget committee, is a first step toward rational organization. Nonetheless it remains unclear whether the new system will quickly be able to overcome the traditions of petty jurisdictional squabbles. On matters involving science and technology more than half of the committees of both the House and the Senate have some significant jurisdiction. [13] About a third of the committees have a major concern with environmental quality. [14] As many as eighteen committees have jurisdiction over one or more programs of aid to education. [15] There is no single committee with any overall coordinating or unifying responsibility in these areas. As a matter of practical fact, each of the committees is extremely zealous in

its efforts to prevent encroachment on its own narrow historic preroga-
tives, while seeking to stake claim to new areas related to its historical
role. An example of such accretion of function is the jurisdiction of the
House Committee on Interstate and Foreign Commerce over public
health. Arising out of an original mandate to provide health care for
seamen, this committee now authorizes programs of hospital construction and health care for the nation, research in biomedical areas, and
education of health personnel. The most hopeful effort to try to end
this competitive free-for-all and rationalize the division of responsibility was the Bolling committee reform of 1974, which attempted to
consolidate the diffuse and overlapping substantive responsibilities of
the committees in the House of Representatives. This plan unfortunately offended too many traditional seats of power and was sup-
planted by a much weaker measure, leaving most responsibilities still
widely dispersed.

In the social programs—education, health, housing, poverty,
hunger, mass transportation—the situation is even worse than in the
scientific and technical program areas. In the latter areas there has
been a generally unified and powerful program sponsorship in the
form of the national security establishment—sometimes known as the
military-industrial complex—which has enjoyed a generation of
unparalleled legislative support. Such is not the case for social programs. Here the role of the national government is controversial, and
each move invokes a potent mythology centered around the meanings
of "freedom" and "democracy" and involves contending political
forces of great power. Great battles have ensued between these forces
as Congress moved forward into the areas of full employment, housing
and urban renewal, federal aid to education, medicare, and so on.

Efforts to provide Congress with at least a minimum data base and
analysis of needs and priorities in the social program area moved
forward slightly in recent years when the Senate passed (in September
1970) S5, the Full Opportunity and National Goals and Priorities Act,
which proposed establishing a Council of Social Advisors in the executive office of the President and required an annual social report by the
President to the Congress. This, of course, would parallel the steps
taken by the Employment Act of 1946, which set up the Council of
Economic Advisers and the annual Economic Report of the President.
Title II of S5 proposed establishing within the Congress an Office of
Goals and Priorities Analysis, which would also "submit an annual

report to the Congress setting forth goals and priorities in the general
context of needs, costs, available resources and program effectiveness."[16]

The need for more adequate information upon which to base social
policy in an era of startling rapid change was testified to by numerous
witnesses at the 1970 Senate hearings on S5.   Joseph Califano, former
special assistant to President Johnson, testified: "The disturbing truth
is that the basis of recommendations by an American Cabinet officer
on whether to begin, eliminate, or expand vast social programs more
nearly resembles the intuitive judgment of a benevolent tribal chief in
remote Africa than the elaborate sophisticated data with which the
Secretary of Defense supports a major new weapons system."[17] Unfortunately, the House took no action on S5 in the Ninety-first Congress
or subsequent Congresses, and though some planning provisions
emerged in the Budget Act, the Califano characterization remains
predominantly correct.

IV

The general picture I am trying to convey here is that of a Congress,
and to a lesser extent an executive branch, bound by tradition and
conventional wisdom to procedures and programs inadequate to the
social problems created by modern scientific and technological
developments. These problems can be solved if the Congress and the
executive are willing to solve them, and if they are willing to provide
themselves with the tools necessary for analysis, planning, and program execution. Today the major executive departments generally
have had some experience with sophisticated planning, programming,
and budgeting systems geared to their departmental mandates,
although confidence in their efficacy has somewhat waned. The
departments most oriented toward science, technology, and hardware
(Defense, NASA, AEC) probably have had the best systems. The
departments oriented toward social programs have had the least effective systems. The President himself has no comprehensive system of
goals and priorities, nor the mechanism for achieving such a system,
which would allow for the development of coordinated plans for the

national welfare, properly encompassing all of the competing departmental programs. This remains the bastion of political obfuscation at worst, or the province of statesmanship at best. The Congress has no goals, no priorities, no plans, inadequate information, jealously guarded committee fiefdoms, and anachronistic procedures.

At the heart of this country's difficulty in solving the problems created by change—particularly scientific and technological change—is our unwillingness as a nation, or as a government, or as a Congress, to accept the need for rational, comprehensive, democratically controlled planning for the public welfare. Our mythology holds that the common good will arise out of the competitive struggle of each individual toward his own goals. While our national practice has long deviated from the standards this mythology would require, we are not ready to defend the principle that we need comprehensive national goals and priorities, and national planning to achieve them—national planning that can only be carried out by the national government, even though such planning must of necessity encompass equally comprehensive local and regional plans. And in the absence of such planning for the total public good, the great governmental bureaucracies, which do plan, and the great corporate bureaucracies, which do plan, are able to make their goals and their priorities appear to be the goals and priorities of the nation.

The debate over technology assessment and the debate over S15 (The Full Opportunity Act) moved us very slightly toward the concept of comprehensive planning, based upon the analysis and evaluation of a scientific data base and guided by democratically determined goals and priorities. Keifer says, "Thus it seems likely that much as laissez-faire economics become socially and politically untenable in the latter half of the 19th Century, so laissez-faire technology may become outmoded during the final decades of the 20th Century."[18] And further on, "What is new, then, is not just the label on the concept but the idea that decisions regarding the exploitation of technological developments must rest on more than simple self-interested analysis. The stakes are too high for innovation to be dictated merely by affirmative answers to the traditional questions: Is it technologically feasible? Is it economically profitable? The profit motive and the market mechanism no longer suffice, at least in the classic manner."[19]

A number of able economists, as well as many other public figures, have come to the conclusion that the profit motive and the market mechanism, even under the prod of Keynesian monetary and fiscal manipulation, no longer adequately ensure the public welfare in large areas of the economy. The simple reason for this is the predominant influence of controlled, or bargained, prices and wages in some of the most important sectors of the U.S. market and the invulnerability of the multinational corporations to either market or other controls in much of their operations. In these sectors the kind of planning and control implicit in Keynesian theory must be supplemented by a more direct program of planning and control.

V

I am well aware that this type of action would arouse a great hue and cry about tampering with the operation of the free market or infringing on the fundamental precepts of democracy. Here we enter the realm of mythology. There is no "free market" when great corporate or labor bureaucracies bargain, or plan, a wages and prices policy extending for years into the future and unresponsive to any market condition. Likewise, the government today, as it has for nearly two generations under both Democratic and Republican administrations, engages in semiconcealed economic planning and control through the exercise of fiscal and monetary tools. The choice is not between planning and regulating a free market, or not doing so. The choice is between *effective* planning and regulation of an already *controlled* market (and *controlled* by power groupings not necessarily concerned with the welfare of the public as a whole), and ineffective planning and regulation of an already controlled market.

It must be noted that a parallel force driving the nation and the Congress toward the acceptance of comprehensive national planning as a necessary tool is the growing environmental quality movement. That the problems of environmental quality and technological change overlap is obvious. The need to understand all the ramifications of this overlap is one of the chief challenges of the subcommittee I chair, the Subcommittee on Environment and the Atmosphere of the Science and Technology Committee. In the Senate, one bill that reflected those ramifications was S4044, originally introduced in the Ninetieth Congress by Senators Magnuson and Hart; it proposed an Independent Technology Assessment and Environmental Data Collection Commission, which would have been independent of the three existing branches of government. Carpenter has referred to a similar proposal for an independent evaluative branch of government, as suggested by Nicholas E. Golovin.[20] S4044 was acted on by neither the Senate or House, but it did have some impact in the evolution of ideas for the Office of Technology Assessment noted earlier.

The most imaginative and far-reaching proposal for the incorporation of the planning function into the structure of government is that of Tugwell in his draft of a new constitution.[21] He proposes that "planning" shall constitute one of six separate branches of government. In order to give some flavor of what he suggests, I quote below a portion of Article III, The Planning Branch, from one version of his draft Constitution. Note that the technology assessment function is included:

> Section 5.   It shall be recognized that the six- and twelve-year development plans represent national intentions tempered by the appraisal of possibilities. The twelve-year plan shall be a general estimate of probable progress, both governmental and private; the six-year plan shall be more specific as to estimated income and expenditure.
>
> The purpose shall be to advance, through every agency of government, the excellence of national life; it shall be the further purpose to anticipate innovations, to estimate their impact, to assimilate them into existing institutions, or to moderate deleterious effects on the environment and on society.
>
> The six- and twelve-year plans shall be disseminated for discussion and the opinions expressed shall be considered in the formulation of plans for the succeeding year.[22]

As a part of the concern for the quality of the environment, I should like also to mention the growing amount of legislation at both state and national levels relating to planning for urban renewal, new towns, comprehensive land use on a local, regional, and national basis for coasts and beaches, rivers and estuaries, open space, and for roads, airports, etc. In practically all cases these legislative proposals, and the relatively few enactments, stem from some current crisis, not from a sense of need for bringing order to the changes effecting our total physical and social environment.

Lest it should appear that I am off on a new and uncharted track in my obsession with planning as the necessary ingredient in technological assessment implementation by the Congress, I would like to go back to the history of a generation ago. Probably the first specific recommendation for a continuing technology assessment capability by the national government was contained in the study "Technological Trends and National Policy" by the National Resources Committee.[23] This study was quoted by Chairman Daddario in his statement on technology assessment cited earlier.[24] What interested me in this study, which was really a most comprehensive technology assessment document in itself, was the emphasis on planning throughout the study. For example, the final recommendation of the report was:

6. The most important general conclusion to be drawn from these studies is the continuing growth of the already high and developing technology in the social structure of the Nation, and hence the hazard of any planning that does not take this fact into consideration. This pervasive interrelationship so clearly manifest throughout the pages of this report points to one great need, namely, a permanent over-all planning board.[25]

The effects of future technological developments in each of nine major economic areas were analyzed in detail in the report. A brief look at one of these areas, agriculture, will show how the technology assessment and planning questions were raised at that time. The subject of the mechanical cotton-picker, not yet developed but generally anticipated, was analyzed.

Suppose that a successful mechanical cotton-picker, capable of picking five thousand pounds a day, is, or soon will be, a reality, and that it will be manufactured on a large scale and sold for approximately $1,000.00. What social and economic consequences might we expect?[26]

After considerable discussion, some tentative conclusions were reached, but additional questions were also raised—the questions of second- and third-order consequences.

If we assume that cotton acreage will remain about the same, and that a successful machine will be produced in large quantities and sold to all who can afford to buy, tenant farming as it now exists in the South would undergo change. Some tenants and sharecroppers would still be needed as laborers in the cotton fields, but many would have to turn elsewhere for a livelihood.

Would they pour into the North and seek employment in industry? If so, what would be the effect. . . ?

Will the cotton-picker, necessitating the use of a tractor, force the elimination of a large percentage of the horses and mules, along with the hoe, the one-horse plow, and the great hordes of roving cotton pickers?[27]

Time has answered the questions raised in 1937 about the impact of technology on agriculture. Millions of southern farm tenants and sharecroppers and "great hordes of roving cotton pickers" have moved North and West. They now reside in the central core of our large cities and have a major impact on the statistics of employment, crime, and welfare—the so-called social issues at the root of today's political ferment. Probably today we could reach agreement on the importance of seeking better answers to those questions raised in the 1930s. But intervening years of war, a seemingly unending economic prosperity, and new manifestations of technology's great impact—the space race, for example—obscured the significance of the fundamental changes taking place in agriculture and the need for those better and clearer responses. As the authors of the report put it:

The answers will be difficult to find and will necessitate reconciliation between many conflicting attitudes. The prospect of more rapid technological advances in coming years emphasizes the need for the early valuation of the social gains and social costs that are likely to arise out of each course.[28]

As a nation, and as a Congress, we failed to heed the warning. As a consequence, many of the great cities of the nation are now on the verge of social and economic collapse. Our most massive efforts seem to avail little. At a time when our wealth and power are unique to history, we grope for solutions to the problem of achieving a tranquil society.

Amazingly enough, the same committee, the National Resources

Committee, which produced the technology assessments I have quoted above, also produced at the same time a study of the problems of the cities. Both studies are being revived because of their pertinence to modern problems. The closing paragraphs of this report on urban problems with its final exhortation for more effective planning on all levels of government are especially pertinent:

Provided the urban community possesses a fundamentally sound economic base and has a site the disadvantages of which are not too costly to overcome, the Committee is of the opinion that the realistic answer to the question of a desirable urban environment lies not in wholesale dispersion, but in the judicious reshaping of the urban community and region by systematic development and redevelopment in accordance with forward-looking and intelligent plans. In this, advantage would be taken of the natural trends in the shifting of industry between established industrial areas and its diffusion within such areas, of the drift of population from congested central districts to outlying sections, of the improved means of transit and the general fluidity of the population—to loosen up the central areas of congestion and to create a more decentralized metropolitan pattern. Such a moderately decentralized and yet integrated urban structure should have greater stability and should offer economies in production and in the provision of public facilities and services. It may be expected to extend the material and cultural advantages of urban life to a larger number of the population; to allow them to enjoy the benefits of a more healthful environment and a richer personal and communal life; and to offer to the lower income groups the possibility of the somewhat less tenuous existence afforded by village and small-town living.

A reasonable set of conditions for attainment of a desirable urban community sketched in these broad terms would doubtless include a sound, well-balanced industrial structure; a rather compact community pattern but with ample light and air and adequate streets, recreational and other public spaces available in all sections; a balanced development free of building, population, or traffic congestion; a relatively stable and reasonable level of land values without excessively high or falling values, and with all the land in efficient and socially desirable use; and a minimum of

obsolescence. The realization of a community with such characteristics can be furthered, among other means, by the organization of the urban area as a whole into neighborhoods and satellite
communities, each of which provides for a maximum of opportunity to care for the daily activities and needs of its inhabitants, each
of which possesses a social and political coherence which can
arouse and hold community loyalty and participation, inspire
responsible civic leadership, and can perform effectively its
specialized function in the metropolitan region. Thus, the
economic and cultural advantages of the great city will be further
enhanced by the physical and social stability and unity which
some have thought was obtainable only in a simple society. Thus
also, the benefits of modern civilization which the great city has
brought to an ever-increasing proportion of our people may be
extended and increased.

The approach toward this type of urban community and a more
satisfactory urban life will require much better appreciation and
understanding of the city and its distinctive problems, greatly
improved governmental organization and wider powers, and far
more fundamental and much more effective planning on all levels
of government.[29]

VI

I believe that Congress is equipping itself with the information
resources adequate for technology assessment. The Office of Technology Assessment has become another servant of the committee chair-
men, providing them with additional resources. However, it does not
ease jurisdictional barriers, and it cannot provide any compulsion or
even substantial inducement for a comprehensive approach to any
particular problem or set of problems. Despite this, the process of
analysis in itself may help force a recognition of the interrelationship of
broad problem and program areas.

But what of the next step beyond analysis? By what process will the
fundamental conflicts of interest produced by policy choices be resolved? How can the political power of economic and social interests
deeply involved in alternative courses be subordinated to the national

interest? Examples of these difficulties abound in Congress today, and examples of their successful resolution are rare indeed.

We in Congress make decisions today that generally favor the most powerful sponsors of new technological developments, with the power measured in terms of the scientific, economic, and bureaucratic resources of the sponsor, which generally are transmitted into political terms. Hence, the automobile, oil, and highway forces traditionally have prevailed over citizen groups interested in clean air, unpolluted beaches, and well-planned communities; the chemical and drug interests have won victories over those who complain about the threats of life and health created by our dependence on additives and pills. Congress plays the role of arbiter of contending forces, with those in support of a more humane and enlightened existence almost always being in the weaker position. Just when environmental concerns have begun to gather strength due to the obvious horror of environmental degradation, the energy crisis has emerged to tempt us to think again in terms of "quick-fix" expedients.

Effective implementation of technology assessment demands that Congress change its role from weak umpire to strong leader. Congress must have its own plan, its own goals for the public welfare, its own strategy for achieving the goals, its own feedback and monitoring devices to measure its success and its failures. Perhaps we are moving closer to that role, but my fear is that the rate at which we are moving is inadequate to cope with the pressures of change. I hope that I am wrong.

NOTES

1. Richard A. Carpenter, "Technology Assessment and the Congress," Science Policy Research Division, Legislative Reference Service, Library of Congress (February 19, 1969).

2. David M. Keifer, "Technology Assessment," *Chemical and Engineering News* (October 5, 1970): 42-54.

3. U.S., Congress, House, Committee on Science and Astronautics Technology Assessment, 90th Cong., 1st sess., August 1968, "Technology Assessment Seminar," opening statement by Emilio Q. Daddario, vol. 129, no. 7, pp. 1-2.

4. U.S., Congress, House, Committee on Science and Astronautics, 91st Cong., 2d sess., 1970, H. Dept. 91-1437.

5. Carpenter, "Technology Assessment."

6. Friedrich G. Juenger, *The Failure of Technology* (Hinsdale, Illinois. Henry Regnery Co., 1949), p. 20.

7. M. King Hubbert, "Energy Resources for Power Production," *U.S. Geological Survey* (August 1970): 20.

8. Juenger, *Failure of Technology,* p. 28.

9. John Kenneth Galbraith, *The New Industrial State* (Boston: Houghton Mifflin, 1967).

10. For example, in an article in *Saturday Review* ("The False Ideology of Schooling," October 17, 1970, p. 56), Illich says, "Underdevelopment is the result of a state of mind common to both socialist and capitalist countries. Present development goals are neither desirable nor reasonable. Unfortunately, anti-imperialism is no antidote. Although exploitation of poor countries is an undeniable reality, current nationalism is merely the affirmation of the right of colonial elites to repeat history and follow the road traveled by the rich toward the universal consumption of internationally marketed packages, a road that can ultimately lead only to universal pollution and universal frustration." See also his *Tools for Conviviality* (New York: Harper & Row, 1973) and *Energy and Equity* (New York; Harper & Row, 1974).

11. George E. Brown, Jr., "A Nightmare of Numbers," *War/Peace Report,* (December 1967).

12. Bernard J. Eastlund and William C. Gough. *The Fusion Torch—Closing the Cycle from Use to Re-use* (Washington, D.C.: U.S. Atomic Energy Commission, Division of Research, 1969).

13. Library of Congress, Legislative Reference Service, "Congressional Organization for Science and Technology," (1969).

14. Library of Congress, Legislative Reference Service, "Committee Concerned with Environmental Quality and Productivity" (1969).

15. Richard Bolling, *Power in the House* (New York: E. P. Dutton & Co., 1968), p. 263.

16. U.S., Congress, Senate, Committee on Labor and Public Welfare, *Full Opportunity Act,* 91st Cong., 2d sess., 1970, p. 2.

17. Ibid., p. 9.

18. Keifer, "Technology Assessment," 43.

19. Ibid., 44.

20. Carpenter, "Technology Assessment," 15.

21. Rexford Guy Tugwell, "Constitution For A United Republics of America—Version XXXVII," *The Center Magazine* 3 (September 1970).

22. Ibid.

23. U.S., Congress, House, *"Technological Trends and National Policy, Report of the Subcommittee on Technology to National Resources Committee,* 75th Cong., 1st sess. July 22, 1937, H. Rept. 1284.

24. U.S., Congress, House, Subcommittee on Science and Astronautics Technology Assessment, 90th Cong., 1st sess.

25. Ibid., p.X.

26. Ibid., p. 141

27. Ibid., p. 143.

28. Ibid., p. 105.

29. U.S., Congress, *Our Cities—Their Role in the National Economy, Report of the Urbanism Committee to the National Resources Committee, June, 1937,* Hearings before the Ad Hoc Subcommittee on Urban Growth of the House Committee on Banking and Currency, Part 2, (91st Congress).

Index